D0147974

The Art of Piano Playing

HEINRICH NEUHAUS

HEINRICH NEUHAUS

The Art of Piano Playing

Translated by
K. A. LEIBOVITCH

KAHN & AVERILL
London

This edition published in 1993 by
Kahn & Averill
9 Harrington Road, London SW7 3ES

First published in Great Britain in 1973 by
Barrie & Jenkins Ltd

English translation copyright © by Barrie & Jenkins Ltd

Music examples numbers: 1-50, 52, 53, 82-85, 89-95, 97-100
reproduced by kind permission of Musikverlag Hans Gerig, Cologne

All rights reserved

Reprinted 1997, 2001, 2002, 2006

British Library Cataloguing in Publication Data

A catalogue record for this book is available from the British Library

ISBN 1 871082 45 5
ISBN 9781 871082 45 6 (from Jan 2007)

Printed in Great Britain by
Halstan & Co Ltd., Amersham, Bucks

This book is dedicated
to
my dear colleagues,
the teachers and the pupils
who are studying
"the art of piano playing".

Contents

Introduction

Heinrich Neuhaus was born in 1888 in Elizavetgrad (now Kirovograd) into a family of musicians. Both his father and mother were piano teachers. The father, Gustav Neuhaus, born in 1847 in the Rhineland, had studied under Ferdinand Hiller who, in turn, as a young man had known Beethoven. His mother, Olga Blumenfeld, was the sister of Felix Blumenfeld, a distinguished pianist, conductor and teacher, first in Petersburg, and then in Moscow; Horowitz was one of his most famous pupils. Through his maternal grandmother he was related to Karol Szymanowski who became a lifelong friend.

Since his parents could rarely spare the time to teach their son, Heinrich Neuhaus was, strictly speaking, self-taught, playing the piano and improvising passionately since early childhood. The main formative influence on his musical development came from Felix Blumenfeld, on his rare visits to his sister's home.

Heinrich Neuhaus made his first public appearance at the age of eleven, playing some Chopin Waltzes and an Impromptu. In 1902 he accompanied Misha Elman in a recital in Elizavetgrad. His first solo recital took place in Germany in 1904 and from then he gave several concerts in Germany and Italy while studying under Godowsky, first in Berlin and then in Vienna, from where he returned to Russia at the outbreak of the First World War.

In 1922 he began teaching at the Moscow Conservatoire and helped to create in 1932 the famous Moscow Central Music School for specially gifted children. From 1934 to 1937 he was Director of the Moscow Conservatoire, a post he relinquished so as to be able to devote himself entirely to teaching, for the sake of which he had already sacrificed most of his career as a concert pianist.

Amongst his pupils were Radu Lupu, Emil Gilels and Sviatoslav Richter who called him an artist of unique genius, a great teacher and friend. Seldom have artistic gifts been so closely matched by the qualities of selfless devotion, deep humanity, true culture and a great capacity for bestowing and winning friendship. He died on 10th October 1964. This book bears witness to his achievements as man, musician and teacher.

THE EDITOR

Preface to the Second Edition

I wrote my book a little at a time, in between my work (my work being teaching and concert playing) and before sending it off to the publisher I condensed what I had written so thoroughly that not more than half my original manuscript reached the printer. But now I do not feel the energy to rewrite or add to my book; let it come out in the "unpolished" state in which it first appeared.

At the beginning I did not give much thought to the publication of my notes. It was rather an unconstrained conversation with acquaintances and pupils; hence the discrepancy between the style of my book and what is usually expected from a work on methodology. But then I am not a theoretician and never shall be.

Several persons considered that I should not have made such frequent use of foreign words and expressions. They are probably right. All of this could have been said in Russian. The fault lies in the conversational style of these pages, for I have since my childhood known several languages and been accustomed to use certain expressions in one particular language; and in writing this book I put down my thoughts just as they came to me.

On page 124 I have definitely made a misstatement (beginning with the words "A few words more about octaves"). Here—may I be forgiven!—I simply prevaricated and I confess it freely. I prevaricated in the sense in which one poet uses the word, taking it to mean not an untruth, but rather a superfluous addition to truth. I can only explain this regrettable incident by the fact that I suffered so much from "sympathetic" fingers (the middle fingers which catch on the keys between the thumb and fifth finger when playing an octave) that I exaggerated the meaning of the "hoop" and in spite of my own practice, I misrepresented the position of the wrist which should be *slightly raised*. This is how all pianists play, including myself. My "prevarication" was due to a desire to avoid the cacophony caused by the middle fingers, but I overdid it and the result was a false statement. I beg the reader to take this correction into account.

One of the faults of my book is the insufficient number of examples and of the considerations and advice that they would have called forth. This is particularly true of the chapters on rhythm, tone, and even technique. I could have given hundreds of examples that could have been useful to learners. But the reader has doubtless noticed that I tried rather to prompt him to think further and independently and felt that this small book should and could only guide the reader's thinking.

Another fault of my book is that I have not indicated by a single word my attitude towards modern music, with the exception of some cursory references to Shostakovich, Prokofiev, Szymanowski and a few others. In our rapidly changing times it is very difficult to come to any final conclusions—even for oneself—that do not claim to be of general significance. My own perception of certain phenomena and my opinions of them are often contradictory. For instance, the phenomenon of dodecaphony and serial music often seems to me to resemble in its basic principles a complicated and interesting game of patience. For some moments this music can give me a certain particular kind of pleasure, but only for a few moments (for instance in Webern). Thinking of the weaker adepts of this trend I cannot help feeling that for them this is a means of inventing music (or rather something similar to music) although they have no talent nor even a musical ear. Thanks to generous patrons, propaganda and advertisements, they achieve a certain standing in the world which they would not have achieved otherwise. But the question of dodecaphony is closely related to many general problems of twentieth-century music; it is very complicated and to be quite honest still not quite clear to me.

Now a few more words about the way this book was written. I wrote it for about three weeks a year! Usually when I was on holiday. In winter when I was submerged by my teaching work and in addition gave recitals which I had to prepare, I had neither the time nor the inclination to put down on paper my views on the art of the piano, particularly since I spoke about it in some form or other all day and every day in class. Now the situation has changed. The trouble with my hand, the result of acute polyneuritis, is becoming increasingly serious and it is now two years since I have had to stop playing altogether. Even at home, for myself, I no longer play; I am too distressed by my helpless hand and after all one can read music with one's eyes, or listen to the radio or to records. To be quite honest I think that even teaching is now inadvisable for me and I am thinking of retiring very soon. To work with pianists only as a conductor, unable to demonstrate my intention and advice by showing what I mean on the piano, as I used to before, is really too upsetting and can satisfy neither me, nor (probably) my pupils. But having said good-bye to the piano (but not, of course, to music) and partly also to teaching, I do not feel very inclined to write about it. In my book I tried most of all (as in all my teaching work) to awaken a love of music. I do not know how far I have succeeded, but still I decided not to add anything substantial to my book and to allow the second edition to appear in the same "unpolished" state as the original, merely correcting a few mistakes. So much has been written on this subject that one book more or less does not really matter.

I shall end with a slightly amended version of the Latin saying: (*Non*) *feci quod potui, faciant meliora potentes* (I did (not do) what I could, let those who can do better).

Anyway I am preparing a new book and hope that it will be more "polished" than this one.[1]

H. NEUHAUS

[1] Heinrich Neuhaus died on 10th October 1964 before being able to carry out this intention.

THE ART OF PIANO PLAYING

In Lieu of a Preface

To begin with—a few simple statements which I shall develop later.

1. Before beginning to learn an instrument, the learner, whether a child, adolescent or adult, should already be spiritually in possession of some music; he should, so to speak, carry it in his mind, keep it in his heart and hear it with his mind's ear. The whole secret of talent and of genius is that in the case of a person so gifted, music lives a full life in his brain before he even touches a keyboard or draws a bow across the strings. That is why Mozart as a small child could "at once" play the piano and the violin.

2. Every performance—the problems of performance will be the main subject of these pages—consists of three fundamental elements: the work performed (the music), the performer and the instrument. Only a complete mastery of these three elements (and first of all, the music) can ensure a good artistic performance. The simplest example of the "triple" nature of performance is the performance of a piano composition by a solo pianist (or a sonata for violin solo, or cello solo, etc.). These simple things have to be said because in actual teaching there are very frequent cases where emphasis is channelled in some particular direction as a result of which one of the three elements is bound to suffer; but specially (and this is saddest of all) one sees that the content, i.e. the music itself (what we call, "the artistic image") is not given its due, attention being focussed mainly on the technical mastery of the instrument. Another error—true, much less frequent among instrumentalists—consists of underestimating the difficulty of completely mastering an instrument

in order to serve the cause of music[1]; this also inevitably leads to imperfect playing from the "musical" point of view, playing tainted by amateurism.

3. A few words about technique. The clearer the goal (the content, music, perfection of performance), the clearer the means of attaining it. This is an axiom and does not require proof. I shall have occasion to refer to it more than once. The "what" determines the "how", although in the long run the "how" determines the "what" (this is a dialectic law). My method of teaching, briefly, consists of ensuring that the player should as early as possible (after a preliminary acquaintance with the composition and mastering it, if only roughly) grasp what we call "the artistic image", that is: the content, meaning, the poetic substance, the essence of the music, and be able to understand thoroughly in terms of theory of music (naming it, explaining it), what it is he is dealing with. A clear understanding of this goal enables the player to strive for it, to attain it and embody it in his performance; and that is what "technique" is about.

Since in these pages there will be frequent references to the "content", as hierarchically the most important principle of performance, and since I foresee that the word "content" (or "artistic image" or "poetic sense", etc.) can with frequent use irritate the young pianist, I imagined a possible protest on his part: "Content, everlasting content! But if I can manage to play well all the double thirds, sixths and octaves and other technical difficulties in the Paganini-Brahms Variations without forgetting about the music, then I shall have 'content', but if I splash or play wrong notes there won't be any 'content'."

Quite right! Golden words! One wise writer[2] said about writers: "To perfect a style is to perfect ideas. Anyone who does not at once agree with this is past salvation." This is the true meaning of technique (style). I often tell my pupils that the word "technique" comes from the Greek word τεχνε and that τεχνε means art. Any improvement of technique is an improvement of art itself and consequently helps to reveal the "content", the hidden meaning; in other words it is the material, the real body

[1] In other words, the prevalence of musical development over technical and professional development.
[2] Nietzsche, ED.

of art. The trouble is that many who play the piano take the word "technique" to mean only velocity, evenness, bravura—sometimes meaning "flashing and bashing"—in other words, separate elements of technique and not *technique as a whole*, as it was understood by the Greeks and as any artist understands it. Technique = τεχνε is something infinitely more complex and difficult. Such qualities as velocity, precision and even faultless reading of the notes do not in themselves ensure an artistic performance which is achieved only by real, thorough and inspired work. That is why with very gifted people it is so difficult to draw a distinction between work at technique and work at music (even if they happen to repeat the same passage a hundred times). It is all one. The ancient truth: repetition is the mother of tuition, is a law for the weakest as well as the strongest talents; in this sense they are on an equal footing (although the results of their work will, of course, be different). It is well known that Liszt would sometimes repeat a particularly difficult bit over a hundred times. When Sviatoslav Richter played me Prokofiev's Ninth Sonata (dedicated to him) for the first time, I could not help noticing that one very difficult, polyphonic and very lively bit (in the third movement, some ten bars, not more) came off particularly well. He said to me: "I practised this bit without interruption for two hours". This is the right method for it gives splendid results. The pianist works at attaining the best possible result, without putting it off till some later occasion. Once, in talking with a pupil, a girl who worked rather languidly and wasted a lot of time, I used the following metaphor from daily life: suppose you want to boil a kettle of water. You have to put the kettle on the stove and not take it off until it boils. But you bring the water up to a temperature of about 40° or 50°C, then turn off the flame, do something else, then you remember the kettle—the water having cooled in the meanwhile—you begin all over again and so on several times until you are so fed up with the whole thing that you wait the time required for the kettle to boil. In this way, you lose a lot of time and lower considerably your "working vitality".

Mastery of the art of working, of learning compositions—which is one of the reliable criteria of a pianist's maturity—is characterized by an unwavering determination and an ability

not to waste time. The greater the part played in this process by
willpower (going straight to the goal) and concentration, the
better the result. The greater the passivity and inertia—the
greater the time needed for learning a composition, while
interest in it inevitably flags. All this is well known, but to
repeat it is not useless. (On technique, see Chapter IV as well as
many other pages in this book. We did agree that τεχνε is art.)

4. In order to speak and to be entitled to be heard it is
essential not only to know how to speak, but first of all to have
something to say. It is as simple as twice two makes four, yet it is
not difficult to show that hundreds and even thousands are
constantly guilty of breaking this rule.

A scholar[1] once said that in Greece everyone could speak well
and that in France everyone can write well. Yet the truly great
Greek orators and French writers can be counted on one's
fingers and in this case they are the ones we are interested in.
Anton Rubinstein used to say (not without a certain wistfulness)
that in our day "everyone" can play well. Well, why not? It is
by no means a bad thing; it is better that "everyone" should be
able to play well than to play badly. But Rubinstein's words,
with their wistful scepticism, have by no means lost their
meaning.

I have since my youth had a feeling which persists to this day:
every time I come in contact with a very great man, whether a
writer, poet, musician or painter, Tolstoy or Pushkin, Beethoven
or Michelangelo, I am convinced that for me the most important
thing is that this man is great, that through his art I see a man
of tremendous stature and that to some extent (in a way of
speaking) it is immaterial to me whether he expresses himself in
prose or poetry, in marble or sound. When I was about fifteen I
was sorry that Beethoven had not turned his music into
philosophy for I thought such philosophy would be better than
that of Kant or Hegel[2], more profound, more right, more
human.

I should like to tell here about one of my childish whims,
which coincided in time with the thoughts I have just described

---

[1] Nietzsche, ED.
[2] I need hardly say that at the time I knew very little about Kant
and specially about Hegel, whereas my knowledge of Beethoven was
fairly good.

(when I was about fifteen). Thinking about art and science, about their mutual relationship and contradictions, I came to the conclusion, for some reason or other, that mathematics and music are situated at the extreme poles of the human spirit, that these two antipodes limit and determine the whole spiritual and creative activity of man and that situated between them is everything that mankind has created in the field of science and art. I was so carried away by that thought that I began to write a "treatise" on the subject. I mention these childish thoughts because (I crave the reader's indulgence) it seems to me even now that mathematics and music are two poles of the human spirit and perhaps, if my life had been different, I would have continued to reflect and wonder on the subject.

In spite of the fact that this is merely a childish fancy, there is a particle of truth in it and I only mentioned it because now, with my tremendous teaching experience, I know too well how often even talented pupils, able to cope with their task, fail to realize with what tremendous manifestation of the human spirit they are dealing. Obviously this does not make for an artistic performance; in the best of cases they stagnate at the level of good workmanship.

I hope that in seeing such words as "great", "of tremendous stature", the reader will not suspect me of being a follower of Carlyle (*On Heroes, Hero-Worship and the Heroic in History*). The old theory of the hero and the crowd died, along with many past delusions. We know too well that the so-called great man is just as much of a product of his time as any other man but we also know that if such a "product" is called Pushkin or Mozart, he belongs to what is highest and most treasured among all our sinful earth has born. Moreover, there is in the whole world nothing more complex than this "product". It is more complex than the structure of the galaxies or of the atom's nucleus. In saying this, I want to emphasize the importance of impressing upon every pupil from the very beginning, just how precious is the stuff with which he will be dealing all his life if he really devotes himself to the service of art. I never fail to feel that I am in the presence of a miracle as I explain to my pupils the works of genius of the great musicians, and we strive together to the best of our abilities to fathom their depth, probe their mysteries, understand their structure and raise ourselves to their lofty

CHAPTER I

The Artistic Image of
a Musical Composition

I confess that this title arouses some doubt in my mind, in spite
of the fact that the conception it expresses is generally accepted
and that everyone takes these words to signify something
completely reasonable, understandable and real. But what is
"the artistic image of a musical composition" but music itself,
the living fabric of sound, musical language with its rules, its
component parts, which we call melody, harmony, polyphony,
etc., a specific formal structure, an emotional and poetic
content? How many times have I heard pupils who have had no
real musical or artistic schooling, i.e., no aesthetic education,
who are musically insufficiently developed, attempt to render
the compositions of great composers! Musical language was not
clear to them; instead of speech, they achieved only some sort of
muttering; instead of a clear idea—only some meagre fragments
of thought; instead of a strong emotion—some abortive pangs;
instead of profound logic—"effect without cause", and instead
of a poetic image—a prosaic shadow. And, of course, so-called
technique was consequently also inadequate.[1] This is the kind of

[1] On one occasion in my class, a pupil (who subsequently gave up
music and became an excellent engineer) played the last two
shattering "outcries" in Chopin's First Ballade in such a way that I
could not help saying to him: "This sounds just like a guard on an
underground station shouting 'Mind the doors!'."

playing you get if the artistic image is distorted, or is not at the core of the rendering, or is altogether absent.

Diametrically opposed, for instance, is the performance of Sviatoslav Richter. When sight-reading a piece for the first time—whether a piano composition, an opera, a symphony, anything—he immediately gives an almost perfect rendering, both from the point of view of content and from the point of view of technical skill (in this case, one and the same thing).

What is the point of this comparison? First, everything that has been said and written on the subject of the "image" (with the exception of certain things said by some very great men) has been mainly tailored to some general idea of an imaginary average learner, whereas we know from experience that those who study music (i.e. who have to work on the "artistic image") are real, flesh-and-blood people, representing every degree of talent from the mediocre to the genius, with hundreds and even thousands of variations and deviations one way or the other, depending on their personal ability. The conclusion is clear: in each particular case, work on the musical image will be different.

Secondly, the greater the musician, the greater his capacity to approach music like an open book, the less the problem which working on the image represents for him. For such as Richter, it is practically nil; in his case all the "work" amounts merely to "learning the piece". But, this is precisely the starting point of that tremendous work, the profound, passionate labour which in the lives of great artists is known as "the agony of creation". If the painter Vrubel[1] painted the head of his "Demon" forty times, it was precisely because he was a genius and not because he was ungifted.

I shall, of course, be asked why I speak of Richter, whose gift is unique, for we teachers, "methodologists", should have in mind the average, or even below average, person; we should not concern ourselves with such as Richter; his is the spontaneous, natural, gift. I emphatically reject such a point of view.

In so thinking, in lulling ourselves with words such as: talent, genius, natural gift, etc., we are avoiding the most burning problem of all, the problem which should be the primary concern of the searcher and teacher. I am convinced that a

[1] Russian painter 1856-1910, ED.

dialectically designed method and school must encompass all degrees of talent—from the musically deficient (since such, too, must study music, for music is a vehicle of culture just as any other) to the natural genius. If methodological thinking is concentrated on a small segment of reality ("the average"), then it is defective, it is impaired, undialectic, and consequently not valid. If one is a methodologist (and a methodologist must probe reality), then one has to be a methodologist to the end, encompassing the whole horizon, and not keep on running around in the vicious circle of some narrow system. Of course this is difficult; very difficult. Every great pianist-artist is, for the research-minded, something akin to an unsplit atom for the physicist. A lot of spiritual energy is needed, a lot of intelligence, sensitivity, talent and knowledge in order to fathom this complex nature. But that is precisely what methodology should deal with; then it will emerge from the nursery and finally stop arousing boredom in every true pianist and musician. All artistic methodology should be interesting and educational both for the teacher and the pupil, for the beginner and the accomplished performer, otherwise it can hardly be justified.

For the sake of convenience, I agree temporarily to ignore my doubts concerning the appropriateness of the expression "work on the artistic image" and accept it at its face value. Then let us agree on the following: work on the artistic image begins in the very first stages of studying music and learning to play an instrument. The best teachers in our music schools for children know full well that in teaching a child to read notes they must use the signs just learned by the pupil to make up a melody (not just a dry exercise), preferably a familiar one (this is a more convenient way of combining sight with hearing—the ear with the eye), and teach him to reproduce this melody on his instrument. Such elementary "music-making" is, of course, accompanied by the first simple exercise, the purpose of which is technical—to make the acquaintance of the piano; these are the first steps on the long road of getting to know an instrument and mastering it. I insist on the following dialectic triad: thesis, antithesis, synthesis: music is the thesis, the instrument is the antithesis and the synthesis is the performance.

Music lives within us, in our brain, in our consciousness, our emotions, our imagination; its "domicile" can be accurately established: it is our hearing. The instrument exists without us; it is a particle of the objective outside world and as such must be studied, must be mastered and made to comply with our inner world, and obey our creative will.

Work on the artistic image should begin at the very first stage of learning the piano and note reading.[1] By this I mean that if a child is able to reproduce some very simple melody, it is essential to make this first "performance" expressive, in other words, that the nature of the performance should correspond to the nature (the "content") of the melody; for this purpose, it is especially advisable to use folk tunes in which the emotional and poetic element is much more apparent than even in the best educational compositions for children. The child should be made, at the earliest possible stage, to play a sad melody sadly, a gay melody gaily, a solemn melody solemnly, etc. and should make his musical and artistic intention completely clear. Experienced teachers of children's schools report that children of average talent are much more enthusiastic in rendering folk tunes than the educational children's literature which is concerned with purely technical or "intellectual" problems (for instance: the playing of minims, crotchets, etc., rests, staccato, legato, etc.); such problems, which help to develop a child's fingers and brain, his effective "working" energy, and are consequently *absolutely essential and irreplaceable,* leave his feelings and imagination completely unaffected.[2]

Everything that I am saying here is as old as music and the study of music; it is known to all. I merely wish to highlight some of the aspects of this problem, and to dot the "i"s.

We all know that the development of the whole wealth and variety of pianistic skills, their accuracy and fineness, which are essential to a pianist for rendering the tremendously varied and

[1] Naturally, I do not mean that this should happen at the first lesson. An intelligent teacher will find the appropriate moment in each individual case. What is important is that it should happen as early as possible.

[2] Of course, besides folk tunes one should also use the simple melodies of Haydn, Mozart, Weber, Tchaikovsky, Glinka and others, to say nothing of the marvellous volumes of Schumann and Tchaikovsky specially meant for children and young persons who have reached a higher level of development; their content is purely artistic.

immeasurably rich piano literature can be achieved only by studying that same literature, that is, by means of real, living, specific works.[1]

When a child plays an exercise or study, a piece which is purely instructive and devoid of artistic content, he may, at will, play faster or slower, louder or more softly, with or without nuances; in other words, there is in his performance an inevitable element of uncertainty, an arbitrary quality; it will be "just playing" without any clear aim (playing for the sake of playing and not playing for the sake of music); it will be "playing as it comes" (and very often it doesn't "come"). In order that it should "come", in order to derive real use from this technical instrumental work (I mean work aimed at mastering the instrument and the player's movements), it is essential to set the pupil very clear aims and tasks and not to depart from them until they are fully met; for instance: to play the study or exercise at a given speed and none other; with given strength, and neither louder nor softer. If the aim of the study is to develop an even sound, then not a single accidental accent should be tolerated; similarly, not a single acceleration or slowing down. If they happen, they should be corrected immediately, etc. (It is assumed that an intelligent teacher will not set his pupil an impossible task.)

What happens when, instead of an educational exercise or study, the child plays a real musical composition, even though a very simple one? First (and that is the decisive moment in this work), his emotional state will be quite different; it will be heightened compared to when he is practising "useful" exercises or dry-as-dust studies. Secondly, it will be much easier to show him—since his own intuition will tend that way—the tone quality, the tempo, nuances, acceleration, etc. (if justified by the piece) and consequently the ways of playing that are required for performing the composition so as to make it clear, meaningful and expressive, i.e. in a manner *adequate to its content*.

This work, the work of the child on the musical-poetic content of a composition (i.e. on the artistic image and its

---

[1] Of course, any intelligent pianist, as he goes along, will evolve for himself special technical exercises to master the particular difficulties of the style, composer, or piece, he may be learning; this is the result of proper deductive thinking.

embodiment in sounds produced on a piano) will be the embryonic form of that type of work which I mentioned earlier in speaking of the work of a mature pianist—rich, determined, unwavering, directed at a specific aim and accurate and varied in its methods of approach.

I think that it is easy to guess my intention in repeating these well-known and perhaps even worn-out statements. I want to appeal to teachers to make unswervingly and directly for their goal, without delaying too much on the way. And that goal is the musical performance of musical literature, the embodiment in sound of the soundless printed note.

Here I should like to say a few words about Leopold Godowsky, the famous pianist.

Godowsky, my incomparable teacher and one of the great virtuoso pianists of the post-Rubinstein era once told us in class that he never practised scales (and, of course, that was so). Yet, he played them with a brilliance, evenness, speed and beauty of tone which I believe I have never heard excelled. He played the scales he encountered in musical compositions in the best possible manner and in this way learned to play ideally "scales as such".[1] A small, but significant detail.

What was Godowsky's method of teaching? As everybody knows, he was reported to be "a wizard of technique" (*ein Hexenmeister der Technik*, as he was dubbed unanimously by the German and indeed the world press). For this reason numerous young pianists from all over the world flocked to him, mainly in the hope of getting his recipe for attaining "virtuoso technique". Alas for them! Godowsky hardly ever said a word about technique in the sense in which these youngsters understood it; all his comments during a lesson were aimed exclusively at music, at correcting musical defects in a performance, at achieving maximum logic, accurate hearing, clarity, plasticity, through a scrupulous observance and a broad interpretation of the written score.

In his class, he valued above all the real musician and approached with obvious irony those pianists whose fingers were fast and agile while their brains were slow and dull (and there

---

[1] Please note: this is a case of deduction instead of the more usual and generally accepted—though much less reliable—induction consisting of first learning "the scale as such" and then playing it in a piece.

were several such in my time). He would immediately lose all
interest in a pupil whose hearing was inaccurate, who memorized
wrong notes or showed bad taste. Thus, he once "failed" at the
very first lesson a lady who was already a concert pianist merely
because, in the penultimate bar of Chopin's Etude op. 10 in
C major, she introduced a superfluous note (a major third) in a
chord of the left hand:

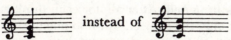

At Godowsky's repeated requests to play the right chord, she
couldn't understand what he wanted of her, shrugged her
shoulders and assured him that she was playing the chord
"without smudges". After the lesson in the corridor, Godowsky
asked me, with a devastatingly ironic smile what I thought of
"the famous pianist, Miss X". (As was to be expected, Miss X
turned out to be a rather feeble pianist, though with a very great
gift for hysteria.)

Godowsky's comments on the method of playing the piano
were usually a few bare words on *Gewichtsspiel* (weighty playing)
and *Vollständige Freiheit* (complete freedom). What need was
there of words? *Sapienti sap.* But two or three times he did
recommend some of his pupils to work at Clementi's Eighth
Etude (F major, edited by Tausig) in thirty-three different ways,
which he demonstrated briefly. Obviously, he assumed that
pupils who were interested not only in virtuoso technique in
general, but in his own (unheard of) achievement, would be
bound to know his arrangements, particularly his *50 Chopin-
Studien*, his fifty arrangements of Chopin études (some of which
are absolutely transcendental in their difficulty and incomparable for musical humour and inventiveness), arrangements in
which not only the musical score, but also the accompanying
comments amount tó an exhaustive school of modern virtuoso
technique—of course in the style of Godowsky.[1]

[1] Obviously, the famous arrangements of the Chopin Etudes are
on a much lower artistic level than the originals. The original works
of genius, these pianistic poems, these vehicles for learning music and
piano by every single means which their author modestly called
"études", Godowsky transformed into real studies, mere studies
thus depriving the term "étude" of the high poetic and artistic
content bestowed on it first by Chopin, then by Liszt, Scriabin,
Rachmaninov, Debussy. But just try playing Godowsky's studies. . . .

I repeat, that during the lesson Godowsky was not a teacher of piano, but first and foremost a *teacher of music*, or exactly what any real artist, musician, pianist, becomes the moment he begins to teach.

I think that everyone will understand why, in this context, I give a brief idea of Godowsky's method of teaching.

I hope I may not be accused of lack of modesty if I now say a few things about myself. After all, for each thinking individual, the self is not only the subject, but also one of the objects of his comprehension of the world around him, true, a somewhat particular object, which it is sometimes more difficult to approach "objectively" than any other object. But I should like to say a few words about myself in connection with the "work on the artistic image".

I was contaminated by music in my earliest years; the musical bacillus raged through both my father's and mother's families (both were music teachers, i.e. piano teachers in the provincial town of Elizavetgrad, now Kirovograd).

From childhood, earlier than I can remember, I heard music; and I heard an incredible amount of the worst possible music thanks to my parents' lessons (nine-tenths of their pupils were the most ordinary, musically ungifted children who studied music as they would any grammar book), whereas really good, first-class music I hardly heard at all. The "nutrient medium" for my abilities was more than meagre.

The greatest musical and family events were the visits of my uncle, Felix Blumenfeld, my mother's brother, who lived in Petersburg. I shall never forget how, as quite a small child, I would listen for whole evenings on end, late into the night (during his visits, we were allowed to go to bed very late) to his magnificent playing. He played a tremendous number of piano compositions, especially Chopin, Schumann, Liszt, his own compositions, Glazunov, Balakirev, Liadov; but most of all I was impressed at the time by some of the Wagner operas: *The Mastersingers, Tristan and Isolde, Siegfried*, which, to our great delight, he would sometimes play in their entirety in one evening.

Thanks to him, I heard for the first time *The Queen of Spades, Boris Godunov* and the operas of Rimsky-Korsakov. Of course, my sister and I had to play to him and we listened reverently to his observations. Happy, unforgettable days! Life seemed a holiday, and the feeling of happiness and joy did not leave us from morning till night.

But, alas, this happened no more than once every three or four years and lasted no more than two to three weeks. Then life went back to its everyday pattern and we had to fill the days and brighten them by our own efforts.

When I was eight or nine, I began to improvise on the piano, at first a little, then more and more, getting more and more worked up. Sometimes (this was somewhat later) I would be like one possessed: I was hardly awake when I would hear music inside me, *my* own music, and almost all day. But, for some reason, I concealed this (particularly from my father) and improvised on the piano only when my parents were out (later, they took pity on my sister and myself and we heard the pupils' tinkering less frequently, but we ourselves began practising more).

I remember as if it were yesterday that when I went for a lesson to my Uncle and Aunt Przyzykhowsky (who taught me mathematics, history, geography and French) I would sometimes literally choke with the music which filled my head: when I heard in my head some solemn "adagio", I would walk slowly and with an important air; when it changed to "allegro con fuoco" or "presto furioso", I rushed at a gallop through the empty streets while multi-coloured mongrels shot out of their yards like cannon balls and rushed after me barking fiercely. It was an unforgettably happy, exciting time which lasted, with all sorts of vicissitudes, of course, with unprecedented ups and downs (*himmelhoch jauchzend, zu Tode betrübt*[1]) till the age of about sixteen or seventeen, when I finally "locked the chest and threw the key into the sea", gave up my own music and devoted myself exclusively to that of others. There began a terrible crisis which lasted several years; a hard, aching period. It was as if I had fallen from heaven to earth and almost killed myself. I was very slow in recovering. Subsequently I took a complete course of theory and composition with Professor Paul F. Juon in Berlin.[2] He considered me gifted and insistently tried to persuade me to devote myself to composition, but I was true

[1] Quote from Goethe's drama *Egmont* (3rd Act, 2nd Scene), ED.
[2] A pupil of Taneyev and brother of the painter K. F. Juon.

to my decision the reasons for which I do not want to discuss here. It is amusing that when after a few lessons I brought him some of my compositions—complicated canons and fugues in contemporary style, a sonatina in classical style (well constructed from the point of view of form, but otherwise characterless, for I wrote rather as an exercise and not "on inspiration") and two or three songs and some small things for the piano, in addition to my school work, Juon listened to all this and said: "In actual fact, you know everything I could teach you. But if you like we could, by way of mental gymnastics, do some strict counterpoint; it is always useful." I agreed and for ten months without interruption I wrote, in addition to exercises, motets, madrigals, even a piece for twelve vocal parts in strict counterpoint on a Latin text.

As for the piano, I was left to my own devices practically from the age of twelve. As is frequently the case in teachers' families, our parents were so busy with their pupils (literally from morning until late at night) that they hardly had any time for their own children. And that, in spite of the fact that with the favourable prejudice common to all parents, they had a very high opinion of my gifts. (I myself had a much more sober attitude. I was always aware of a great many faults although at times I felt that I had in me something "not quite usual".) But I won't speak of this. As a pianist, I am known. My good and bad points are known and nobody can be interested in my "prehistoric period". I will only say that because of this early "independence" I did a lot of silly things which I could have easily avoided if I had been under the vigilant eye of an experienced and intelligent teacher for another three or four years.[1] I lacked what is known as a "school". I lacked discipline. But it is an ill wind that blows nobody any good; my enforced independence compelled me, though sometimes by very devious ways, to achieve a great deal on my own and even my failures and errors subsequently proved more than once to be useful and

[1] How much better off are modern children who study in children's music schools, particularly in the Central Music School! I could tell a long story on the subject! (Central Music Schools are affiliated to conservatoires; particularly gifted children, aged seven to eighteen, can receive there an integrated education in music and general subjects, ED.)

educational, and in an occupation such as learning to master an art, where if not all, then almost all depends on individuality, the only sound foundation will always be the knowledge gained as the result of personal effort and personal experience.

I wanted to give this autobiographic information—for which I hope the reader will forgive me!—precisely here, in the chapter dealing with the artistic image. I think that it will explain to the reader why I find it difficult to speak about working on the artistic image outside the general context of music and the pianist's work. Of course, as a professional, I frequently made this difference, particularly when I grew older and more conscious of what I was doing; as many another, I sometimes repeated for a long time not only some particularly difficult technical bits, but sometimes even the simplest phrase (for instance, out of a Chopin mazurka, or a Mozart sonata) in order to render its musical intent as clearly and eloquently as possible.

I described earlier the manner in which a truly great musician "acquaints himself" with a work. There, apparently, an instantaneous and subconscious process of "work at the artistic image" takes place; this is clearly shown by his performance. (To avoid confusion of concepts I should perhaps mention that one may frequently come across a pianist who is a "past master", who can sight-read without a single mistake or wrong note the most complicated composition, but his performance is apt to be of the most ordinary kind, even rotten. Such pianists should not be confused with Richter, whose most striking feature is precisely the excellence of his performance.) We have heard of Liszt's achievements; once, for instance, he played at sight (and played magnificently) Schumann's *Carnaval*[1] before an audience.

I give this instance of an "instant" mastery of music (and consequently of the artistic image) and could give many more, at will, from reliable reports about many great musicians, not in order to mention yet again their genius which is well known to

[1] There is no rose without a thorn. Clara Schumann says that Liszt played her husband's Quintet in their home so abominably that only her good manners prevented her from leaving the room in disgust. But we shouldn't forget that Clara was far from objective on the subject of the great Franz.

all, but to ask a question: what, in actual fact, happens? What lesson from the point of view of method, can we draw, from these real-life cases that might help the average pupil, and indeed all learners?

I believe that, in spite of the mysterious nature of the gift of "genius", it is possible not only to describe it, but also to study and analyse it. There is a widespread belief among the teachers of our profession that the average pupil should on no account imitate a great talent: *quod licet Jovi, non licet bovi*. Imitation, and particularly blind, unreasoned imitation (a fairly widespread phenomenon) is of course only harmful; but to *learn*[1] from someone who knows more is always useful. I think this is clear. Every teacher knows from experience that the stronger pupils "haul up" the weaker ones; this is a form of competition which comes about quietly and spontaneously but also—because of pride—consciously. Our methodological reasoning should help this process and not hamper it. And I consequently believe that from the point of view of teaching, not only is it not harmful (even in the case of a most mediocre pupil) but, on the contrary, it is extremely useful not to lose sight for a single moment of the summit to which musical talent attains and which—whether we want it or not—determines the development of music and musical life, including our own everyday educational efforts. In short, I believe (and I hope I may not be accused of unfounded optimism) that by attempting to the best of our ability to fathom the "mechanics" of the highest musical gift we shall always extract something useful that can be applied even to the most average pupil. And on the strength of this conviction which, incidentally, is purely intuitive I have never, in my teaching career, adapted a composition to the pupil, but always attempted to adapt the pupil to the composition, whatever efforts it may have cost the pupil, and also myself.

There lives in my mind, in my heart, a certain image of, let us say, Beethoven; I love him, I worship him, I experience him as a most significant event in my life. I feel and I know that he expressed something, that he created something which had never existed before him; I know within the limits of my ability that it has to be rendered in a certain way. Can I abandon this

[1] And this concept includes compliance, adaptability and hence a certain degree of imitation.

perfectly clear, perfectly real image? Can I agree to any kind of compromise, any concession to satisfy a weak pupil? Never. It would mean a lack of respect for myself and for the pupil. More than once my colleagues, hearing me teach, have hinted to me that I was being quixotic, that all the same it will never "come out" the way I want it. I replied to them: "My dear business-men, you want 100% profits, whereas I shall be overjoyed if I get 10%".[1]

Such is the inevitable "optimistic scepticism" of an experienced teacher. The sense and the usefulness of such work lies in the fact that, as anyone can see, the pupil is given a very clear, lofty and difficult objective (in the light of his possibilities and understanding) which in turn determines the direction and intensity of the work—the only way of achieving *development* and *growth*. And I am perfectly aware that these 10% sometimes yield a much richer crop than the 100% of "grammatical gloss" which, in spite of Mayakovsky[2] and myself, poor sinner, some people still value above all else.

And so, the lower the musical and artistic level of a pupil, i.e. the lower his intellect, imagination, ear (!), temperament, etc., as well as his purely technical abilities, the greater, the more complex the problem which work on the "artistic image" sets both him and his teacher; in other words, the harder it will be, even if he has a good technique, to get him to give a performance that satisfies musically, that is interesting, emotional, that holds the attention and carries away the listener, an interpretation that provides food for heart and intellect. And if that is lacking then to perform, to play for someone, is pointless. And this, incidentally, is what led Anton Rubinstein to lament: "Everyone knows how to play!" meaning: "Everyone knows how to play but only a few know how to perform." I am not speaking of such pianists as Rachmaninov. Even I, poor sinner, can grasp the substance of any composition at a first reading and the difference between this first acquaintance and a real performance after learning the piece is merely that "the spirit is clothed

---

[1] There is no contradiction with what I have said above. I can in no case lower my requirements—although I know full well that the results are sometimes vastly different.

[2] Russian poet 1893-1930; Neuhaus refers to his poem "100%" written in 1925, ED.

in flesh", that the image conjured up by imagination, emotion, inner hearing and aesthetic and intellectual understanding becomes a performance. I do not mean by this that work on a composition does not add anything to one's initial perception and intent; far from it. The relationship between these two events is the same as between a law and its implementation or between willing and carrying out. I only want to say that if there is no "law", no "will", there is no reality, no implementation. This is the crux, the nerve centre which the teacher, guide and educationist must try to influence; obviously, if the pupil is filled with this creative will the role of the teacher is merely that of counsellor, a sort of elder colleague. Sometimes it is even advisable to refrain entirely from interfering and to maintain a friendly neutrality.

The conclusion to be drawn from all these considerations is obvious: "work on the artistic image" can be successful only if it is the result of the pupil's continuous development musically, intellectually and artistically and consequently also pianistically; without this there can be no "implementation", no "embodiment". And that means developing his ear, giving him a broad knowledge of musical literature, making him live with one composer for a long time at a stretch, until he has thoroughly assimilated him (the pupil who knows five Beethoven sonatas is not the same man as the one who knows twenty-five sonatas; here quantity turns into quality); it means making him memorize music by reading the score without touching the piano, in order to develop his imagination and his ear; teaching him from childhood to distinguish the form, the thematic material and the harmonic and polyphonic structure of the composition he is performing (my own unwavering rule is that if a talented pupil, nine or ten years old, can play a Mozart or Beethoven sonata well, he should be able to tell, in words, a great deal that is substantive about what goes on in that sonata from the point of view of musical and theoretical analysis). It means using every means to arouse (if necessary, i.e. if this quality is not inherent to the pupil) his professional ambition: to be equal to the best; developing his imagination by the use of apt metaphor, poetic similes, by analogy with natural phenomena or events in life, particularly spiritual, emotional life. It means supplementing and interpreting musical language (but without, God forbid!, falling into banal "Illustrations"); using every means to develop in him a love of other forms of art, particularly poetry, painting and architecture, and, most important of all—making him feel (and the earlier the better) the ethical dignity of the artist, his obligations, his responsibilities and his rights.

Having read this chapter so far, the reader might perhaps ask: "Well, he hasn't said anything specific about working on the image after all". My reply is "Come to my class, sit with us a month or two and you will get such a helping of the 'specific' that it will last you a long time". In order to give these notes the desired specific quality, I should supplement them with numberless musical examples, detailed descriptions of the work done with the pupil or pupils on any particular composition (for sometimes I can sit with a pupil for one and a half to two hours over a single page of score; this usually happens at the beginning of my work with a pupil), but then this chapter would grow to the size of a thick volume. I cannot quote here even a small portion of the advice I give a pupil for learning and mastering a composition; such advice naturally comes before the artistic image. But I will mention two or three things I tell my pupils.

I suggest to the pupil that he should study a piano composition, i.e. the notes, as a conductor studies a score, that is, not only as a whole (this should be done first of all, otherwise there can be no complete idea of the composition, no complete image) but also in detail, taking the composition apart to see its component elements, the harmonic structure, the polyphonic structure; taking separately the main elements—for instance, the melodic line, the "secondary" elements—for instance, the accompaniment; to dwell particularly on the decisive "turnings" of a composition—such as (in the case of a sonata) the transition to the second subject or to the recapitulation or coda, in other words *on the main landmarks of the formal structure*, etc. Working in this way, the pupil discovers amazing things; there stands revealed to him a beauty not recognized at first but which abounds in the works of great composers. Moreover, he begins to understand that a composition that is beautiful as a whole is beautiful in every detail, that each such detail has a sense, a logic, an expressiveness, for it is an organic part of a whole. I recommend that much more effort should be devoted to such work than to the usual practising of the left and right hands separately, which I admit in certain special cases; (it is necessary just as "emergency exits" in a building are necessary in case of fire or some other trouble.)[1] If a composition has been learned, mastered, memorized, in fact if, as pupils call it, it "comes off", what is the particular work which remains to be done to give the performance a true artistic value? What must be done to make the performance emotionally moving, interesting, to make it reach the hearer? (I would remind the reader for the third or fourth time that some people can achieve this immediately, while others have to work hard to achieve it within the limits of their ability.) I know the answer will be: "it is a question of talent; some can and others can't, that's all there is to it". So long as I go on teaching I shall stop my ears so as not to hear this reply.

So what is it that the performer needs in order to "burn the hearts of men by his speech", to quote Pushkin's "Prophet", or if not to burn, at least to warm and move them somewhat?

Some say: patience and work; others—suffering and privations; others still—self-sacrifice and a great many other things besides. Everybody knows the importance for young artists of success—accidental or deserved recognition. All this is true, all this is inevitably part of the biography of a man who has something to say to others, but at this moment I am not looking so far ahead and I do not want to discuss "psychological problems".

Our purpose is modest, and at the same time vast; it is to play our amazing, our magnificent piano literature in such a way as to make the hearer like it, to make him love life still more, make his feelings more intense, his longings more acute and give greater depth to his understanding. . . .

Of course, everyone knows that teaching which sets itself such an objective ceases to be mere teaching and becomes education. Yet it is not always the kind of teaching one finds even among outstanding teachers. Amazing and inimitable as was Godowsky, yet with some pupils (particularly private pupils who paid in inverse ratio to their talent) he worked in a

[1] Of course, there are pupils whom I strongly urge to practise each hand separately—an "emergency exit" is there to be used—but only in addition to the work I have described above.

completely formal, not to say, formalistic manner. Frequently in the course of such a lesson Godowsky only wrote a few dynamic and tempo indications on the music, or indicated the fingering in a couple of cases, made a few comments that resembled prescriptions and set the work to be done for the next time. All this in a dispassionate, cold, businesslike manner. There was no attempt to see deeper into the heart and mind of the pupil, to alter him, to shake his tedious guts, to set before him some difficult emotional or musical problem; none of this. He showed neither joy, nor grief, neither anger nor approval; only at times when a pupil's playing was really too uninteresting or unintelligent, he would let fall a sarcastic remark or make a joke not devoid of venom. But his prestige and authority were such that the pupils accepted even such a lesson as something significant and precious. "He was great today!" exclaimed a delighted American after Godowsky had indicated the fingering on two notes and seen him to the door with a pleasant jocular remark.

True, at the *Meisterschüle* lessons which were attended by many people, including really talented pupils (eight to nine "players", i.e. real *Meisterschüler* and about twenty *Hospitanten* who were only entitled to be present but not to play), he was quite different. But I never noticed him attempting to "liberate the atomic energy" of a pupil or anything of the kind; apparently in his heart of hearts he did not greatly believe (and here we must admit a certain degree of wisdom) in the almightiness of teaching. And in spite of my boundless admiration for Godowsky, that great master, I believe that to teach as he sometimes did is no longer possible in our country nowadays. (I have in mind, of course, the teacher who is a great master musician, one who has received the gift of knowing.)[1]

I believe that the task of consolidating and developing the talent of a pupil, and not merely of teaching him to "play well", in other words, of making him more intelligent, more sensitive, more honest, more equitable, more steadfast (I won't go on!) is a real task which, if not fully attainable, is none the less dictated by the times we live in and by art itself, and is at all times dialectically justified.

[1] May my incomparable late teacher forgive me for criticizing him; the criticism is prompted not by me, but by our times.

In actual fact, I had already said all this when I spoke of the "10% profit" which I was willing to accept, but I wanted to make my meaning clearer. But, to come back to my question: is it possible (and, if so, how?) to make a pupil who "plays well" play like an artist, that is, make his playing infectious, make it reach his audience, make it "outstanding" (meaning, different from the average), etc.? I would reply: yes, it is possible; it is possible to a certain extent, it is possible at times to make him achieve exceptional results; let us recall Stanislavsky's excellent comment on actors who can be geniuses once in a blue moon— "surely better once in a blue moon than never at all!" How? By aiming not only at his intellectual but also at his emotional reactions.

Talent is passion plus intellect. The main error made by the majority of pedagogues, "methodologists in art" is that they understand only the intellectual aspect of artistic activity, or rather the process of reasoning which is part of it, and their reasoning and intellectual advice is aimed at influencing that side alone, while completely forgetting the other side, this inconvenient X, which they simply discard, not knowing what to do with it. That is why all methodology is (or at any rate, was, up to now) so empty, that is why it inevitably brings an ironic smile to the lips of the really well informed, those who are actively engaged in art.

One of the main demands I make for achieving beauty in a performance is for *simplicity* and *naturalness* in expression. These two small words, so well known and apparently so obvious, I ought to decode, for they are complex and their meaning is manifold. But this would again take up several pages, so I shall refrain in the hope that the reader will disentangle them himself and will feel their tremendous and decisive importance when they are put into effect.

All the work that is done in my class is centred, to the utmost of our ability, on music and its embodiment in piano playing, in other words, on the artistic image and on piano technique. That teacher is worthless—however clever he be—who is content to talk about "image", "content", "mood", "idea", "poetry" and fails to insist on the concrete, material embodiment of his sayings in tone, in phrase, nuance, and perfection of piano technique. Similarly worthless is the teacher who sees only the piano playing, piano technique, and has but a vague idea of the music, its sense and its structure.

To give at least some specific example of our work in class on the "artistic image" plus music, plus piano technique, I shall describe how I worked with a pupil studying Beethoven's Sonata quasi una Fantasia op. 27 in C sharp minor. One short page of Beethoven is amply sufficient to give the reader a clear picture of similar work in connection with any piano composition.

And so the pupil is playing the so-called "Moonlight" sonata.

Usually it is the second movement, Allegretto in D flat major, which gives rise to specially different views and the reason is obvious: the first movement, which is an expression of utmost sorrow, and the third, which is an expression of dispair (*disperato*) are more clearly defined, stronger in their shattering expression than the fleeting, "modest", refined and at the same time terribly simple, almost weightless Allegretto. In the rendering of insufficiently sensitive pupils the "comforting" (in the sense of consolation) mood of the second movement easily turns into a jolly scherzando, which is radically opposed to the sense of the composition. The cause of this is an excessively dry staccato:

Ex. 1

(and the same in similar places) and also excessively fast tempo.

I have heard such an interpretation dozens, if not hundreds, of times. In such cases I usually remind the pupil of Liszt's apt description, now famous, of this Allegretto: *une fleur entre deux abîmes* and attempt to show him that this image is not accidental,[1]

---

[1] After all, he could have said: a smile amidst a flood of tears or something similar.

that it renders with amazing accuracy not only the spirit, but also the form of the composition since the first bars of the melody:

Ex. 2

recall the opening of a flower, and the following bars (see mus. ex. 1) the leaves drooping on the stem.

Please remember that I never "illustrate" music, i.e. in the case in point I do not say that the music represents the flower; I say that it can create the spiritual and visual impression given by a flower, it can symbolize it, and call forth in imagination the image of a flower. Any music is that particular music only, A = A, by virtue of the fact that music is a complete language, a clear expression, that it has a definite immanent meaning and hence its perception and understanding do not need any additional explanations or interpretations in word or picture. Our understanding can be helped by a number of disciplines: theory of music, harmony, counterpoint, form analysis, and these disciplines are constantly developing and their ramifications increase as is the case for every type of knowledge which increases with every new matter learned. But we have in our brains a "photocell" (I think that everyone knows this miracle gadget) which can translate the phenomena of a given world of perception into another. After all, the curve traced on a film produces a sound! Surely the human spirit is not poorer or duller than the apparatus it has created! That is why for people who have the gift of creative imagination all music in its entirety is programme music (even the so-called pure music devoid of programme) and at the same time does not need any programme, since it expresses in its own language the whole of its content.

Such are the antinomies of our art.

Let us go back to the lesson. Sometimes Liszt's words—*une fleur entre deux abîmes*—would make me ponder over the role

of the flower in art. I would give pupils examples from architecture, sculpture and painting. I would show them musical
phrases and melodies in which the image of the flower could be
perceived through the nature of the music, as in the Beethoven
Allegretto. For the flower lives also in music as in other arts,
since it is not only the "experience" of the flower, its fragrance,
its enchanting poetic quality, but its whole form, its structure,
the flower as an image, as a phenomenon that cannot fail to be
expressed also in the tonal art, since that art gives expression
without exception to everything that man can experience, live
through, think and feel.

Many regard it as a paradox and even smile contemptuously
when I, as a musician, express my attitude to knowledge by
saying that everything that can be learned is musical.[1]

They argue: can it be said that Mendeleyev's[2] periodical
tables are musical? Of course, the periodical tables are a law of
chemistry, whereas a Beethoven sonata is music, the expression
of musical signs, $A = A$. But surely it is clear that the periodical
tables as a discovery, as a tremendous achievement of the
human mind, as a method of knowing nature (to which artists
are sometimes more closely bound than the scientists who probe
it) go far beyond the strict limits of chemistry and the musician
who has mastered them if he has an inclination for "associative
relationships", for thinking in broad analogies (without yielding
to the temptation of thoughtless amateur comparisons—which
is as in identical with "illustration")—such a musician will more
than once remember them, while probing the boundless laws of
his art (such, too, was my case when I was sixteen or seventeen).

But this is not all! The power of music over the human mind,
its omnipresence, would be unexplainable if it were not rooted
in the very nature of man. For everything that we do or think,
whether the most insignificant action or the most portentous,
whether it is buying potatoes in the market or studying
philosophy—everything is tinted by the colours of a subconscious spectrum, everything without exception is endowed
with emotional overtones which may even be undiscernible to

[1] Of course only in the case of people with a musical ear; this does
not apply to the rest.
[2] Russian chemist (1834-1907) who discovered the Periodic Law,
ED.

the protagonist but are unfailingly present and easily identified when such actions come under the scrutiny of a psychologist. This emotional quality (let us agree to call it the subconscious state of the spirit) is not absent even in the most reasoned, to all appearances unemotional, actions or thoughts. All the greater then, the emotional content, for any thinking musician, of any knowledge—whether philosophy, moral and political problems, pure science, natural science, etc., etc. It is not by accident that all outstanding musicians, composers and performers, have always been noted for their broad spiritual outlook, and have shown a very lively interest in all questions affecting the spiritual life of humanity. It is true that many great musicians have been so obsessed by their art that they had hardly the possibility (or the time!) to acquire a profound knowledge in other domains of spiritual life, but the potentials for acquiring such knowledge have always been within them. I recall the remarkable saying of Rachmaninov: "I am 85% a musician; there is only 15% man in me." (We shall come back to this later.) What the musician acquires in knowledge, he expresses in his compositions or his performance. And hence I am entitled to express the following paradox: all knowledge is musical (for a musician, of course). Or, more accurately (and more boringly), all knowledge is at the same time an experience. Consequently, like every experience, it belongs to the sphere of music and inevitably enters its orbit. The absence of such experience, and still more of any experience whatsoever, results in soulless, formalistic music and an empty, uninteresting performance.

Everything that is "indissoluble", inexpressible, untranslatable that lives in a man's soul, everything "subconscious" (frequently it is "supraconscious") is the domain of music. This is its source. (I cannot refrain from recalling Pasternak's wonderful words: "hearing is an organ of the soul"). That is why we can speak of the philosophical content of many compositions, particularly of Bach, Beethoven and others (I would recall Chopin's conversation with Delacroix about the possibilities of expressing philosophical thought in music).

More than once I had such conversations with my pupils in an attempt to penetrate as deeply as possible into the content of a composition and the natural desire to probe the limits of musical *expressivity*, and of everything within its reach.

But if I were to confine myself to these "pleasant conversations" in connection with some musical composition and with the pupils' faulty playing, then I think my proper place would be at the gatherings of the "Free Aesthetics" groups[1] and not in Class 29 of the Moscow Conservatoire where I teach. After such, or similar, conversations we begin our meticulous work on the composition, to overcome its technical difficulties, until we have achieved the desired result.

It goes without saying that the less developed the pupil, the more numerous the conversations and explanations of every sort and the more thorough and insistent the pianistic work. There were pupils to whom I would say two or three words about this Allegretto. But there was a case—and I remember it perfectly—when I spent three exhausting hours with a pupil on the Beethoven page described above. And even then we only managed to get beyond the front door, take off our raincoats and rubber shoes and put the wet umbrella in the stand.

I think this is sufficient to give the reader an idea of the way we work on the "artistic image" and on solving the pianistic problem in the laboratory which goes by the name of "Professor Neuhaus' class".

In conclusion I would say this: whoever is moved by music to the depths of his soul, and works on his instrument like one possessed, who loves music and his instrument with passion, will acquire virtuoso technique; he will be able to recreate the artistic image of the composition; he will be a performer.

[1] This was the name, before the Revolution, of an association which devoted its meetings to airing philosophical opinions on the arts.

CHAPTER II

A Word or Two About Rhythm

Am Anfang war der Rhythmus
("In the beginning there was rhythm")
Hans von Bülow

Music is a tonal process and being a process and not an instant, or an arrested state, it takes place in time. Hence a simple logical conclusion: these two elements, tone and time, are fundamental also for mastering music, for mastering its performance; they are decisive and determine all the rest.

A great deal, both good and bad, has been written about rhythm (this periodization of unlimited time, essential to music) and it is not my intention to explore in depth this extremely complex question. I merely want to say a word or two about rhythm in music as one of its most essential elements.

The rhythm of a musical composition is frequently—and not without reason—compared to the pulse of a living organism. Not to the swinging of a pendulum, or the ticking of a clock or the beat of a metronome (all this is metre, not rhythm), but to such phenomena as pulse, breathing, the waves of the sea, the swaying of a wheat field, etc.[1] In music, it is in a march that rhythm and metre are closest to each other, though never identical, just as the marching of soldiers comes closest to the mechanical, precise beat of metre, i.e. of equal segments of time.[2] The pulse of a healthy person is regular, but accelerates or decelerates under the stress of physical or psychological

[1] I take the concept of rhythm in its broad sense, i.e. as meaning an equal parcelling of time; metre I consider here to be a particular case of rhythm—its mechanical regularity.

[2] Also in compositions such as a *perpetuum mobile, toccata*, etc.

experience.[1] The same applies to music. But just as every healthy organism has a regular rhythmical pattern for its vital functions, which is close to metre, so, too, in performing a musical composition, rhythm should, in general, be nearer to metre than to arrhythmia, more like a healthy pulse than a seismographic record of an earthquake. One of the requirements of a "healthy" rhythm is that the total of accelerations and decelerations, and indeed of all rhythmic changes in general throughout the work, should be equal to a constant so that the arithmetic mean of the rhythm (i.e., the time needed to perform the work, divided by the unit of time, for instance, a crotchet) should also be constant and be equal to the basic metric duration. There is an interesting rhythmic analysis by S. S. Skrebkov of Scriabin's Poem op. 32 as performed by the composer; this shows that in spite of very real changes in tempo—rubato—the arithmetic mean (in this case the duration of a crotchet), remains completely identical to the initial metronome indication. I have frequently had occasion to tell my pupils when confronted by a rubato, that *rubare* is the Italian for stealing and if you steal time without returning it soon after, you are a thief; if you first accelerate the tempo, you must subsequently slow down; remain an honest man: restore balance and harmony.[2]

I must confess that for me a musical performance devoid of the rhythmic core (i.e., of the logic of time and of development in time) is just musical noise, so that for me the musical language becomes distorted beyond recognition and is, in fact, simply lost.

A sequence of uncoordinated moments and convulsive movement brings to mind the catastrophic nature of a seismographic record and not the majestic waves of a calm sea swayed by the wind. Of two evils, metric regularity or rhythmic performance, I prefer the former. But a performance that is real, living, artistic and felt is, of course, equally removed from either of these. The constant and unjustified acceleration and deceleration of some performers, their rubato (in quotation marks!) give

[1] To consider that rhythm equals metre is nonsense; an absolutely metrical pulse would be possible only in a corpse.
[2] Incidentally, rubato almost always means first an acceleration; passionato (especially in recitative) very frequently requires first a ritardando, followed by an accelerando.

an even greater impression of monotony and boredom than an excessively metric execution, although it is obvious that the performer is striving to give a varied, an "interesting" perform- ance. Here time (rhythm) avenges the crime committed against it, it "periodizes" the unrhythmic, convulsive performance and convulsion becomes chronic, constant, "regulated"; convulsion squared.

But how beautiful the real rubato of a great artist! This is the true kingdom of dialectic: the greater the pianist's awareness of the rhythmic structure, the more freely, the more logically does he depart from it at times and thus the greater the intensity with which he conveys its powerful regulatory force.

Remember Rachmaninov, Cortot and some of the others. I believe that rhythm, just as art as a whole, must be governed by harmony, concordance, joint submission and relationship, a supreme coordination of all the parts. But, what is harmony? It is, first of all, a sense of the whole. I consider harmonious the Parthenon, the Church of the Ascension in Kolomna, the monstrously fantastic Vassily Blazhennyi in Moscow, the incredible Doges' Palace in Venice, and disharmonious the house at 14-16 Tchkalov Street in which I live.

It is very difficult to speak of rhythmic harmony although it is extremely easy to feel it. It is irresistible. When it is achieved in a performance, it is felt by literally everyone. When I listen to Richter, very often my hand begins spontaneously to conduct.

The rhythmic element in his playing is so strong, the rhythm so logical, so organized, strict and free and is so much the result of his total conception of the work he is performing that it is impossible to resist the temptation to take part in it by gesture, although such participation is somewhat ridiculous and reminds one of Faust's *Du glaubst zu schieben und du wirst geschoben* (You think you push but you are being pushed). Strictness, co- ordination, discipline, harmony, sureness and mastery, this is the real freedom! With a performer such as Richter, two or three departures from strict rhythm are more effective, more expres- sive, more meaningful than hundreds of "rhythmic liberties" in a pianist in whom this feeling of harmony, this total concept is absent.

I will say a few words about the way in which we work at rhythm (the organization of time) in our class.

Whether this is good or bad I don't know, but when I want to show a pupil the proper rhythm, tempo and departure from tempo, such as a ritardando, accelerando, rubato, etc. I cannot refrain from conducting as if there were an orchestra in front of me. Sometimes a simple gesture, a wave of the arm can explain much better than words. Nor is this contrary to the nature of music, in which one is always conscious of latent movement, gesture (muscle work), a choreographic germ. I have already said that to my mind the word "pianist" includes the concept of "conductor". True, this conductor is concealed, but he is none the less the motive force. I urge pupils when studying a work and in order to master its most important aspect, the rhythmic structure, or the ordering of the time process, to do just what a conductor does with the score: to place the music on the desk and to conduct the work from beginning to end as if it were played by someone else, an imaginary pianist with the conductor trying to impress him with his will, his tempo first of all, plus, of course, all the details of the performance. This method which is particularly necessary in the case of pupils who have not the gift of organizing time, is also rational because it is an excellent way of dividing labour and makes it easier to master a composition. A pupil who has not completely grasped the tempo and rhythm of a composition as being its foundations,[1] often— because of technical difficulties or some other reasons—changes the tempo without any musical reasons (in other words he plays "what comes out" and not what he wants and thinks, or— most important of all—what the composer wants). Even such a virtuoso as Egon Petri when playing the "Faust" Waltz by Gounod arranged by Liszt (and in several other compositions) suddenly played the octave passages slower than the rest, although this was by no means due to the demands of the music, but merely to the fact that his octaves were weaker than the rest of his technique, a fact which he himself admitted. In that case he was demanding towards himself as a pianist (everything had to be played!) but not sufficiently demanding as a musician and artist.

In short, I recommend that in studying a composition the

[1] Let me recall! Bülow's saying which heads this chapter: "The musician's bible begins with the words 'In the beginning there was rhythm'."

organization of time be separated from the rest of the process of learning; it should be studied separately so as to enable the pupil to achieve with greater ease and confidence full concordance with the composer and with himself concerning rhythm, tempo and any departures from them or changes. I need hardly say that it is essential for that kind of work that the pupil should be able to hear the music in his head without hearing it physically. That is why it is better to carry out this experiment with music that is already familiar, i.e. that has already been played on the instrument and at least slightly practised.

This feeling for time is very apparent in some pianists, for instance when sight-reading four-hands. One who is only a pianist will, when faced with a difficulty, slow down, stop, correct himself, repeat; while the musician who feels that "everything flows" (Heraclitus) will rather leave out some detail, omit playing something but will never stop, will never lose the rhythm, or lose his place. (It should be said, incidentally, that practice plays an enormous part in this: good sight-reading is something that is acquired and requires not only talent but also exercise and experience. The decisive factor is, of course, interest in and love of music.)

Here some frequent and hence typical mistakes in rhythm and metre must be mentioned which lead me to believe that there must be some metres and rhythms that are more difficult than others. Of course, it is more correct to consider all the mistakes which follow as metrical, but since the concept "metre" is merely a particular instance of the concept "rhythm" I think we could perhaps use it in order to conform with the generally accepted musical jargon.

1. All teachers and all conductors, too, are well aware how difficult it is sometimes for a performer to render accurately the rhythmic figure $\frac{9}{8}$ ♩. ♫ ♩ ; typical examples are the last number of the "Kreisleriana", the fifth variation in the Etudes Symphoniques by Schumann, the first movement of Beethoven's Seventh Symphony, etc. In a fast tempo this figure tends to become a simple $\frac{2}{8}$ ♫ ♩ or ♫. ♫ ♩.

Even such a wonderful pianist as Cortot played the last number of the "Kreisleriana" quite frankly in 2/4 instead of 6/8.

Perhaps this was intentional? Personally I cannot admit that a three-part rhythm should be changed into a two-part rhythm.[1]

Those who want to hear an ideal rendering of this rhythm should listen to a recording of Beethoven's Seventh Symphony conducted by Toscanini.

If a pupil just cannot get this rhythmical figure right, which is especially difficult in a fast tempo, I recommend making use once more of the method of exaggeration—this time rhythmically and not dynamically—dwelling longer on the first beat as if it had a small fermata 𝄐♩♩♩ and also play it several times perfectly regularly, in order to grasp better its three-beat character. It is also a good idea to play simply ♩ ♩ ♩ | ♫♫ leaving out the semiquaver (or quaver if it is in 3/4) ♩ ♩ | ♩ ♪ then playing ♩ ♪ | ♩ ♪ deliberately turning the semi-quaver (or quaver) into a grace note (another exaggeration).

I hope the reader will not think that I am splitting hairs; I swear that I have had to do this sort of exercise with some of my pupils and the results were positive. I deliberately dwelt at length on this small rhythmic detail.

The method I have described can be adapted to any rhythmical problem that may arise (for instance in the first movement of Tchaikovsky's Fourth Symphony).

A figure which is closely related to ♩.♪♪ is ♫♩.♪ (a characteristic example is the continuation of the secondary subject in the first movement of Chopin's Sonata in B minor).

Pupils very frequently play it as ♫♪ in other words

---

[1] A memorable instance from my own experience. I was playing Beethoven's Fifth Piano Concerto with a rather indifferent orchestra. In the last movement, the bassoon simply could not play the figure

⁶⁄₈ ♪ | ♩.♫♩ ♪ | ♩.♫♩ ♩ correctly. He played not

♩.♫ but worse still ♫♫ ♩ etc. So I sang for him several times "Klem—perer, Klem—perer" and "Ams—terdam" on these notes, with a very energetic accent on the first syllable (a well-known method used by conductors) and he got it right. Of course, I also played it on the piano.

again turning a three-beat rhythm into a two-beat with
syncopation. There the temptation is particularly great because
of the quadruplet figure (four semiquavers) in the left hand.
Again, it is sufficient to remember and feel that in a three-beat
figure the accent is always on the first beat (not taking into
account exceptions such as the mazurka, etc.) and to play
first simply ♩♩♩ , then[1] ♩♩. and it is bound to
come out right. As in the case of "Klemperer", here, too, I
sometimes use words to help the pupil and make him sing an
appropriate word; like beautiful or idiot (never beautiful or
idiot). Incidentally from an educational point of view, the
second word is particularly effective.

2. Among the more primitive metrical mistakes is that of
sometimes turning the figure ♩. ♪ into ♩ ♪ ♩ ♪ or a
two-beat figure into a three-beat figure.

Some thirty years ago I heard a certain student in the
Moscow Conservatoire play the Funeral March from Chopin's
Sonata in B flat minor as follows:

Ex. 3

instead of

Ex. 4

[1] Incidentally, here the accent on the first quaver is more agogic
than dynamic (>, but not ∧).

unaware that he was turning a majestic funeral procession into a tedious waltz.[1]

This three-beat temptation sometimes assails pupils when performing the Largo from Chopin's B minor Sonata (first subject): instead of a "march for the gods", instead of an Apollo leading the Muses one thinks of a very dreary young lady looking out of the window at a very dreary street and humming a very dreary ballad. (I may be exaggerating but only slightly. There are cases where rhythm determines everything.) There is no need to speak of remedies; they are obvious.

3. Yet another example of inaccuracy which is widespread and which, in actual fact, is only indirectly related to rhythm. It is well known that immature pupils very often increase the tempo when increasing the volume of tone, and in decreasing the volume they slow down. With them crescendo equals accelerando and diminuendo, ritardando. It is essential to get the pupil to separate them in his mind and in his actions. Crescendo: the sound approaches, comes nearer, grows; with a diminuendo, it becomes more distant, decreases, dies off.

In actual music there are as many cases of "crescendo ma non accelerando" as of the contrary: "crescendo ed accelerando". In most cases composers indicate this clearly but sometimes it is only implied, and since the meaning is entirely different one has to be particularly careful not to make a mistake.

Just as frequent, obviously, are the cases when a change of volume must not be accompanied by a change of tempo, and *vice versa*. The concepts of morendo, smorzando, etc., are in many cases contrary to the concept of ritardando or rallentando; yet pupils are fond of mixing the two.

I write of all this here, in the chapter on rhythm, because the deeper a performer's awareness of the time structure, the

[1] To make the picture complete the left hand should have been changed to:

Ex. 5

"flowing architecture" of a work, the more rarely will he make a mistake of this nature.

4. Changes of tempo are subject to certain laws that are well known to good conductors but of which pupils are frequently unaware. For instance, no gradual change of tempo (ritardando, accelerando) or of volume (crescendo, diminuendo) can begin at the beginning of a phrase or bar; it must begin somewhat later and preferably on a weak beat. Disregard of this rule turns a ritardando into a "meno mosso", and an accelerando into a "più mosso"; the gradual effect ("poco a poco") becomes sudden (súbito). It is particularly difficult to avoid this pernicious suddenness when the ritardando or accelerando applies to a very small segment of music or time. In the course of my teaching life I have put a lot of work into making pupils render correctly certain short phrases as, for instance, at the end of Chopin's First Ballade in G minor:

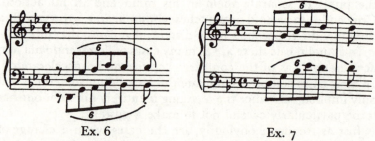

Ex. 6   Ex. 7

This tragic cry which precedes the final catastrophe, the collapse and the destruction, is almost comic if played presto instead of accelerando (this is the second time I mention this sad case). In actual fact, this short segment must encompass a ritardando, accelerando, più accelerando. I am sure there is no need to show that the emotional content and significance of a gradual or a sudden effect is entirely different and hence that to confuse them is to allow a serious musical fault.

5. The fermata, too, requires attention: it is frequently misinterpreted. It is easiest to determine the duration of a fermata after a ritenuto, mentally continuing the slowing down on the notes held by the fermata, in other words without increasing the duration indicated (and without continuing to count units of

time, e.g. crotchets, in the fundamental tempo of the composition which preceded the slowing down). The fermata is thus the
logical culmination of the ritenuto and "piú ritenuto" ("ancora
piú ritenuto": a geometric progression) which led to it and
is made to last to the ultimate moment of audibility of the note
or chord in question. This is only one kind of fermata. A
fermata which occurs suddenly without a previous retarding or
acceleration should be counted in the fundamental normal
tempo and the value of the note under the fermata should be
doubled, trebled or even increased fourfold according to need.
Incidentally, it is extremely important to distinguish at what
particular structural point in the composition the fermata
occurs; whether at an important or less important turning point,
i.e. whether it coincides with a basic or secondary section of
form. Example: Beethoven's Seventh Sonata op. 10 no. 3 in
D major: in the first movement I suggest that the first two
fermate should be only doubled—before the bridge—whereas
the fermata at the end of the development, which is on a
dominant seventh (first inversion) before the recapitulation
should be held four bars, i.e. four times longer than written,
although the composer has put notes of the same duration under
each of these fermate. This is a requirement of form and
structure. In the last movement of the same sonata, it is best to
render the fermata in the fourth bar thus:

Ex. 8

(As you see, this case contradicts the rule I mentioned above
concerning the fermata after a ritardando.)

I recommend to those interested to seek out several similar as
well as different fermate and to determine their accurate
duration in each case.

Not only the fermata but also pauses between the movements of a composition in several parts are far from unimportant for the "logic of musical time". Every teacher who has seen a thing or two in his time will remember the pupil who plays in public and who, either from stage fright or a businesslike approach begins the second movement—a sombre adagio—when the sounds of the first jolly allegro have hardly died away. Thus, entirely different and perhaps even contradictory moods and emotions knock into each other as a result of such haste. Or on the contrary, the performer seems to go into a very long brown study; the pause between movements becomes an interval; you can smoke a cigarette or talk to the friend next to you. My advice to pupils: silence, pauses, etc., should be heard; they, too, are music. The act of listening to music should not be interrupted for a single second. Then everything will be convincing and true. It is also useful to "conduct" such pauses mentally.

6. I am often forced to repeat a well-known truth to my pupils; a performance can be good only when all the infinite variety of means available to the performer are made to concord fully with the work performed, with its meaning, its content, and first and foremost with its formal structure, its architecture, its actual *composition*, with that specific organized tonal material which we are to turn into a performance. Someone once said to me of an extremely egocentric performer: "He puts so much of himself into the music". "Quite right", I said, "and takes so much of what the composer put in out of it." However right Busoni's statement that "every performance is already a transcription", a transcription (just as a translation) can be extremely close to the original, it can be "good"—or it can be very far removed from the original and be "bad". One of the most popular mottoes adopted in my class is: "Long live individuality! Down with individualism!"

The most pernicious departures from a composer's text and intentions are caused by a "rethinking" (it would be more correct to call it "unthinking") of the fundamental content of the work and a distortion of its time structure. The mistakes made by a musician performer in the organization of time are akin to the mistakes of an architect in solving problems of space in architecture. It is obvious to anyone that these are *cardinal* mistakes.

7. There are conductors and pianists who find it difficult to set the correct basic tempo from the start. An irresolute or mistaken tempo at the start may leave its mark on the whole performance. Sometimes the tempo evens out, and finds its proper channel, but the unity of the performance has already been destroyed. This is an evil difficult to overcome. But it is not impossible. The much despised metronome may be of help. It is a good thing to experiment during work, and by means of repeated changes and departures from the starting tempo, to establish its extreme limits from the slowest possible to the fastest. Before beginning the performance it is useful to compare mentally the starting tempo with some part of the work nearer the development. It is particularly important—and I frequently give this advice to my pupils—before beginning some broad adagio or largo (where for some reason or other such mistakes are particularly apt to occur), to sing mentally the opening in the tempo which is considered as the most suitable and correct, in order to get into the proper rhythmic mood before beginning the performance. This method considerably reduces the elements of chance and approximation in establishing the starting tempo.

But there is no point in concealing the fact that the main reason for this lack of precision as far as tempo is concerned is due, roughly speaking, to an artistic inadequacy in the performer, an insufficient receptivity to the mood, intent and emotional content of the music. Hence the teacher must, in this as in all "serious" cases in general, resort to panacea: he must arouse the spiritual qualities of the pupil, he must stir his imagination, his impressionability, he must make him feel, think and experience art as the most real, most unquestionable *ens entium*, the very substance of life.

8. Complete mastery of polyrhythmia is as complex as the full mastery of polyphony. In one case—time, in the other—tone; the difficulties are similar. I could quote an enormous list of various instances of polyrhythmia which represent exceptional difficulties for learners. I shall confine myself to a few examples and a few recommendations which I believe to be useful. It is obvious that only the most simple examples of polyrhythmia

admit of an arithmetic approach, as for instance 2 against 3. The common denominator of the fractions 1/2 and 1/3 is 6. It is easy for those who cannot get it immediately to calculate precisely when a note should be played. But for the next problem—that of playing correctly 3 against 4 and getting the precise duration for each 1/3 and each 1/4 the arithmetic approach is already unsuitable. After all, you are not going to take the common denominator 12 and calculate that each note of the quadruplet falls on 1, 4, 7, 10 and each note of the triplet falls on 1, 5, 9. It is inconvenient, clumsy and silly.[1]

The complete unsuitability of the arithmetic method becomes immediately obvious in cases when you have to play simultaneously and evenly, in the same unit of time, 11 against 7, 5 against 9, 17 against 4, etc. And such examples abound, particularly in Scriabin. Even the case of 3 against 5, so frequently met in Liadov and Scriabin, makes it impossible to use the common denominator. If the pupil finds such simple examples of polyrhythmia difficult, I usually advise him to play the right hand and the left hand alternately (twice or several times each); for instance, if we take the Scriabin Etude op. 8 No. 4:

Ex. 9a

[1] I can remember only one case when such a calculation is warranted: it is the first subject of the second movement of Rachmaninov's Second Concerto:

Ex. 9

The common denominator 12 in the quaver triplets will help a not too bright pupil to solve the rhythmic problem.

In so doing the duration of the crotchet should be mathematically exact, as also the divisions within the crotchet, into triplets in one case, into quintuplets in the other. And so on in every similar case.

I know from experience that when playing the Chopin Sonata in B flat minor (development of first movement) 90 % of the pupils play not as it is written, in other words, four crotchets in the right hand and six in the left hand,

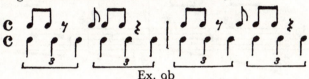

Ex. 9b

but simply

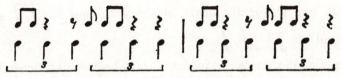

Ex. 9c

This is "more convenient", the rhythm in the right hand coincides with the rhythm in the left (6/4 and 6/4). There is no need to think of a difficult combination of four crotchets and six crotchets, everything goes smoothly and the composer's text is mauled about and the rhythm distorted. I know from experience that in studying this piece the method I have just indicated is a sure means of giving a rhythmically precise and correct rendering. But in this case, I would recommend playing two bars with the left hand and two bars with the right, repeating this many times and mentally conducting this *alla breve*, 2/2. With this method, even the clumsiest (rhythmically speaking) pupil will overcome this difficulty.

If the polyrhythmic figure is written for one hand only (which is much rarer), I recommend playing each voice separately in the way just indicated, for instance the right-hand duet in Chopin's Nocturne in E flat major, op. 55, which represents a complete fusion of polyphonic and polyrhythmic difficulties.[1]

[1] It is obvious that the first method I indicated, namely the arithmetic method, which is suitable only for the simplest cases of polyrhythmia is a method of reasoning and analysis, while the second method is one of wisdom and synthesis.

9. Frequently, passages that are not difficult rhythmically are distorted by pianists because of their technical, "acrobatic" difficulty. For instance, the following passage from Liszt's "Mephisto" Waltz:

Ex. 10

What one frequently hears in the left hand is:

instead of: ♩ ♫ ♪.

It is enough to note this inaccuracy, to hear it, in order to find the means of remedying it. One of them, though not the best, is the following variant:

Ex. 11

The reason for this inaccuracy is understandable: it is the difficulty of two almost simultaneous leaps: the right hand upwards from left to right, the left hand downwards from right to left.

10. Hundreds and hundreds of times have I heard pupils perpetrate a rhythmic inaccuracy which consists of playing a slow broad melody or theme, especially in Bach, in such a way that any shorter metrical units that it contains (for instance quavers and semiquavers in a melody made up generally of crotchets and mimims) are suddenly played in a hurried way,

faster than the others. How many times have I had to hear and correct the following:

J. S. Bach, Fugue in B flat minor

Ex. 12

J. S. Bach, Fugue in G sharp minor

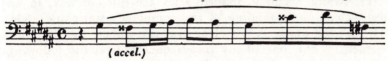

Ex. 13

J. S. Bach, Fugue in D sharp minor

Ex. 14

These dear little accelerations of quavers and semiquavers in slow tempo have been the cause of much damage to my liver throughout the long years of my teaching career.

The cause of this mistake, which is so widespread among pupils of average level, is to be found first of all in the inability to listen to the singing of the piano in faster motion; secondly, in the fact that the sight of "long" notes arouses in the pupil a conditioned reflex: "slowly"; whereas, the sight of shorter notes arouse the reflex "faster", to which he indiscriminately succumbs.

In such cases I insist that the shorter notes be played especially deliberately as if it were difficult to part from each sound; my antidote is the following rendering:

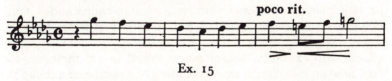

Ex. 15

Moreover, I urge my pupils to listen to good singers, violinists, cellists who have a perfect mastery of cantilena and know how to extract the full cantabile quality out of short notes and are consequently more inclined to slow down over them, than to hurry.[1]

I wrote the whole of this section mainly because I wanted to show how inextricably tone is bound up with rhythm and how a mistake in tone quality can result in a mistake in rhythm. Again and again: everything is part of the same entity.

11. Many rhythmic inadequacies are due, in fact, to an insufficient understanding of the composer's spirit and style. The artistic image is not clear and this affects the rhythmic element. Thus, one of my pupils once played the following passage from Liszt's Twelfth Rhapsody:

dolce con grazia

Ex. 16

so evenly, metrically, with such careful accents on the first semiquaver of each phrase group that the result was a series of typical Bach trochee:

Ex. 16a

I suddenly saw, in my mind's eye, Liszt, the rhapsodist of Hungarian folklore, wearing Bach's wig and dressed as the eighteenth-century organist of the Leipzig Church. The same girl played the C sharp minor Prelude out of the First Book of the *Wohltemperiertes Klavier* with such elegiac rallentandos and such excessively tender expression that instead of Bach, I saw a provincial lady playing a tear-jerking ballad.

I cite this example, one of many stored in my memory, to show how an insufficient understanding of a composer's thought

[1] Remember the rendering of Rachmaninov's "Vocalise" by Nezhdanova. (Famous operatic soprano, ED.)

or of the style of an era, can have an adverse effect on the main elements of music: tone and rhythm.

12. When a big cyclic work has not been felt and thought out as one single whole, the performer inevitably falls into errors of tempo and rhythm. In my own experience as a teacher, a particularly prominent place in this respect is held by two popular Beethoven sonatas, op. 57 ("Appassionata") and op. 53 ("Waldstein").

Almost always the first movement of the "Appassionata" is played with excessive agitation and much too fast in relation to the Finale, and the Finale (Rondo) of the "Waldstein" is usually played too fast in relation to the first movement. The result is a certain sameness of mood and character,[1] whereas the general pattern of the two sonatas is by no means A—B—A, but A—B—C, which together give a certain D. After all, with all its passion, the first movement of the "Appassionata" is first of all majestic and grandiose, while the Finale is a whirlwind of passion, a hurricane, a tidal wave, with, above it, a passionate, pathetic voice.

In the "Waldstein", the Rondo ("allegretto moderato") is a rosefingered dawn; gradually the sun rises, the dew disappears, and a beautiful day is born. . . . Is it possible to play this music with the businesslike animation with which I have too often been regaled by eager youngsters? Particularly since the composer has clearly indicated: "allegretto moderato", in other words almost an Andante, but on no account, God help us! an Allegro or, worse still, "allegro vivace". But the final Presto should be played "prestissimo possibile", *so schnell wie möglich und schneller* (as fast as possible and still faster) to use Schumann's terminology, otherwise there won't be any popular holiday, the Bacchanalia will have flopped! Yet some pupils, in spite of Beethoven's indications, or to spite him, play the Allegretto faster than necessary and the final Prestissimo slower than necessary. The result is that this poetic Finale, this superlative work of genius, is made to sound like an exercise.

In such pieces as, for instance, Chopin's First Scherzo in B minor or his Fantasie in F minor, I have frequently had to point

[1] Not of the music itself, of course, which is quite different in the extreme movements, but its performance.

out that the threefold occurrence of the main subject loses its
meaning if rendered according to the pattern A—A—A. Anyone who feels and understands the whole will, without a doubt,
render it as A—A1—A2. It is even better to show it as A →
A1 →A2, particularly in the First Scherzo. In the Fantasie, I
personally imagine the pattern according to the graph:

$$\boxed{\begin{array}{c} A \quad A_2 \\ {\scriptstyle\searchly}A_1{\scriptstyle\nearrow} \end{array}}$$

Of course, I am now referring to the pattern of the performance,
in other words, the emotional, expressive rendering in accordance with the structural pattern of the composition.

13. I have in my time known excellent virtuosi pianists who
had marvellous hands, but did not have what we term a feeling
of entity and who were consequently incapable of playing a
single big work (Beethoven or Chopin sonatas, or a single
concerto) satisfactorily from the point of view of form. In their
rendering any big composition is split into a number of more
or less enchanting moments—whereas trifles, such as waltzes,
études, preludes, nocturnes (particularly trifles by other than
front-rank composers, for instance Saint-Saëns, or Moszkowski,
etc.) were dazzling and left nothing more to be desired.[1]
  Roughly speaking, the more intelligent the pianist, the better
he can manage a large-scale composition, and the more stupid
he is—the less well he can manage it. In the first case it is
perspective thinking—i.e. horizontally; in the second case it is
short-term thinking—i.e. vertically. That is why I so much
admire the rhythm of Richter's performances: one feels clearly
that the whole work, even if it is of gigantic proportions, lies
before him like an immense landscape, revealed to the eye at a
single glance and in all its details from the eagle's flight, from a
tremendous height and at an incredible speed. I ought to say
once and for all that such unity, such structure, such a wide
musical and artistic horizon as his I have never encountered in
any of the pianists I have known, and I have heard all the great
ones: Hofmann, Busoni, Godowsky, Carreño, Rosenthal,

---

[1] A typical example was Vladimir Pachmann who was a famous
pianist in his time.

d'Albert, Sauer, Essipova, Sapelnikov, Medtner and a lot of
others (I am not speaking of the younger generation). Unfortunately, there are two that I have not heard but whom I
would probably have loved more than any others; they are
Rachmaninov and Scriabin.[1]

I did not write this to praise Richter (there are pianists whom
I like almost as much), but in order to focus attention on the
great problem of performance, namely Time-Rhythm, with
capital letters, where the unit for measuring the rhythm of the
music is not the bar, the phrase, the period or the movement,
but the composition as a whole, where the musical work and its
rhythm are almost identical.

There is an apocryphal letter of some alleged acquaintance of
Mozart which tells that Mozart was asked how he composed
and what he replied. I will only quote the most important part.
Mozart said that sometimes, when composing a symphony in
his head, he became more and more elated and finally reached
such a state that it seemed to him that he could hear the whole
of his symphony from beginning to end at once, simultaneously,
in a single instant! (It is before him like an apple in the hollow
of his hand.) He then added that such moments were the
happiest in his life for which he was prepared daily to thank his
Maker.

I read this saying of Mozart for the first time when I was
about twelve or thirteen years old, in an old and very thick
German book of anecdotes about great composers and their
sayings. Even then, Mozart's words made an unforgettable
impression on me and you can imagine my amazement and
delight when quite unexpectedly some twenty or thirty years
ago, I read in a volume of *De Musica*[2] the profound and
detailed considerations of I. Glebov (Boris Asafiev[3]) on the
subject of this apocryphal, uncertified letter, which is nowhere
to be found. To Glebov and to me it was clear that such a
statement could not be invented, that it is founded on truth, the
Mozartian truth which does not contradict the image of Mozart

[1] I know them only from records.
[2] Title of collection of essays edited by Asafiev Calias Glebor
published in 1923 and also of *Yearbook* published in Leningrad in
1925, 1926 and 1927, ED.
[3] 1884-1950; most outstanding Russian music critic and author of
books on Russian music and composers, ED.

that we have evolved on the strength of his work and his life, but which confirms it and is in complete harmony with it. For anyone who knows anything at all about the psychology of the creative process, what Mozart said here is an example of the highest gift of the human spirit, that gift which defies words and before which we can only bend our heads in wonder and adoration.

Speaking of Mozart's apocryphal letter, my thoughts, as usual, crowd each other out and this is where I should like to write about musical time, rhythm, the creative process, etc., but this would take me too far afield. I mentioned Mozart's apocryphal letter because it can help the pianist in his main problem, namely, grasping the work as an entity and in ordering the time process.

14. I could conclude here but I should like to add a few small observations, purely as a teacher, and offer some advice on the subject of rhythm. Among some teachers, the view is very widespread that many even passages in pieces should be practised with all sorts of rhythmic changes. For instance, if a passage is written in even semiquavers, it should be practised as

Ex. 16b

or in some similar manner.

I accept this method only when practising exercises (including those taken from some difficult bit in a piece), but in learning musical compositions this method should be used only in exceptional cases. Indeed, why practise the Fifth Prelude in the First Book of Bach's Forty-Eight, with dots and other rhythmic mannerisms, when the main purpose is to achieve maximum equality and evenness, keeping accurately the figure of each crotchet, which dots and rhythmical delays would only hamper? But if it is essential to practise some sharply divided rhythm like the following

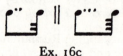

Ex. 16c

then take the Second volume of the Forty-Eight, open it at the Sixteenth Prelude and slog at it until you get it right. I cannot imagine anything more futile than playing the F minor Prelude out of the First Book as:

Ex. 17

and the G minor Prelude out of the Second Book (if we follow this nonsense to its "logical" conclusion) as:

Ex. 18

whereas the object is to achieve exactly the opposite, namely: what was written by Bach. I want to recall my constant advice: as far as possible make straight for the goal, holding course as the Red Arrow train from Moscow to Leningrad, on a straight line, or better still, as a plane flying by compass. (Of course, the engine and the driver, the plane and the pilot have to be in perfect condition.) As for the various "methods", variants, means, I am very much in favour of using them when dealing not with musical, artistic material, but with its molecules, its atoms, i.e. with exercises. (The classical example is the first exercise in the First Book of Liszt's Exercises, edited by Winterberg.) But not for children! Only for adults! This is useful, analytical, technical, craftsman's work, and nobody can shirk it.

If a pianist who is not yet fully mature encounters in a piece difficulties he has never met before and in which he gets bogged down, he will merely show his intelligence and inventiveness if he is able to turn these difficulties into useful exercises

which he will play again and again until the new becomes
familiar, the inconvenient convenient, and the difficult easy.
I have invented for myself and for my pupils, many such
exercises based on the technical problems met in music, and I
will give some examples of them in the chapter on technique.
One thing only is important: one must remember that after the
temporary fragmentation of living musical matter into molecules
and atoms, these particles, having been duly processed, must
once more become living parts of the musical organism.

It is no secret that a gifted pianist who knows how to work
properly can transform an ordinary étude into an artistic
virtuoso composition, whereas one who doesn't know how to
work, i.e. how to reason correctly, will turn an artistic work into
an exercise.

15. To speak of the complete interdependence of tone and
rhythm is almost superfluous. If a syncopation, which is of such
tremendous rhythmic importance, is played more softly than
the non-syncopated note preceding or following it, or simultaneous with it but in another part, it ceases to be a syncopation.
In other words, it loses its rhythmic and dynamic characteristic.
Strange as it may seem, it is sometimes necessary to mention this
even to advanced and talented pupils. Of course in their case,
or in the case of the less advanced pupils, this is due to the fact
that, because of some technical difficulty they have not yet
mastered, they play not quite what is written but what they can
manage. For instance, eight out of ten pupils who studied
Beethoven's Sonata in D minor (no. 17) played in the first movement (just before the development) the left hand as follows:

Ex. 19

instead of:

Ex. 20

which is correct.

Sometimes I used to get so fed up repeating again and again about syncopation that I would suggest to the pupils to remember once and for all that syncopation, Mrs. Syncopation, is a definite person, wherever she may appear, with her own expression, her own character and significance and may never on any account be confused with anyone else.[1]

16. The link between tone and rhythm becomes specially clear in rubato. It is impossible to determine the degree of rhythmic freedom of a phrase if the correct nuances have not been found. Tone and rhythm go hand in hand, help each other and only jointly can they solve the problem of ensuring an expressive performance. I repeat: the things I say are so well known that it is almost embarrassing to write them, and yet . . . how many times have I seen in class that a pupil has solved only half of the performer's problem and that the entity is "wobbly" (or *vice versa*). That is why it is so essential to keep harping on the need to harmonize all the elements of a performance and to insist on it in everyday practice. Again and again: everything is part of one whole. With the very talented, this unity comes, as it were, of its own accord; the less gifted can do a very great deal by means of learning, straining their will, by steadfast persistence. . . . Read the books of Stanislavsky[2]; there is much about this in them, beautifully said.

And never forget that the musician's bible begins with the words: "In the beginning there was rhythm".

[1] The same applies to dynamics: one may not confuse Mary Parsons (*mp*) with Mary Fields (*mf*), or Peter (*p*) with Peter Peterson (*pp*) or Fred (*f*) with Freddy Frost (*ff*). These childish jokes, believe it or not, are sometimes very useful even with adults.

[2] Famous director and co-founder of the Moscow Arts Theatre (1863-1938), ED.

CHAPTER III

On Tone

Music is a tonal art. It produces no visual image, it does not speak with words or ideas. It speaks only with sounds. But it speaks just as clearly and intelligibly as do words, ideas or visual images. Its structure is governed by rules, just as the spoken language, the composition of a picture or the architecture of a building. The theory of music, the study of harmony, counterpoint, and form analysis help us discover these rules which were created by the great composers in accordance with the nature, history and development of mankind.

Performers do not analyse music, or dismember it; they re-create it in its organic unity, its integrity materially concretized in sound. From these simple and well-known premises the pianist must draw all necessary and even obvious conclusions; yet very frequently he does not.

Since music is a tonal art, the most important task, the primary duty of any performer is to work on tone. You might think that nothing could be more obvious. Yet frequently a pupil's preoccupation with technique in the narrow sense of the word (i.e. velocity, bravura) predominates, relegating tone, that most important element, to the second place.

The mistakes made by teachers and pianists with respect to the perception and production of tone on the piano can, roughly speaking, be divided into two contradictory trends: the first consists of underrating tone, the second—of overrating it. The first is more widespread. The player does not give sufficient

thought to the extraordinary dynamic wealth and diversity of
tone which the piano provides. His attention is focussed mainly
on technique (in the narrow sense) about which I spoke earlier
(velocity, evenness, bravura; that dazzle and crash), his ear is
insufficiently developed, he lacks imagination, he is incapable of
listening to himself (and of course to the music). In fact, he is
more *homo faber* than *homo sapiens*, whereas the artist has to be both
(with the latter slightly predominating). The resulting musical
web is as drab as army khaki. To such pupils I never cease
repeating what Anton Rubinstein said about the piano: "You
think it is one instrument? It is a hundred instruments!" Carl
Czerny, "the dry and methodical genius" who has tortured
generations of pianists with an inexhaustible stream of studies
and exercises, established that it is possible to render on the
piano one hundred dynamic gradations encompassed between
limits which I shall term "not yet tone" and "no longer tone".
How curious that two such entirely different personalities as
Rubinstein and Czerny should have arrived at the same figure
of 100. *Cela donne à penser.* (It makes you think.)

This, briefly, is the first mistake: underrating tone.

The other mistake is overrating tone. This occurs with those
who have an excessive admiration of tone, who savour it
excessively, who in music perceive first of all the sensuous beauty
of tone, and do not see its entity: in other words, who don't
see the forest for the trees. Such pianists—and their numbers
include teachers, pupils and "accomplished" pianists, have to
be told the following: The concept of beauty of tone is not
sensuously static but dialectic; the best tone, and consequently
the most beautiful, is the one which renders a particular
meaning in the best possible manner. It may happen that a tone
or series of tones taken out of context and, so to speak, relieved
of all meaning, may appear to some ugly or even unpleasant
(let us recall the effect of muted trumpets or the rasping of the
double bassoon in the lower register, the shrillness of the E flat
clarinet and the jangle of a broken-down old piano, etc.). But if
these sounds, with the exception naturally of the old piano, are
used for a definite purpose by a good composer who is an able
orchestrator, they will, within the context, become the most
expressive, the most necessary; they will be right. It is not for
nothing that Rimsky-Korsakov used to say that all the sounds

of the orchestra are good and beautiful; one should merely know how to use them and to combine them. If the adepts of beautiful tone as an end in itself were right, how could we explain the fact that we prefer a singer with a physically less good voice to one whose voice is better, if the former is an artist and the latter a blockhead? How could we explain why a good pianist plays so well on a bad piano and a bad pianist plays badly on a good piano; why a good conductor with a bad orchestra can create an incomparably greater impression than a bad conductor with a good orchestra? I suppose the reader could continue the mental exercise of finding more examples.

There is an incident in the life of Liszt which applies to this whole question of the role of tone in a piano composition. When Liszt heard for the first time Henselt, who had an extra-ordinary "velvet" tone, he said: *Ah, j'aurais pu aussi me donner ces pattes de velours!* (I, too, could have given myself these velvet paws!) For Liszt, with his immense horizon as composer-performer, the "velvet touch" was merely a detail in his technical arsenal, whereas for Henselt it was the main purpose. I write all this in order to stress once more that tone (together with rhythm) is the first and most important among other means of which a pianist should be possessed, but that it is a means, and not the purpose. I have so often heard piano teachers say that "the most difficult thing is to teach a pupil to acquire a beautiful tone, and that everything depends on the pupil him-self". I am interested not in the difficulty of the problem but in its importance, and the need to solve it as completely as possible. Of course, work on tone is the most difficult work of all, since it is closely connected with the ear and—let's face it—the spiritual qualities of the pupil. The less refined his ear, the duller the tone. By training his ear (which can be done in a variety of ways), we directly influence his tone. By working at the instrument, persevering relentlessly in an attempt to improve the quality of tone we influence the ear and develop it.

Briefly and clearly: mastery of tone is the first and most impor-tant task of all the problems of piano technique that the pianist must tackle, for tone is the substance of music; in ennobling and perfecting it we raise music itself to a greater height.

In my work with my pupils, I can say without exaggeration that three-quarters of all work is work on tone. It may be said that the sequence, the causal relationship in our work naturally falls into the following pattern: first—the image (i.e. the meaning, content, expression, the what-it-is-all-about); second —tone in time[1]—the embodiment, the materialization of the image, and finally, the third—technique as a whole, as the sum total of all means essential for solving the artistic problem of piano playing as such, i.e. mastery of the muscular movements of the performer and of the mechanism of the instrument.

This is my general pattern of study. I repeat myself, but do so deliberately. *Repetitio est mater persuadendi* (repetition is the mother of persuasion). In practice, of course, this pattern is constantly fluctuating according to the requirements and needs of the moment and of the specific case, but though sometimes concealed, it is always present as a hierarchical principle ordering the work. In order to acquire a so-called "good", beautiful tone (I shall subsequently attempt to unravel this somewhat superficial definition) what is needed is particularly hard, persistent, long-term, constant, obstinate work at the instrument. If in his *Conversation with a Finance Inspector*, Mayakovsky says that to become a poet, to write poetry you have to eat a *pood*[2] of salt, then for the piano you have to eat a whole ton of salt, and the reason is obvious: a poem can be carried in one's head, when walking in the country or riding in a bus[3]; but piano playing (not music in general) can be done only at the piano; the piano is, after all, only a mechanical box, a wonderful, an amazing box, on which it is possible to express anything one wants, but a box, and to "humanize" it requires infinitely more effort than does the lovely, living, flexible, ever-ready and infinitely expressive, most human and marvellous invention of man—the human word.

Since, in this chapter, we are dealing not with sound in general, but with tone produced by the pianist's hand on the piano, I must discuss the most simple things that a pianist should know just as any literate person knows his multiplication tables or his grammar.

[1] It would be more accurate to say: working at "time tone", since rhythm and force are inseparable.

[2] Pre-revolution weight = 20 kg roughly.

[3] Richard Strauss conceived some of his operas while playing cards.

Each phenomenon in this world has a beginning and an end. So, also the tone of the piano. The usual indications which range from *pp*, seldom *ppp* or *pppp* to *f*, *ff*, and more seldom *fff*, very seldom *ffff* (mainly in Tchaikovsky) in no way correspond to the real dynamic range of which the piano is capable. In order to probe this real dynamic range, I suggest that the pupil should with complete precision obtain the first appearance of tone (*ppppp*), the softest possible tone which immediately follows on what is not yet a tone (a certain zero which is obtained if the key is depressed too slowly, when the hammer rises but does not strike the string); by gradually increasing the force of the action—*F* and the height at which the hand is raised—h^1 we come to the upper limit of volume (*ffff*), after which we get not tone but noise, since the mechanical (lever) arrangement of the piano does not allow excessive speed (*v*) coupled with an excessive mass (*m*), and especially not a combination of these two excessives.[2] This test can be carried out either on one note (the "atom" of the musical substance) or on two-, three- or four-part chords (the "molecule"). This very simple experiment is important because it gives an accurate knowledge of the tonal limits of the piano. By depressing a key too slowly and softly, I get nothing, zero; it is not yet a tone; if I let my hand fall on the key too fast and with too much force (the forbidden excessive "*v*" and "*h*"), I get a noise; it is no longer a tone. Between these limits lie all the possible gradations of tone.

"Not yet tone" and "no longer tone", this is what whoever has to do with piano playing must probe and experiment. Just as any workman knows the limits of power and productivity of the machine he is operating, so also a pianist who "operates a piano" must know his instrument, his machine. Some people may object, saying: "What dry and boring examples. Even if this is approximately so, what has it got to do with the playing of the great virtuoso pianists who give us such spontaneous

[1] The symbols *F* (force), *m* (mass), *v* (velocity), *h* (height) I have borrowed from physics and mechanics. They are a great help for understanding and using the physical possibilities of the piano, considered as a mechanism.

[2] I will not go into the purely mechanical reasons for this phenomenon. Any good piano tuner can explain this just as well, and perhaps even better.

delight?" I agree. The highly gifted seldom give such matter a
thought; they just do their job. They are much more capable of
creating laws than of analysing them. But, on the other hand,
the lesser talents, or the totally ungifted don't think of such
things at all, yet the resemblance (a very superficial one at that)
between them and the highly gifted is not to their advantage
and of no use to them. "Cold reason and a warm heart"—this is
my educational slogan, and cold reason will not despise this
mite of precise knowledge gathered and tested by experience.

Almost all my technical considerations, advice and exercises
are the result of deduction. For instance, the procedure I have
just described (first appearance of tone, etc.) occurred to me
when I was playing Scriabin or Debussy which at times require
the tone to melt away, to disappear almost completely (yet still
be there). Here is an exercise which I sometimes recommend as
equally useful for developing the ear and for getting to know the
keyboard:

Ex. 21

The significance of the exercise lies in the fact that each
consecutive note is played at the same level of volume as that
to which the previous note has dwindled at the time and not
at which it was originally struck—(detestable word!). This
exercise, which is a protest against the percussive quality of the
piano (for one must first of all learn to make the piano sing, and
not only "strike" it) occurred to me when I was trying on the
piano to get as close as possible to the human voice in the
inspired recitative of the first movement of Beethoven's Sonata
in D minor op. 31, no. 2:

Ex. 22

My advice: play beautiful melodic passages (for instance from
Chopin) much slower than they should be played; for convenience I call this slow motion. This advice was born of my love
for the beauty and melodic line of a passage—and hence its

expressiveness—of a desire to examine it at close quarters, as one can examine a beautiful picture, in close-up or even with a magnifying glass, in order to penetrate, however slightly, its mysterious concordance, its harmony and the accuracy of the brush strokes of a great painter. The slowing down of a process in time is the exact counterpart of the enlargement of an object in space.

Almost all the details of my "methodology" are the result of such deductive thinking.

In my forty-four years of teaching (unofficially, longer still!) hundreds of pupils passed through my hands, representing all the degrees of talent—from the musically defective (there was a time when I didn't scorn even such pupils; you have to try everything) to the geniuses, with all the intervening degrees. The experience of a lifetime, the encounter with this great wealth and variety of human nature led me to methodological conclusions which differ somewhat from the usual schoolbook methods.

It is essential to understand in the fullest possible manner that, on the one hand, the teaching of music, and musical literacy— for which purpose the piano is the best, the irreplaceable, if not the only, means—is part of general culture, that the study of music is just as essential for a cultured person as the study of languages, mathematics, history, sociology, natural sciences, etc. (if I had my way, I would introduce the compulsory study of music by means of the piano, in all secondary schools). Even the musically defective, those who have absolutely no ear for music—and these are not so numerous, for the population of our planet is mostly musical—may acquire a theoretical knowledge of music which is bound to be useful to them in their spiritual life. For music is just as much the product of human thought as all else that was created by man, and is governed by the same laws. As in any other aspect of spiritual life, the dialectics of art, and consequently of music is a continuation and development of the dialectics of nature.

On the other hand, musical education encompasses also those who are exceptionally gifted; the elect, who are destined to be the masters of music, its creators, its performers. It is obvious that instilling general musical knowledge as one of the facets of culture and educating the few great talents, is as different as the role of the piano itself in our "social" life; on the one hand it is the most popular, widely used instrument played by millions of people, for the piano is as essential to any musician or amateur as a tongue, words and speech to any man; on the other hand it is the most difficult, individual instrument in the hands of a great pianist, and great pianists come in dozens compared to the many millions that use the piano.

Who, then, is such a pianist, such a great pianist? I cannot fail to recall the simple but beautiful words of Alexander Blok[1]: "What sort of a person is a poet? Some one who writes in verse? No, of course not; he writes in verse because he is a poet, because he brings words and sounds into harmony. . . ." This idea can be paraphrased to say: "What sort of a person is a pianist? Is he a pianist because he has a good technique? No, of course not; he has a good technique because he is a pianist, because he finds meaning in sounds, the poetic content of music, its regular structure and harmony."

That is what technique is needed for; a technique that is adequate to the force, height and clarity of the spiritual image; that is why pianists work at it until the end of their days and constantly set themselves new aims and solve new problems. That is why great men are always hard workers; that is why so many have said that genius is diligence. Pushkin said that prose needs, first and foremost, ideas. A pianist playing to an audience needs, first and foremost, meaning. And in order to reveal that meaning, he needs technique and more technique.

This is as old as art itself. But young people are frequently unaware of it and make the mistake of attempting to master art "from the other end". A speaker in whose speech beauty of language prevails over depth, truth and passionate thinking is not a very good speaker.

This is something the concert pianist must remember. After all, he, too, is an orator and is engaged in propaganda. For pianists who have virtuosity on the brain there is nothing better than to listen to great composers play their own compositions. They are not specially concerned with piano technique, yet their rendering of their music is magnificent. The reasons are obvious and I need not dwell on them.

So I, too, have a methodology if you can call "methodology"

[1] Russian symbolist poet 1880-1921, ED.

something which remains essentially true to itself, yet is always changing and developing in accordance with the general rules of life, the life within me and without. Methodology is knowledge gained by deduction and by experiment; its source is a definite will, a relentless striving towards a goal which is determined by the artist's character and his outlook on life. Textbook methodology, which mainly lays down prescriptions, so-called hard and fast rules (even if they are tested and reliable) will always be but a primitive, primary, simplified method, which at any moment when coming into contact with reality needs development, rethinking, clarifying, livening up, in short —a dialectic transformation.

Teaching (and I have in mind a good teacher-performer) where the ways of influencing a pupil change constantly and are infinite in their variety while unwaveringly pursuing one aim, fully bears out this statement.

After a short excursion into general methodology, I come back to the particular question of tone and how to produce it on the piano.

We teachers inevitably and constantly use metaphors to define the various ways of producing tone on the piano. We speak of the fingers fusing with the keyboard, of "growing into the keyboard" (Rachmaninov's expression) as if the keyboard were resilient and one could "sink" into it at will, etc. All these extremely approximate definitions are without a doubt useful, they arouse the pupil's imagination and when accompanied by illustrations at the piano they help to develop his ear and his motor-sensory mechanism, what we call the "touch".

One of my favourite pieces of advice is the following: play a note, or several notes simultaneously with a certain amount of force and hold them until the ear ceases to detect even the slightest vibration of the strings, in other words until the tone has completely died away. Only those who clearly hear the continuity of the piano's tone (the vibration of the strings) with all the changes in volume, can, first of all, recognize all the beauty, the nobility of the piano (since this continuity is in part much more beautiful than the original tone when struck)[1];

---

[1] Of course, everything in its proper place. The piano is also adapted for all sorts of toccata effects and even "xylophone" effects, just as much as for a moving cantilena.

secondly, they will be able to master that essential variety of tone which is necessary not only for playing polyphonic music, but for any clear rendering of harmony, the relationship between melody and accompaniment, etc., but especially, in order to create tonal perspectives which are just as real for the ear in music as for the eye in painting. Everyone is aware of the fact that visual and auditive perspective are identical; the only difference being that they are created and perceived by two physically different organs, the eye and the ear. How often the playing of a great master makes us think of a picture with a deep background and varying planes; the figures in the foreground almost leap out of the frame whereas in the background the mountains and clouds are lost in a blue haze. Remember for instance, Perugino, Raphael, Claude Lorrain, Leonardo, our own great painters, and let them influence your playing, your tone.[1]

At least twice a week I remind my pupils (because I have to!) of Anton Rubinstein's saying which I mentioned earlier: "You think the piano is one instrument? It is a hundred instruments!" Of course, I doubt whether anyone will be sufficiently daring to attempt to catch up with and even surpass the great Anton, but these words of his must be borne in mind.

In his book *Von der Einheit der Musik* (The Oneness of Music), Busoni devoted about one and a half pages to the piano under the heading: *Man achte das Klavier* (Respect the piano!). In a highly laconic and perfected style he gives such a clear and accurate description of the piano's characteristics that it is all I can do not to give it in full. I shall confine myself to a few extracts. After pointing to the obvious defects of the piano, its impermanent sound, the implacable division into semitones, Busoni speaks of its qualities: its exceptional dynamic range from an extreme pianissimo to the greatest fortissimo, its tremendous compass from the lowest to the very highest notes, its equality of timbre in every register, its ability to imitate any other instrument (a trumpet can only be a trumpet, and a flute can sound only like a flute, and a violin like a violin, etc., while in the hands of a master, the piano can represent practically any

[1] One very knowledgeable person once called my playing "stereoscopic" and this gave me very sincere satisfaction; so my efforts had, apparently, not been in vain.

instrument). In conclusion he mentions that magic means of expression which is the attribute of the piano alone—the pedal.

In addition I often say to my pupils that the piano is the best actor of all the instruments for it can play the most varied roles. Compared to the sound of other instruments that are emotionally much more specific, much more expressive, as for instance the human voice, the French horn, the trombone, the violin, the cello, etc., it is a certain abstract quality in the sound of the piano—perhaps precisely this abstract, cerebral quality—that gives it its incomparable tone, its unquestioned individuality. It is the most intellectual of all instruments and hence it embraces the widest horizons and encompasses boundless musical vistas. For apart from the immeasurable quantity of indescribably beautiful music written for the piano "personally", one can perform on the piano everything that is known by the name of music, from the melody of a shepherd's pipe to the most gigantic symphonic and operatic works.

This description of the piano (for which I used Busoni's admirable page) was essential in order to arrive at certain deductions concerning the piano's tone. Just as I said that the piano is the best actor of all the instruments,[1] I have to remind pupils constantly of the orchestra to give them an idea of orchestral sounds; I cannot work otherwise! Although I am a pianist, I consider that the orchestra[2] is the first solo instrument, with the piano as second in importance. I think that this cannot be taken as an offence for either the piano or the pianists.

Because the piano is, as I believe, the most intellectual instrument and is not endowed with the emotional substance of other instruments, the player's imagination should, indeed must, be peopled by the most expressive and specific musical images, by every existing variety of shade and timbre contained in the human voice and in every instrument on earth in order to reveal fully all the wealth of the piano's potential. But the main

[1] I should like to call it "inter-instrumental"; forgive the clumsy word.

[2] Of course, only under the baton of a great conductor. The PERSIMFANS for instance has never been a solo instrument.

PERSIMFANS (PERvyi SIMFonicheskii ANSambl First Symphonic Ensemble) functioned in Moscow from 1922 to 1932 and achieved international fame. It was an experiment in musical "collectivism" —an orchestra without conductor, ED.

reason why it is absolutely essential for the pianist to know and feel all this—and a pianist who does not understand this is wearing blinkers, to say nothing worse—is because the pianist, on his own, on a single instrument, without help from anyone, gives an absolutely complete image, creates something full and perfect—a piano composition; the whole of music is in his hands and his hands only, he is at once master and servant, "both Tsar and slave, both worm and God".[1]

When speaking to my pupils, I often make use of a very simple metaphor which even kindergarten pupils can understand but which is equally useful for advanced pupils and even pianists who have completed their studies. I say to them: the pianist and the piano, they are at the same time: (1) the conductor (the head, heart, hearing); (2) the players (both hands with ten fingers and both feet for the two pedals); and (3) all the instruments (a single piano or, in Rubinstein's words, a hundred instruments, which is as many as there are in a symphony orchestra).

All this is very simple and very well known, and honest to goodness I wouldn't repeat these truisms if . . . well, if I did not feel daily more convinced of the fact that not only pupils, but even many accomplished pianists, are not aware of this.

I am afraid that my many references to the orchestra, the conductor, etc., may be misunderstood and so I shall try to explain myself.

I don't at all demand of a piano pupil that he should, at the piano, imitate an orchestra, thinking of it all the time, considering the piano as a sort of poor copy of another, better sound. First of all, the piano has its own individual beauty of tone, its own "ego" which cannot be mistaken for anything else in the world. Secondly, you have to know and love this individual, particular "ego" of the piano in order to know and master it fully. Anyone who has ever heard how some conductors or singers treat the piano (not knowing it) will know once and for all how not to play it.

I hope that this apparent contradiction will be understood correctly, that everyone will understand the dialectic of this phenomenon and why I speak, practically in the same breath,

[1] From the *Ode to God* by Derzhavin (1743-1816), a poem translated into most European languages, ED.

of the piano being the image of the orchestra, and of the piano as such.

It is only by demanding the impossible of the piano that you can obtain from it all that is possible. For the psychologist this means that imagination and desire are ahead of the possible reality. A deaf Beethoven created for the piano sounds never heard before and thus predetermined the development of the piano for several decades to come. The composer's creative spirit imposes on the piano rules to which it gradually conforms. That is the history of the instrument's development. I don't know of any case when the reverse occurred.

I shall not repeat all that has been known so well and for so long; that polyphony is the best way of obtaining a diversity of tone, that melodic cantabile pieces are indispensable for learning to sing on the piano,[1] etc., etc., that it is essential to develop the strength of the fingers, a strong attack in order to play rapid passages with all the necessary clarity and accuracy and to be able to tackle the toccata-type literature of the piano.

From the locomotor point of view, "good" tone is always accompanied by fullest flexibility (but by no means weakness),[2] relaxed weightiness (in other words, an arm which is relaxed from the back and shoulder to the fingertips touching the keys, for all accuracy is concentrated in the fingertips!) and a sure, adequate control of this weight from a hardly perceptible contact in quick, extremely light notes[3] to a tremendous pressure using if necessary the whole body in order to obtain the maximum tone. All this mechanism is not at all complicated for anyone who can hear well, has a clear purpose, is able to realize the flexibility and freedom of body with which nature has endowed him and knows how to put in a lot of stubborn work on the piano.

I frequently tell my pupils, half seriously, half in jest, that to get inside an over-crowded trolleybus is a much more difficult problem from the locomotor point of view than settling down at

---

[1] Although it is much more accurate to say: you must be able to sing on the piano in order to play a melodic cantabile piece. The same applies to polyphony.

[2] *La souplesse avant tout*, as Chopin and Liszt used to say and as all knowledgeable people still say to this very day.

[3] That excellent French expression: *jeu perlé*.

the piano. By the way, it is perfectly natural and quite legitimate that I should occasionally dash into another chapter, in this case the chapter on technique. All the phenomena grouped under the heading "piano playing" are indissolubly linked with each other. That is why when speaking of tone it is impossible not to speak of the way it is produced, i.e. of technique; speaking of technique it is impossible not to mention tone, just as one cannot speak of the pedal separately from tone, or of all these components of piano playing separately from their origin, which is the musical intention.

Each master pianist has his own individual palette. I feel this so strongly that it sometimes seems to me that the lighting or architectural appearance of the Great Hall of our Conservatoire varies with the performance of the pianist (for instance, Richter, Sofronitsky, Gilels). I know that this is just my fancy, but a fancy which recalls reality to a remarkable degree.

There is no tone "in general", just as there is no interpretation "in general", or expression "in general"; nothing is "in general". In this connection I would recall those pages of Stanislavsky's book in which he refers to the expression "in general" as a very great misfortune.

Someone asked Anton Rubinstein if he could explain the tremendous impression which his playing made on the audience. He said roughly the following: "Perhaps it is due partly to the very great volume of sound, but mainly because I have put in a lot of work in order to succeed in making the piano sing". Golden words! They should be engraved in marble in each classroom in each school or conservatoire where piano is taught.

And here I shall go back to something I said earlier: since the basis of all audible music is singing and since piano literature is full of cantabile, the first and main concern of every pianist should be to acquire a deep, full, rich tone capable of any nuance, with all its countless gradations, *vertically and horizontally*. An experienced pianist can easily give three or four dynamic nuances simultaneously: for instance

$$f$$
$$mp$$
$$pp$$
$$p$$

to say nothing of using horizontally every possibility inherent in the piano's tone. The mistaken idea born out of the no less mistaken trend of the adepts of so-called *neue Sachlichkeit* (new objectivity) that the piano is only a percussion instrument, is contradicted by the whole history of piano literature and applies only to the few works by these *sachlich* "businesslike" composers.

In actual fact "work at tone" is just as inaccurate an expression as that of work on the artistic image. We are too enslaved by our inaccurate words and expressions, we trust them too much. People always say of any good pianist: What a beautiful tone! How wonderful it sounds! etc. But what gives us the impression of a beautiful tone is in actual fact something much greater; it is the expressiveness of the performance, or in other words, the ordering of sound in the process of performing a composition. I am convinced that you could never say of a not very musical performer that his playing sounds wonderful, even if he knows hundreds of ways of producing tone and has gone through the whole business of working at tone quality. In the best of cases, it will sound good in places, but not throughout. With a really creative artist and pianist "a beautiful tone" is a most complex process combining and ordering the relationship of tones of varying strength, varying duration, etc., etc., into a single entity. All this proves yet again what I have just said: tone is one of the means of expression available to the pianist (like paint, colour and light for the painter), it is the most important means, but still only a means and nothing more. It is obvious that a good pianist with a bad tone is a *contradictio in adjecto*—an impossibility. It is possible to work effectively at the tone quality only when working at the work itself, the music and its components. And this work is, in turn, inseparable from work on technique in general.

The difference and variety of the tonal picture presented by various great performers is infinite because of the differences in their personalities, just as the paint, colour and light of great painters differ. Compare, for instance, Titian and Van Dyke, Velasquez and El Greco, Vrubel and Serov,[1] etc. And remember, similarly, the tonal pictures of Busoni and Hofmann, Petri and Cortot, Richter and Gilels, Sofronitsky and Oborin, etc. The lower the artistic level of the performer, the less the

[1] Russian painter 1865-1911, ED.

personal, individual element in his playing, the more monotonous and similar to that of other, like performers is the tonal picture he produces. A concert given by above-average pupils, for instance, clearly demonstrates that it is extremely difficult to distinguish one pupil from another even if all of them play "very well".

It is obvious that all piano playing, since its object is to produce tone, is inevitably work at tone, or with tone, regardless of whether the "thing played" is an exercise or a great musical composition. To play scales with a "bad" tone is just as wrong as to play the Chopin Nocturnes with a bad tone. When a great pianist is working at some technical problems, what strikes one first of all is not the velocity, accuracy or force, etc., but the tone quality.

I assume that when working at tone quality, each pianist —if he sets himself that task specially—does so his own way, according to his own personal characteristics. It would be hard to imagine, for instance, that Chopin, whose ceiling of tone according to his contemporaries was about mezzoforte (*mf*), worked in the same way as Rachmaninov whose ceiling was incomparably higher (five or six fortes). But at the same time we should not forget that according to these same contemporaries Chopin had, within the limits of an extreme pianissimo and the mezzoforte referred to, such a variety of sounds, or nuances, such a rich palette as no other pianist endowed with much greater absolute strength ever dreamed of. This needs to be stressed quite particularly because this, precisely, is more important than anything else.

I could confine myself to the considerations about tone and work at tone quality that I have set out in this chapter. I will just add some of the advice I have to give my pupils when there is something wrong with their tone.

1. As I have already said, the condition *sine qua non* for a good tone is complete freedom and relaxation of the arm and wrist from the shoulders to the tips of the fingers which should always be at the ready, like soldiers at the front. (After all, the decisive factor for tone quality is the contact of the fingertips on the keys; the rest—hand, wrist, arm, shoulders, back—that is "behind the lines" and must be well organized.)

2. At the very first stage of pianistic development, I suggest the following very simple exercise for acquiring variety of tone, essential for all playing but particularly for performing polyphonic music:

Ex. 23

Then do the same thing on four- and five-part chords; it is sufficient to do this in some three or four tonalities. The following elementary exercises are also useful:

Ex. 24

They should be practised in several tonalities, slowly, then in moderate tempo and fast, alternately playing one part legato, the other staccato.

3. If in polyphonic music a pupil cannot manage to reproduce the polyphonic web with sufficient relief, or plasticity, the method of exaggeration will be useful, as for instance playing the following difficult passage from the Fugue in E flat minor out of Bach's *Wohltemperiertes Klavier* (Book I, no. 8) with the following dynamic indications:

Ex. 25

(for greater clarity I have written the two top parts on separate staves). For the inexperienced pupil the difficulty lies in the crossing of parts.

4. A very frequent mistake among pupils (even among the advanced ones) to which one has to draw attention frequently, is the dynamic "similarity" between melody and accompaniment, the lack of an "air cushion" between the first and second levels or between different planes, which is just as unpleasant for the eye in the case of a picture, as for the ear in the case of a musical composition. Here, too, an exaggeration of the dynamic distance between melody and accompaniment can explain a great deal and help the pupil to understand. This is a fault of which many conductors are guilty, when they allow the wind instruments, specially the brass, to play too loudly in places where they should only supply the harmony.

5. It is very often necessary to repeat that time-worn truth that when the score indicates crescendo one should (at that place) play piano and if the indication is diminuendo one should play forte. An exact understanding and rendering of the gradual dynamic changes (i.e. their perspective) is vital for a true musical image. Yet with many pianists and conductors a protracted crescendo immediately turns into an outright forte; this weakens the growth and culmination which the composer had intended; the mountain summit becomes a plateau. To drive the point home I usually remind my pupils of the difference between an arithmetic and a geometric progression; this applies also to a rendering of ritenuto and accelerando.

6. It is told of Tausig, the famous pianist, that when he came home after a concert he would play the whole of his programme all over again, very softly and not too fast. An example worth following! Softly—that means with utmost concentration, carefully, conscientiously; accurately, painstakingly, with a beautiful tender tone; an excellent diet not only for the fingers but also for the ear, an instant correction of any inaccuracies or accidents that inevitably occur during an impassioned, temperamental concert performance!

7. It has to be frequently repeated that since the piano does not have a lasting tone like other instruments, it needs much richer and more flexible shading not only of the melodic parts but also of runs and passages (exaggerated if compared to other instruments) in order to render clearly the *intonation* (rising and

falling) of the music.[1] Of course there are exceptional cases
when what is needed is a completely even sound devoid of any
shading, as for instance the dead, monotonous sound in the
Organ Fugue in E minor, arranged by Busoni (in the Supplement to the First Book of the *Wohltemperiertes Klavier*) or, as
frequently happens, a protracted, powerful and even *f*, etc.

8. What very gifted pupils achieve by instinct (though, of
course, with the help of hard work)—a complete coordination of
the fingers and hand, the whole locomotor system, with the
demands of the ear, the musical intent—can, to a great extent,
also be explained to and developed in much less gifted pupils.
Let me give two examples of this coordination: every experienced pianist knows that to get a tender, warm, penetrating tone
you have to press the keys very intensively, deeply, keeping the
fingers as close to the keys as possible, with "*h*" at a minimum,
or in other words "*h*" equal to the height of the key before it is
depressed. But to get an open, broad, flowing tone (think of
Caruso or Gigli) you have to use the whole swing of the finger
and hand (with a completely flexible legato). These are but two
small examples but they can be multiplied *ad infinitum*; it is
important to know, and to know from experience, that the
anatomy of the human hand is ideal also from the point of view
of the pianist and is a convenient, suitable and intelligent
mechanism which provides a wealth of possibilities for extract-
ing the most varied tones out of a piano. And the mechanism of
the hand is, of course, in complete harmony with the mechanism
of the piano. In good pianists there is a complete symbiosis
between hand and keyboard. But that this does not always
happen—and not only with pupils but also with mature
pianists—that, too, we know full well. Sometimes, when
playing a protracted *f* or *ff* some pianists get excited, they boil
and pant and apparently do not notice that the volume of
sound does not increase, but that the reverse happens, that
their tone becomes weaker and sometimes degenerates into
mere thumping. This is like the man who is beginning to lose
his voice and tries to talk as loudly as possible, instead of which

[1] Compare the excellent indications of Hans von Bülow to the
Adagio in Beethoven's Sonata op. 106 (where the right hand has
demi-semiquavers), or the second movement of op. 111 (fourth
variation with demi-semiquavers).

he merely gets hoarse. With the pianist this happens precisely because there is no coordination between the musical demand and the work of his muscles, which, in such cases, are usually stiff, tense and hampered. As a matter of fact it should never be forgotten that this physical freedom at the piano is impossible without musical or spiritual freedom. A pianist who is unable to render musical expression without hysterics or cramp will inevitably have a hysterical and cramped, in other words an imperfect, technical mechanism and the main components of music—time (rhythm) and tone—will be perverted and distorted. The old Latin adage—*mens sana in corpore sano*—retains all its meaning for the pianist. These simple truths have to be frequently mentioned in class and that is why I repeat them here.

9. The question of tone in compositions which require the use of pedal—in other words almost always—cannot be considered separately from pedalling, just as it is impossible to decide on proper pedalling separately from tone, from tone quality. I have already referred to this. Of course it is useful to play a piece without pedal in order to check the accuracy and clarity of each note, but it is more useful still to study a composition with proper pedalling since it is only with its help that the required tonal effect can be obtained. But I shall take this in greater detail in the section dealing with pedal.

10. One of the most difficult but satisfying tasks for the pianist is to create a multiplane tonal texture. I have already mentioned this when I compared a musical composition to a painting. Any kind of polyphony is in itself a multiplane structure—one has to play expressively and independently the theme and all the other parts that accompany it. The fundamental tendency of polyphony (its "Protoform") is the movement of parts in contrary motion; the purest example—possible only in two-part writing—is the F sharp major Prelude from the Second Book of Bach's *Wohltemperiertes Klavier* (bars 53 and 55) and the bars preceding the end of the Fugue in A flat major, No. 17 in the Second Book. There is also the "mirror" movement of notes and fingers, bars 9, 10, 11 and 12 of the Prelude in D minor (Book 2, No. 6) or the second subject in the second movement of Prokofiev's Fourth Sonata (I have left out the accompanying semiquavers):

Ex. 26

We find a similar example in the concluding part of Prokofiev's Third Sonata. This tendency of juxtaposition, of "mirroring" can be achieved in polyphony with more than two parts, mainly by means of different nuances, or dynamic planes corresponding exactly to the polyphonic texture and its meaning.

This multiplane texture is even more essential in transcriptions of orchestral works (for instance the famous concluding scene from *Tristan*, "Isolde's Death", arranged by Liszt) but also in any piano composition, whether a Chopin fantasie or a Beethoven sonata, a Schumann fantasie, etc. (those who so wish may find their own examples).

Examples of multiplane structure may be found first of all in any polyphonic composition, beginning with the Inventions and Fugues of Bach and Handel and ending with the fugues of Glazunov, Taneyev, Reger, Szymanowski and Shostakovich.

But, of course, examples of multiplane abound in the most varied styles. Here are a few typical instances:

(*a*) Chopin Etude in E flat minor, op. 10 (No. 6). Foreground: melody; second level: bass, long bass notes lasting a whole bar or half a bar; third level: semiquaver movement in the middle part. If this natural three-level structure, which sometimes becomes four-part, is not observed, the whole composition becomes misty and unclear, regardless of the expressive way it may be played.[1] I have had to explain it in class many times; very often the semiquavers of the middle part were played too loudly compared to the bass (see para. 11), the music lost its support and became "legless". It is very appropriate here to remember that Anton Rubinstein called the two fifth fingers "conductors" leading the music. The limits of sound (both upper and lower) are to music what the frame is to a picture;

---

[1] A typical example of this triple-level are the Choral Preludes of Bach in E flat major and C major for organ, arranged by Busoni.

the slightest blurr (which is particularly frequent at the lower limit) in the bass results in a diffuse, shapeless picture; the musical composition then turns (as I sometimes tell my pupils) into either "a headless horseman", if the bass and harmony swallow the melody, or "a legless cripple" if the bass is too weak, or "a potbellied monster" if the harmony swallows both bass and melody (unfortunately the latter frequently happens with the orchestra). Although what I write here is elementary and generally known, yet it has to be repeated in class very frequently. There is obviously a considerable distance between knowing a thing and carrying it out (theory and practice, planning and implementing, knowing and doing).

(*b*) Chopin's Nocturne in C minor, repetition of the first subject (agitato). This is far from easy to render in a clear, plastic manner because of the very full harmony that accompanies it (the "middle"), the octaves in the bass and the fact that the melody is left to the fifth finger alone, and yet must prevail over the rest. If there is here a lurking danger of the "headless horseman" I suggest using the method of exaggeration which I mentioned earlier and attempt to play the melody very *f*, the accompaniment *p* and the bass *mp* (approximately).

A similar difficulty is to be found in the whole of the end of Chopin's Polonaise-Fantaisie op. 61 (after the unison passage in both hands until the end).[1]

(*c*) Scriabin, Fourth Sonata, the whole of the end (*ff*). Same difficulty. In spite of the tremendous *f* with an accompaniment of seven- and eight-part chords and a full bass in octaves, the melody, which is only in the fifth finger, has to predominate:

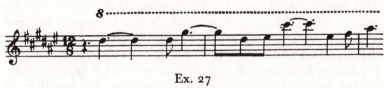

Ex. 27

Poor fifth finger, what a lot is expected of it! Hence the conclusion: develop the little finger in every way, make it into

---

[1] Richter plays this extremely clearly and expressively, not only because of his tremendous musical talent but also because of his tremendous, powerful hands. In such places small hands must always try to "cheat".

the strongest pillar under the dome of the hand. (But fingers will be discussed in the chapter on technique.)

(*d*) Much easier to perform are such examples of multiplane structure as, for instance, the second subject in D flat major in Chopin's Third Scherzo (C sharp minor), not only because of the extreme contrast in register, but also because the various tonal patterns follow each other and are not simultaneous (horizontal instead of vertical).

A similar example—the Debussy Etude *Sonorités opposées* from the Second Book. But here too, though actual execution is easier, it is essential first to predetermine with the ear the finest shade of difference and quality of tone and then execute it with the fingers; but this requires a well-developed ear and touch.

(*e*) In modern music, Scriabin, Rachmaninov, Debussy, Ravel, Prokofiev, Reger, Szymanowski and others, there is an immense number of particularly telling examples of such multi-plane texture. I recommend anyone who is interested to seek out such pieces and passages and then study them in order to perfect tonal technique. There is endless scope for such activity. It is obvious that if the player understands this musically, i.e. if he *hears* this multiplane texture, he will inevitably find the means of rendering it; if, however, he is still too bogged down by technical difficulties and is unable to hear the music mentally, the teacher must help him.

11. Time and again I have to remind pupils that long notes (minims, semibreves, notes lasting several bars) must, as a rule, be played with more force than the shorter notes that ac-company them (quavers, semiquavers, demi-semiquavers, etc.). This again being due to the fundamental "defect" of the piano: the extinction of its tone (with the organ this rule obviously does not apply). I have often been amazed to find that even very talented pupils did not always appear to have a sufficiently demanding ear in this respect and did not render the musical texture with sufficient plasticity. An insufficiently educated ear is also frequently reflected in too much volume in the bass when playing *f* ("booming"). This booming is par-ticularly unpleasant in Chopin, where a rough, thundering bass is definitely not permissible (in Liszt, on the other hand, one can often hear kettle-drums and cymbals in the bass, but this in no way implies that one can thump and bang on the piano).

12. A fault which is very prevalent and which has a fatal
effect on tone quality is found in pupils with small hands
(especially women); it is the dynamic dominance in the right
hand of the thumb over the little finger in chords and octaves.
This is particularly inadmissible in cases when the octave is a
doubling of the melody (for instance the end of Chopin's Third
Ballade) and thousands of similar cases:

Ex. 28

In such a case I advise the pupil to learn each part separately
and thoroughly and, in addition, to play the excellent exercises
for double notes which Godowsky gives in his comments to his
arrangements for the left hand of Chopin's Etude in double
thirds op. 25, beginning with the chromatic seconds, frequently
encountered in such piano literature as Ravel and Szymanowski
and ending with octaves. The main significance of these
exercises lies in the fact that they are taken as exercises in
polyphony in two parts, not just double notes, but two parts
which one must be able to play differently from each other. I
will give these exercises here as Godowsky's arrangements of the
Chopin Etudes are very difficult to get. I shall take as an
example chromatic minor thirds. Exactly the same exercises are
recommended for octaves, sixths, and as I have already said,
for any type of double note.

Ex. 29a

etc., etc., two octaves up and two down. The same may be
played legatissimo:

Ex. 29b

etc. (the fingering remains always the same)

Ex. 29c, d, e, f, g

(glissando from above downwards, as everywhere)

Ex. 29h, i

This exercise is meant to strengthen the third on the spot, and acquire an accurate consonance of the two notes.

And finally simply a chromatic scale in thirds:

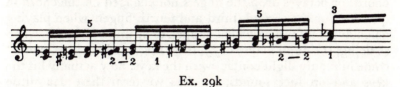

Ex. 29k

(This exercise, as all the others, to be played two or three octaves up and down, at first not too fast, then presto possibile). If the octave exercise were played according to this system, examples (*d*) and (*e*) would look like this:

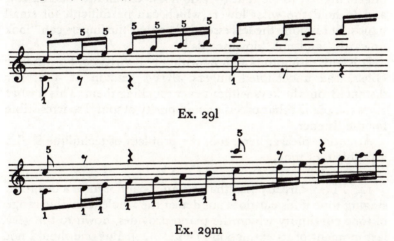

Ex. 29l

Ex. 29m

(play chromatically, also as triads, and chords of the seventh; see Liszt's Exercises in Twelve Books). The purpose of stopping on the first octave is that the hand playing subsequently only one note of the octave should retain the octave stretch and not close "accidentally".

I should like to point out that I could perhaps give these exercises with greater reason under the heading of technique, but I deliberately placed them here since technical exercises are exercises for producing tone. And with this I want to stress once more that work on tone is work on technique and work on technique is work on tone.

13. There is a fault which is closely linked to the one mentioned in the previous paragraph. It is a carelessness very widespread among pupils with small hands, who when playing chords or octaves drop the fingers not engaged on the chord in question (or the second, third and fourth fingers when playing an octave) on the keys which happen to be under them. If, when so doing, the pupil plays f or ff, these fingers which in a "piano" come into only slight contact with the keys, now actually hit the keys and produce sounds. In class we term these dear little fingers "sympathetic".

It is obvious that in order to correct this fault the pupil must first of all be made to listen carefully to the resulting cacophony, and then should be simply advised to hold the unoccupied fingers higher, to see that they do not accidentally touch a key, and to hold the wrist lower (which can be difficult for small hands, but is none the less essential) so that the fingers can "look upwards" and not "downwards".

It is interesting to note how with a real virtuoso, for instance Gilels, the unoccupied fingers always remain at a proper distance from the keys without ever touching them. This is what gives the pianist that precision and purity of sound so irresistible for the listener.

Attention please: here, too, the problem of technique is also a problem of tone.

14. I have already said that a pianist cannot have a beautiful singing tone if his ear does not detect the whole available range of tone continuity which the piano provides, down to the very last moment of its extinction ($f < ppp$ . . .). But one should not forget the amazing brilliance, the sparkle of such pianists, as for instance Horowitz, who make a very sparing use of the pedal, often use a non legato and in general know how to show off the percussive "hammer" quality of the piano to its best advantage (this of course has nothing in common with "dryness" or "banging").

The inference is clear: one must develop one's technique to produce both qualities, particularly since they are essentially needed in piano literature.

I repeat: both the average pianist and the great pianist, if they only know how to work, will acquire their own individual tone quality which corresponds to their psychological, technical and physical make-up, and will never be a warehouse of "universal" tone or of every kind of technical perfection. There are, luckily, no such phenomena. In the case of performers, too, one may only speak of universality in the sense in which it is spoken of generally, i.e. in connection with the history of music as a whole. We have to accept that the highest achievements of the performer's art (for instance the playing of Mozart or Bach, of Anton Rubinstein or Rachmaninov, Paganini or Liszt) come and go, and go for ever. But there is no need to grieve over this. Others are born who take their place. In this respect the life of Art follows Nature very closely.

I am repeating well-worn truths, but I do so deliberately. Because to forget them is to leave room for the mistaken opinions and false demands which one encounters daiiy.

I could quote much additional material concerning work on tone quality, material which comes to light during work with my pupils. I am almost sure that I have forgotten to say something very important and perhaps was wrong to dwell on things of secondary importance. But for fear of boring my hypothetical reader—and myself—I shall draw the line. Besides, it is not my intention to turn these notes into a textbook of piano playing.

And I should like to end these pages on tone with the words I sometimes say to my pupils: tone must be clothed in silence; it must be enshrined in silence like a jewel in a velvet case.

CHAPTER IV

On Technique

1. General Considerations

In this chapter I shall attempt to say something not about what
must be done but about *how* one must do what is known as
artistic piano playing. That, incidentally, is what technique is
about. I repeat once more: the clearer what is to be done, the
clearer, too, how it must be done. The objective is already an
indication of the means of attaining it. This is the secret of the
technique of truly great pianists: they embody Michelangelo's
words: *La mano che ubbidisce al intelletto* (the hand which obeys
the intellect). This is why I insist that musical development
should come before technical development or should at least go
hand in hand.

Technique cannot be created in a vacuum just as you cannot
create a form devoid of any content. Such a "form" is equal to
zero and does not, in fact, exist. The most simple, laconic and
sensible description of artistic technique was formulated by
Alexander Blok. "In order to create a work of art", he says,
"one must know how to." Therein lies the similarity between a
good engineer, airman, artist, doctor, scientist: all of them
"know how to". Chkalov[1] knew how to fly over the North Pole
in the same manner in which Shostakovich knows how to write
a symphony. And it is of this know-how, of how to play the
piano that I want to speak.

[1] Famous Soviet airman of the 1930s, ED.

I have already said that a performance consists, roughly speaking, of three elements: first, the work performed (the music), secondly the performer, and thirdly the instrument. We shall for the time being leave aside the first (the music) and concentrate our attention on the remaining two: the pianist and the piano. A few points I mentioned already in the previous chapters, but I shall examine the whole question in greater detail here. Let me deal first of all with a few simple principles.

1. To acquire a technique which enables you to perform all the existing piano literature, it is essential to use all the anatomical possibilities of movement with which man has been endowed, beginning with the hardly perceptible movement of the last joint of a finger, the whole finger, the hand, the forearm, arm and shoulder and even the back, in fact the whole of the upper part of the body, i.e. beginning with one point of support —the fingertips on the keyboard, and ending with another point of support on the chair. This would appear to be axiomatic. Yet I can prove that very many pianists do not make full use of all the possibilities that our body provides. Feet, too, have a work to perform since they press the pedal. A mature pianist knows full well which of the power installations built into his body he should use and when, and which to disconnect and why. One who is not mature either brings out his heavy artillery to shoot sparrows or uses a toy pistol against a battery of guns.

2. To play the piano is easy. I mean the physical process, and not the summit of pianistic art. It is obvious that to play the piano very well is just as difficult as to do anything else very well, for instance to pull teeth or macadam a road. Let me cite two simple facts to prove that playing is easy: first, the keys move extremely easily, slightly more weight than that of a matchbox will suffice to make a string vibrate; for the finger this is an insignificant effort. Secondly, by raising the hand not more than twenty to twenty-five centimetres above the keyboard and from that height (h) dropping a finger or several fingers on to the key (or keys) with the "pure weight" of the hand without any pressure, but also without any holding back, *come corpo morto cadde* (as a dead body falls) as Dante puts it, you get the

maximum volume of sound, the dynamic ceiling of the piano. Knowing how easy it is to play, i.e. how easy it is to obtain the softest and the loudest tone and to determine the lowest and highest limit of actual piano dynamics, we can also immediately say what, in piano playing, is the most difficult (again only from the purely physical point of view): the most difficult is to play very long, very loud and very fast.[1] Between these two limits (I have already said that I like to establish the beginning and the end of any phenomenon) lies, in fact, the whole technique of the piano considered from the point of view of physical motion.

3. I should like to draw attention to the following exercise (B sharp can also be replaced by B natural):

Ex. 30

I could refrain from adding anything to this and leave everyone to ponder this small well-known piano formula, the far-reaching nature of which reveals its genius. But I must still add a few words.

These five notes: E, F sharp, G sharp, A sharp, B sharp, are the contents of Chopin's first lesson in piano playing. Perhaps not the first he actually gave, but the first from the point of view of systematic teaching.

In time, by no means immediately, I came to the conclusion that it is with these five notes that one must begin the whole methodology and heuristic of piano playing, of learning the piano, that they are its cornerstone, its Columbus' egg, the seed of wheat which yields a thousandfold harvest. This small formula is truly weightier than many heavy tomes. What is it in this formula that so attracts me?

Chopin, as we know, used to place the pupil's hand on these five notes which represent the most convenient, the most natural, the most relaxed position of the hand and fingers on

[1] I suggest that everyone should immediately draw up a mental list of passages from piano literature (and also studies) substantiating my statement.

the keyboard, since the shorter fingers—the thumb and little finger—are on the white keys which are lower and the longer fingers (second, third and fourth) are on the black keys which are higher. You cannot find anything more natural on the keyboard than this position. Anyone can see how much less convenient is the position of the five fingers on only the white keys: C, D, E, F, G.

Chopin made his pupil play these five notes in turn not legato (which could have caused a certain tenseness or stiffness with an inexperienced beginner) but as a light portamento, using the wrist, so as to feel in every point complete freedom and flexibility. Thanks to this simple exercise the beginner immediately makes friends with the instrument, and feels that the piano and keyboard are not an alien, dangerous and even hostile machine but a familiar, friendly being ready to meet you if you treat it lovingly and freely, and yearning for the closeness of the human hand as the flower yearns for the approach of the bee, ready to yield all its pollen.

But instead of this, how many hundreds and thousands of pitiful beginners—and during how many years—when brought by their teachers into contact with the keyboard for the first time tried to turn their living hand with its nerves, muscles, flexible joints and pulsating blood, into a piece of wood with curved hooks, to extract with these hooks such offensive combinations of sound as for instance:

Ex. 31

In truth, there is no better way of educating the ear than to accustom a child from the beginning to such delightful consonances as:

From here the path to formalism is short and straight, but of this our venerable ancestors were apparently entirely unaware. And the exasperated piano bares its decaying teeth at the poor neophyte and emits a barking sound!

As we know from Mikuli,[1] Chopin used to suggest to his pupils that they should first play scales with many black keys (the most convenient to start with is the B major for the right hand and the D flat major for the left) and only then, gradually decreasing the number of black keys, come to the most difficult scale of all, that of C major. This is the reasoning of a realist, a practician, one who knows his stuff not from hearsay, but from inside, from its very substance. And in spite of the fact that this composer, pianist and teacher of genius, Chopin, lived so long ago, after his time (to say nothing of what went on before him!) hundreds and thousands of exercises, études and educational pieces have been written in that beloved C major with an obvious disregard for the other tonalities with many sharps and flats.

Except for an excessive love of ivory and a contempt for ebony it would be difficult to find an explanation for this one-sided approach. Please do not think that I am so naïve as to ignore the logic of the circle around which our scales are built and the centre of which is C. I merely stress that the theory of piano playing which deals with the hand and its physiology is distinct from the theory of music. Chopin, as a teacher of the piano, was a dialectician, whereas the authors of educational compositions were schematists, not to say scholasters.

4. The piano is a mechanism, a complex and delicate one to boot, and man's work at the piano is to a certain extent also mechanical, if only because he has to make his body conform to the mechanism. When producing a sound on the piano the energy of the hand (of the finger, forearm, the whole arm, etc.) is transformed into the energy of the sound. The energy of the blow which the key receives is determined by the force—F—which we apply to the hand and the height—h—to which the hand is raised before being lowered on to the key. The speed of he hand at the moment when it strikes the key (v) varies depending on the value of F and h. It is precisely this figure (v) and the mass (m) of the body (finger, hand, arm, etc.) striking the key that determines the energy which acts on the key.

Many of my pupils have so thoroughly mastered the practical meaning of these values that sometimes I need merely make a brief observation: too much v! and the pupil immediately

[1] A pupil of Chopin who later edited Chopin's works, ED.

decreases the speed at which the hand drops on to the piano and the tone is fuller and softer. Or else I say: not enough F! and the pupil immediately understands that the tone was not sufficiently deep and compact because he deprived his hand of part of its natural weight, he so to speak stopped that weight falling before the hand had touched the keyboard.[1]

But I have already spoken about this in the chapter on tone. I believe that the practical significance of the symbols "m", "v", "h" and "F" is so simple and clear that there is no need to dwell on it further. But as a matter of fact I shall have to come back to it later.

Some may ask me: What is the point of all this mathematical stuff in conjunction with music? Surely, this can all be explained in a less dry and cerebral manner. Here is my answer: I have already said that the better a pianist knows[2] the three components mentioned earlier (namely: first the music, secondly himself and thirdly the piano), the greater the guarantee that he will be a master of his art, and not an amateur. And the greater his ability to formulate his knowledge with precision in statements even remotely akin to mathematics and that have the force of law, the more profound, sound and fruitful will his knowledge be.

And do not let this worry those who hold the "mystery" of art so dear: the mystery of art remains unfathomed, retaining all its force and scope, just as in life. But one should not see the "unfathomable" where common sense, against which we all of us sin so much, can perfectly well understand all there is to understand. And that there is *in principle* nothing that is unfathomable is now known to every child.

2. *Confidence as a Basis for Freedom*

I have already said in the chapter on rhythm what I mean by "freedom". We all know that freedom is a recognized need.

---

[1] There is a pianist who is an excellent musician and a master of his art, but I have one objection to make to his playing: h and v are exaggerated.

[2] Please remember once and for all that when I speak of the "knowledge" of an artist, I have always in mind an active force: understanding plus action. Or simpler still: acting correctly on the basis of correct thinking.

Hence the immediate conclusion: freedom is the antithesis of arbitrariness, the enemy of anarchy, just as the ancient Greeks held cosmos to be the enemy of chaos and just as order is the enemy of disorder, etc., etc.

Those who have not learned to think dialectically and have not had sufficient experience in their working life, frequently confuse these two concepts: freedom and arbitrariness which, in actual fact, are contradictory. This position retains its full significance and is applicable (even indispensable!) to any activity, including that of acquiring an artistic piano technique.

Since confidence is the prerequisite of freedom, it is confidence that one should stubbornly strive for, first of all. Many inexperienced players suffer from an inherent timidity, a sort of "pianophobia" which manifests itself thus: they frequently play wrong notes, make many unnecessary movements, are often stiff, do not know how to use the natural weight of the hand and arm (they hold their arm "suspended" in mid-air), in short, they show all the signs of insecurity with its unpleasant consequences. And although it may seem that this insecurity is purely physical, a question of mobility, you can take it from me it is always first of all psychological: either purely musical or a component of the player's character (shyness, indecision, vagueness, everything that makes it so easy to tell the humble from the impudent). None in whom these faults are deep-rooted can be taught to play the piano well with the help only of technical skill, however good and appropriate. If such a person must become a pianist, it is essential to influence not only his physical but also his pyschological make-up, in other words, to re-educate him as far as this is possible.

I confess that in the many years when I worked with very indifferent pupils (of my own free will, incidentally) and suffered a great deal from it, I comforted myself with the thought that though I would never teach them to play well, that I would never make pianists out of them, I would still, by means of music, by injecting into them the bacillus of art, drag them some way up into the realm of spiritual culture and would help them to develop their best spiritual qualities. . . . This is not being quixotic; with very few exceptions I did manage to achieve something. . . .

It is clear from the previous chapters, especially Chapter I, that I suggest, in all difficult cases, to strive first of all to improve and develop the ear and the musical faculties, the faculty to imagine, to represent, i.e. the artistic ability, in short the intellectual qualities of the pupil. Deficiencies of instinct (i.e. of talent) must be made good by reason. I know of no other way. But if the technical education, the training of the fingers, hand, arm, the whole locomotor mechanism lags behind the spiritual education, we may find that we have trained not a performer but at best a musicologist, a theoretician (one who is able to talk correctly but who is not able to demonstrate).

In short, the greater the musical confidence, the less the technical insecurity. I would not mention these truisms were it not that even today, and frequently, I still meet certain teachers and their pupils who believe that by mere swotting, cramming, by endless training of the mechanism without any musical training and, what is even more important, without constant spiritual development, it is possible to achieve good results and to learn to play well.

No, my friends, you cannot.

Present-day technology is striving to turn the machine into a human being (through the number and variety of operations it can perform), but it is sinful and stupid to turn man into a machine. True, for the last thirty years this deplorable tendency has been on the wane. The principles of Soviet educational methods, which are also applied to piano teaching, are gaining ground increasingly within the teaching profession.

For the highest example of the type of teaching method I have mentioned—the complete coordination of musical and instrumental teaching (with the former prevailing)—we have to go back to the great Bach. All his Inventions, small Preludes or Fugues, the Anna Magdalena Book and even the "Forty-Eight" and the Art of the Fugue were intended in equal measure for *teaching* music and the *playing* of music as well as for the creative study of music, the study of its very nature, which probes the musical cosmos and fashions the inexhaustible wealth of "tonal ore" concealed in our musical universe.

Sometimes the inability or ignorance of a pupil prompted Bach to compose for him there and then an Invention or a Prelude which in his professional modesty he considered mere teaching aids, but which, thanks to his genius, became works of art. A golden age! How great the downward path of teaching aids (exercises) from the Bach Inventions to the exercises of Hanon, Pischna, etc. True, the Brahms exercises, even the Philippe Method in which each purely technical problem is accompanied by relevant examples from musical literature, are a new advance in piano teaching aids. The trend goes from the Bach Inventions through a number of Etudes by Clementi and Cramer to those of Chopin, Liszt, Scriabin, Rachmaninov and Debussy.

It must be thoroughly understood that Bach's method consisted of combining the technically useful (from the loco-motor point of view) with the musically beautiful, and that he managed to reduce to practically nil the antagonism between the dry as dust exercise and the musical composition. I do not doubt for a single moment that Bach gave his pupils all the technical, or, more accurately, the instrumental and anatomical advice they needed (position of the fingers, which fingers to use, position of the hand, how much force to use, tempo, etc., etc.), advice which, in most cases, has not come down to us. But there can be no doubt, also, that he gave that advice without reducing music and piano playing to a mere handicraft. To catch up with Bach and to surpass him, is that not a worthy task for Soviet musical education?[1]

To come back to the question of acquiring sureness let me say that the old principle of *langsam und stark* (slowly and with force) when applied to technique not only has not lost its meaning but has, perhaps, acquired new significance since the growing demands which composers, and consequently also performers, make on the piano's volume of tone (think of Rachmaninov's Third Concerto, the Second Sonata by Szymanowski, Reger's Variations on a Theme by Bach, etc., etc., *ad infinitum*), make these "exercises in force" most essential. Only it should not be forgotten, as is the case with some young

[1] If I were not afraid of making this chapter excessively long I would set down here some considerations as to why teaching of the Bach type is a thing of the past although it has lost none of its value. Let me give just two reasons: the gigantic development of music and of piano literature and its tremendous variety, similar to the variety of science. (Kant taught at the University of Königsberg all the sciences known at the time.) In a certain sense Bach developed virgin land.

pianists, that the principle "slowly and loud" (or, if possible, "fast and loud") is only one of many true principles of technical work. When it becomes a monopoly, or when it has priority over all others, the pianist and his playing inevitably grow dull and stupid. But that it is essential is borne out by fact. As a child and as a young man, Emil Gilels did a great deal of technical work this way. The result, as everyone knows, is brilliant. I would find it hard to name another pianist whose tone is so rich in noble "metal", twenty carat gold, that "metal" which we find in the voices of the greatest singers (Caruso, Gigli, Chaliapin). I have noticed that every great virtuoso—I mean particularly the virtuoso who plays in large halls with very large audiences—at some time or other in his youth was extremely fond of banging and thumping; the future great virtuoso sowing his wild oats, as it were. Richter, too, used to thump away when he began his concert career, and Vladimir Horowitz, when he was seventeen or eighteen used to bang so mercilessly that it was almost impossible to listen to him in a room.[1] True, Gilels never banged, but at that age he was very fond of playing very fast and very loud, and it was only beyond these prominent (though, it is true, captivating) qualities that one could make out the shape of the wonderful artist and virtuoso to be, the Gilels as we know him. I think that I did not point out in vain that the hardest, purely pianistic, task is to play very long, very loud and very fast. The true spontaneous virtuoso instinctively throws himself into this difficulty at an early age, and overcomes it successfully. It requires daring, persistence, temperament, passion, energy, quick thinking; and that, precisely, is talent or the essential elements of talent. That is why we too frequently hear a young virtuoso destined to become a great pianist, exaggerate his tempo and his strength.

Of course this fault is to be found also in young people who are not destined to have such a brilliant future. But they frequently get stuck at this point while the very gifted get over it quickly.

And so the slogan: playing should be intense, strong, loud, deep and precise, is right. And in working this way the following rules should be observed: make sure that the hand and arm, from the wrist to the shoulder, are completely relaxed, that

[1] I am almost certain that Liszt, too, was guilty of this in his young days. Remember what Glinka said of him.

there is no contraction, no "freezing" or stiffening anywhere, that none of the potential flexibility is lost, and at the same time remain perfectly still, making only those movements which are absolutely essential. *Le stricte nécessaire* which is the complete embodiment of the principle of economy, is one of the most important principles of any kind of work and particularly in psycho-physical work. Then: use pressure only when the simple weight of the inert mass is insufficient to produce the desired volume of tone; understand that the greater the height (h) from which the note is played (i.e. the key or keys), the less pressure or effort is needed, dwindling down to nought. And conversely, the less the factor h (its minimum is easily determined: it is the height from which a key is brought from the level of the keyboard, the hammers being at rest, to the position when the key "touches the key-bed" and the hammer is raised so that the finger is already in contact with the key surface before actually depressing it) the more pressure (i.e. F) is required to produce a strong tone. It is equally easy to determine minimum "v" (speed of pressure) of a key to achieve the very first appearance of tone. I have already mentioned this in the chapter on tone but to be systematical I must come back to this important question. The simplest experiment which anyone who is neither a musician nor a pianist can try will show that if you depress a key too slowly—as if it were not the first link of a transmission system but some resistant mass similar to uncooked dough or soft wax—there will be no sound because the hammer will not have received sufficient impetus and though it rises it will not hit the string, which will remain silent. If you depress the key ever so slightly faster you will achieve that first tone which I find so important, and at the same time you will find the exact minimum of "v" required to produce it. It is also not difficult to determine the upper limit of "h" (if one is not absolutely stone deaf, which a pianist is hardly likely to be). By gradually increasing "h" you will inevitably reach the limit when the gradually increasing volume of tone will become its own antithesis: thumping. Now try, with "m" unchanged, to decrease "v" (being guided, naturally, by your ear) and you will get, almost "next-door" to the thumping, an excellent "metallic" tone. That is your upper limit of "F". Similarly, always guided by your ear, you can determine the limits of "F", its maximum and minimum essential in each particular case, and continuing the experiment you will find that "*h*" and "*F*" are mutually replaceable; for instance, you can get practically the same "*v*" (with a slight but important difference in the timbre) using a minimum "*h*" but a very high "*F*" (simply by holding the hand practically over the key surface and striking the note or chord very rapidly) or with a high "*h*" and a low "*F*" (the hand falls on the keyboard from a great height but with much less speed).

For the third time I see before me an imaginary opponent who, this time with irritation in his voice, asks what is the purpose of all this pseudo-scientific abracadabra flavoured with algebra. Since this opponent is so far only imaginary, i.e. invented by myself, I will not hesitate to be rude and shall simply break off this pointless argument.

3. *The Locomotor System*

This is precisely the point where, in connection with force, sureness, etc., a few words should be said about hands and fingers, these living creatures who carry out the pianist's will and are the direct creators of piano playing.

We are all of us constantly saying how essential so-called "finger strength" is for the pianist. This idea needs to be closely examined in order to avoid possible errors.

What we frequently and mistakenly call "finger strength" is in actual fact only the ability of the fingers and hand to support any kind of load. Anyone conversant with anatomy and physiology will tell you that the strength of the fingers, properly speaking, is negligible compared to the force which the pianist is able to develop at the piano in case of need. This is not the place to examine this complex anatomical and physiological process although it is certainly not devoid of interest. Personally, whenever I have to speak of the locomotor system, I do so in metaphors, similes, comparisons, and every kind of symbolism which is a tremendous help to the pupil not only in sorting out his mistakes and insufficiencies, but also in correcting them.

I suggest that we consider the fingers not only as the independent living mechanisms that they ought to be, particularly for *jeu perlé*, *p* "non legato", etc., and all cases requiring clarity, precision, evenness, smoothness without much volume of sound, or cantilena requiring rich singing tone and when, because of the absolute legato, the hand cannot leave the keyboard for an instant; in other words, when we need maximum swing for the finger (with the whole hand helping, of course) since the "*h*" produced by raising the whole hand above the keyboard is precluded because of the absolute legato. All this, and much else (I am not going to give a full list of instances; anyone who is so inclined can do it at his leisure) is the realm of the finger as such, i.e. of the finger from the wrist to the fingertip (the "fingerballs" on the keyboard). The weight of the whole hand and arm will naturally be governed by dynamic requirements and will vary from the minimum to a very considerable weight for playing a melody f ("with a full voice").[1]

But fingers also have entirely different tasks to perform. If we need a very great volume of sound requiring maximum force (sometimes, as I mentioned, the whole body takes part, including its point of support on the chair. Some very temperamental pianists, for instance Artur Rubinstein, go one better and jump up and down on the stool, turning the "point of support" into some sort of peculiar power generator), and so, if we need a great, an enormous volume of sound the fingers are transformed and from being independently active units they become strong supports capable of bearing any amount of weight; they become pillars, or rather arches under the dome of the hand, a dome which in principle can bear the full weight of our body,[2] and all that weight, that tremendous load, these finger-pillars must be able to bear! That is the main task of the fingers! It would of course be more correct to call them arches, but I want to call them pillars because it sounds better!

[1] In such cases many pianists (Rachmaninov) swing their hand, arm and shoulder not only in order to feel full freedom but also in order to get the maximum swing of hand and fingers in a strict legato. Artur Schnabel in such cases even used a vibrato of the hand as if the piano were a bowing instrument. I consider this unnecessary since, as we all know, no amount of shaking the hand after a note has been played can have any effect on the sound.

[2] A pianist ought to be able to do the following gymnastic exercise: place his ten fingers on the floor and raise his body vertically. This is the full load which the fingers should be able to bear (these pillars, columns, arches, supporting a dome).

Unfortunately, one still comes across pianists, particularly lady pianists, who have no idea of weight, load, pressure, swing, and who, whatever the occasion, preferably play with dainty little fingers. Forgive my rudeness, but they remind me of *castrati* who sing only the highest notes. Whenever I happened to be, and specially to play, in their company, I would be reminded of Heine's verse:

> *Doch die Kastraten klagten*
> *Als ich die Stimm'erhob,*
> *Sie klagten und sie sagten,*
> *Ich sänge viel zu grob.*[1]

I think it is worth while discussing the hand and fingers somewhat further. The mechanism of our hand and fingers is ideal as far as piano playing is concerned. (As a matter of fact it is silly even to talk about it. Everyone knows what the hand is and what it means to a human being. I only wrote about it because some people who play the piano seem completely unable to cope with their hands and have no idea of their worth.) I intend to sing many a madrigal to the hand and fingers.

One of the most legitimate demands made upon the pianist is evenness of tone. A good pianist must be able to play evenly anything and everything, from the simplest elements of technique —scales, arpeggios, every kind of passage, thirds, all double notes in general, octaves, up to and including the most complicated combinations of chords. Once upon a time it was thought, erroneously, that because one needs to be able to play evenly, the fingers, too, should be even. How this was to be achieved since Nature has made all five fingers different, remains a mystery. But if we put the question this way: any finger must be able to, and can, produce a tone of any given strength, everything becomes perfectly clear, since it follows from this definition that all the fingers will be able to produce tone of equal strength.

The reader may be surprised that I should state so clumsily something so simple and understandable. But even in my childhood and in my youth, I have heard it said among teachers, as well as pupils, what a pity it is that the thumb is placed so

[1] Heinrich Heine: *Heimkehr aus der Fremde* (Yet the castrati complained / As soon as I raised my voice / They complained and they said / That I sang far too coarsely), ED.

differently on the hand, that it is "so strong" whereas the fourth finger, for instance, is so weak, poor thing, squeezed between the third and fifth which, as a matter of fact, are also in an unfavourable situation; now the second, perhaps, is the one that is well off, and wouldn't it be wonderful if Nature had made all our fingers equal and similarly placed. How easy it would then be to play well!

There is hardly any need to show what nonsense these pious wishes are! A nice outlook for the pianist if this finger equalization were to take place.

This, precisely, is where our luck comes in, that we have five dissimilar fingers, and as a matter of fact not five but all ten since the "mirror" arrangement of the hands on the keyboard (which is similar to the simultaneous appearance in a fugue of the subject and of its inversion) gives us ten different individual positions. Suppose we had two left or two right hands; how much worse off we would be! What an experienced pianist values most of all, in his fingers, is that every one of them is an individual, that each one has certain individual functions which it performs preferably to others, but that every one of them is capable of replacing its fellow in case of need. The well-trained hand of a good pianist is an ideal community: each for all and all for each one; each one a separate individual, and all together—a united community, a single organism!

I do not want to run ahead, since it is my intention to speak about fingering when discussing the properties of the fingers in the second addendum to this chapter. I will merely give, as an example, two fingerings which clearly show the "polar" (opposite) nature of the fingers and their use:

L. v. Beethoven, Sonata Op. 106

Ex. 32

This fingering is recommended by Hans von Bülow in his edition of Beethoven's works, and he calls it the "Chopin fingering", for indeed anyone looking at this passage (with the fingering 5, 4, 5, 4, 3, etc., as indicated) will immediately think of Chopin's passages using the top fingers (3, 4 and 5)—in particular of the Second Etude in A minor, op. 10—and hundreds of other cases. Of course it is perfectly possible and reasonable to use the following, pre-Chopin fingering particularly since this is Beethoven:

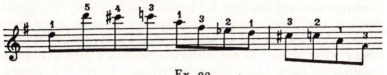

Ex. 33

But it is obvious to anyone that to play this bit with the Chopin fingering is convenient, natural and beautiful.

And here is the second (the "polar") example from Rachmaninov's Seventh Etude-tableau, op. 39 (with Rachmaninov's own fingering):

Ex. 34

In the first example (No. 32) the passage requires that the "thin" fingers (or as I called them earlier, the "weak" fingers) be used; in the second (No. 34) the abrupt, heavy staccato requires the use of the "heavy" thumb (in this case it is truly heavy) as often as possible. The end of the Eighth Etude-tableau in D minor provides an even better illustration; it is a typical solo for the thumb of the left hand. I shall have to come back to this example later on.

Even these two simple examples are eloquent proof of the fact that each finger has its own individuality with its own properties. In class, I frequently refer to the thumb of the left hand as "the cellist" or "the French horn" since in the piano score it is constantly playing the part played by the cello or the horn in an orchestral score.

All that I still have to say about the nature of the fingers is

closely connected with the principles of fingering that I intend
to set out in the second addendum to this chapter.

I have deliberately refrained here from saying much about
the arm—the forearm and upper arm—and have said even less
about the "supinators"[1] and "pronators"[2] for which I have a
hefty dislike, that is not so much for them as for the treatises or
methods in which so much is written about them and which are
of so little use to teachers and pupils alike. I already said earlier
that the decisive moment in piano playing is the contact of the
fingertip with the key and the actual tonal picture, or to speak
plainly, the music which this produces. I must state quite
frankly that if I manage to achieve what I had in mind, if I can
embody my "idea" in my performance, it is a matter of utter
indifference to me to know how my elbow behaved at that time,
what my good friends the supinators and pronators are doing or
whether my pancreas has a part in my work or not. One must
not think that this is mere dullness on my part. It is simply that
the knowledge derived from studying supination and pronation
—and this has been proved—is of no earthly help for the art
of pianoforte playing and, what is more, is to be found almost
always among those who lack that real knowledge with which
this book deals and which does actually help to improve piano
playing. If you do not believe my words, you will perhaps
believe my deeds, I mean my pupils.

I think that the considerations connected with concepts
borrowed from physics and mechanics will help an intelligent
person to understand the role and purpose of the upper arm as
well as of the elbow, etc., in other words, of the whole body, the
ultimate purpose of which in this case is piano playing, good,
correct piano playing.

4. On Freedom

I shall begin at the beginning. When I still taught very little
gifted and sometimes entirely ungifted pupils, I soon noticed that
their main locomotor fault was a terrible stiffness, a complete
absence of freedom. No sooner did such a pupil sit down at the
piano than he would turn to stone, wood, his joints would cease

---

[1] Muscles that turn the palm downwards, ED.
[2] Muscles that turn the palm upwards, ED.

functioning: a normal child who could walk, run, jump, play ball, dance with perfect ease would suddenly be turned into stone. The reasons are obvious: inability to cope with the task, fear of the instrument, utter unmusicality which bred a secret (and sometimes an overt) hatred of music lessons, notes, keys— everything. . . . I was still very young and inexperienced when I taught such victims of compulsory musical education and God is my witness that I was of very little use to them, whereas they made me suffer acutely. I did not know at the time that, as I have learned since, a tunnel has to be dug at both ends, and in order to help the pupils acquire at least some sort of flexibility, I suggested some exercises similar to the following: with the wrist raised and the hand hanging loosely down play a note on the keyboard from above, gradually lowering the wrist as far down as possible, in a quick, measured movement, then raise it again above the keyboard until the finger can naturally no longer hold down the key and is carried away quickly and smoothly, together with the hand and wrist. This to be repeated many times with each finger. This is quite a good system in itself, and, of course, in time the pupil acquires flexibility; but the trouble is that this method is purely technical and I failed to give sufficient attention to methods and means that developed the pupil's intellectual faculties. Of course, I did give him some sort of a musical education since we studied easy pieces and I tried (with tremendous difficulty) to get him to give a decent "musical" rendering. But I think that perhaps during this work my pupil was more influenced by my howls of suffering than by my method which was still in its embryonic stage. In short, I was, in this case, a conscious teacher of piano playing and only an instinctive, unorganized teacher of music.[1]

But I have already spoken on this subject. I only formulated my error because this same error is still perpetuated to this day by some insufficiently qualified teachers.

Subsequently, and even at the Moscow Conservatoire and at times even now, if a pupil did not have full control over his body, in other words when a pupil did not have sufficient freedom, I

[1] More accurately still: I taught freedom of physical movement but did not teach psychological, musical freedom. Inexperienced teacher that I was, this was a task still beyond my capabilities, and hence it was beyond the pupil's.

suggested the following exercises away from the piano: stand, letting one arm drop "lifelessly" like a dead weight alongside the body; let the other "active" hand pick it up by the fingertips gradually raising it as high as possible and having reached the highest point suddenly let go so that it should drop just *come corpo morto cadde* (as a dead body falls).

Would you believe it? This simplest of all exercises was at first beyond the possibilities of many of the frightened and cramped brigade. They just could not manage to disconnect completely the muscles of the arm which was to be the "dead body". It would come down half way but did not drop (probably because the other hand at the time was very active and thus influenced the first "contagiously").

I have several more exercises of this kind but I shall not mention them here since they partially coincide with exercises recommended in eurhythmics and I would therefore refer those interested to a teacher of eurhythmics or of the Dalcroze Method. They can tell and show them much more than I (besides which I find this awfully boring).

It is important, in order to have complete mastery over one's body—and the pianist needs this no less than the ballerina—to know "the beginning and the end" of any activity, "zero effort" (complete stillness) and "maximum effort" (what is known in machine design as theoretical maximum power), and not only to know, but of course to be able to use this in playing. And for this the virtuoso pianist must train by no means less than a prize-winning race horse. I deliberately repeat this well-known truth and I shall be repeating it again, should the occasion arise.

I sometimes tried, as I said earlier, by means of every kind of metaphor, simile, and comparison to help a pupil to understand what freedom is and to feel it. I compared the arm from shoulder to fingertip with a hanging bridge, one end of which is fixed to the shoulder joint and the other to the fingers on the keyboard. The bridge is flexible and resilient, whereas its supports are strong and firm (as soon as the hand and fingers are raised above the keyboard the image of the bridge is no longer accurate and it is better to think of a crane). This same bridge I sometimes made the pupil swing in every direction, to the left, right, up and down but always so that the finger resting on the key never left it for a single instant. This simple experiment showed the pupil in practice how great can be the flexibility, resilience and freedom of movement of the whole arm, while the fingertip rests on the keyboard with full confidence, accuracy and firmness. The finger, or rather its tip, must cling to the key, yet it should be understood that this does not require either much pressure or much force, but only as much weight as is necessary to hold the key down on the "key-bed". There is no doubt that this exercise is useful and, of course, not so much from the purely technical (locomotor) point of view, as from the point of view of understanding how the arm works. It is also a protest against the teaching of some old pedagogues according to which the ideal position of the hand on the keyboard is the one which allows a straight line to be drawn from the tip of the little finger to the elbow or above. Most harmful metaphysics! This is where one can see for oneself how senseless it is to apply "metaphysics" to each and every practical action. I maintain that the best position of the hand on the keyboard is one which can be altered with the maximum of ease and speed. Occasions might arise when the best position is the one where it is possible to draw a straight line from the little finger to the elbow, and that's all there is to it. Why then should this be the ideal?

As a matter of fact, think less about various positions and more about music, the rest will sort itself out, as Matvey, the valet in *Anna Karenina*, used to say. (But we, who have taught for so long and seen so much—meaning pupils—will keep on thinking about positions—or rather situations, and how to get out of them.)

Again and again I am tempted to repeat: *la souplesse avant tout*. From all I have said in the chapter on tone, the reader was able to see what importance I attach to legato playing; a real acoustical and physical legato or, to express it more precisely, playing in such a way that a note (key) is released only after the next one has been played and not an instant sooner. It is well known that Busoni rejected that kind of playing because he considered that legato on the piano was only imaginary due to the impermanent quality of the piano's tone. Legato is unthinkable without flexibility. What then is flexibility and how do we work at it?

So long as the pianist is playing such technical forms as trills, five-finger exercises and all their combinations on the same spot without moving the hand along the keyboard (what, in violin language, is called—in one position), the problem of flexibility hardly arises; the fingers must work well, the arm remain completely still and relaxed, that's all. But the moment we begin figurations, which require the thumb to pass under the hand or move away from it, in other words as soon as we transfer (move) the hand up and down the keyboard (that is to the right and left), the problem of flexibility is there. This flexibility is impossible without the forearm and shoulder (usually the former more than the latter) taking part. We see that already with a simple scale. I have known teachers who used to force their pupils when playing scales with the right hand downwards (i.e. from right to left) to hold the hand permanently sloping towards the index finger and the thumb. This was supposed to be convenient and beautiful. In actual fact, however, one cannot imagine anything more impractical. Or rather, this should be done only in a very few cases as an exception to the rule.

I suggest that anyone interested should play a scale first this way and then the proper way, which is the exact opposite; namely: as you approach the thumb (i.e. playing the fourth, third, second) the hand should be held sloping from the second to the fifth finger and in turning the thumb under, i.e. approaching the next position of three fingers in a row (third, second and first), the hand should describe a small arc over the thumb, a kind of loop, and at that moment, of course, the hand (more precisely, the line of the knuckles, "where the fingers start growing") slopes from the fifth towards the second finger (for an instant!) and the next instant it straightens out and the instant after it takes up once more the first position, sloping towards the fifth finger.[1] If you play a scale this way, loud and fast, the eye will plainly see the wavy line ∼. This wave will be particularly large in a scale played on white keys only (the reader will understand why).[2]

---

[1] How difficult it is to describe accurately this very simple process, and how easy it is to show it on the piano with just a few words of explanation!

[2] The greater the volume of sound the more swing is required.

What I am leading to is quite obvious: the concept of "turning the thumb under the hand" is replaced by the more viable and natural concept of bringing the hand over the thumb. And concentrating on the basic element of this movement we get the following exercise which I recommend very warmly:

Ex. 35

Play this beginning very slowly and gradually bringing it to maximum speed.

For the arpeggios the corresponding exercise is:

Ex. 36

At the beginning it is better to play the quavers on black keys; subsequently also on white keys.

In this movement the forearm plays a part (the "wave" is achieved thanks to the natural function of that excellent bone, the radius, and the corresponding muscles), whereas in the first case, when the hand is constantly sloping from the fifth to the second finger the upper arm becomes artificially immobile, almost atrophied.

With experienced, well-schooled, pianists all these movements (waves, loops) are hardly perceptible to the naked eye, but they are there, they exist, and retain all their force through proper, well-organized work.

And so, here is one of the simplest examples of flexibility, that sister of freedom. It is easier to show what the mechanism of this flexibility consists of, taking as examples widely spaced passages when the forearm, the elbow and shoulders inevitably come into play in the movement of the hand from note to note (from one key to the next).

These are Chopin-type passages (there are thousands of them in Chopin), as for instance:

Ex. 37

as distinct from Bach or Beethoven arpeggios:

Ex. 38

If we could make a slow-motion film of such a passage as the one in Example 40 being played (at the proper tempo) by an experienced pianist, we would see that the forearm is in constant and smooth motion, the wrist turns when and as needed, and thanks to this the fingers strike the keys they need and are always, at every instant, in the most favourable and convenient position for so doing. This position is taken care of by the whole of the "hinterland" beginning with those directly connected with the "frontline", that is: the hand, wrist and arm, and ending, as I have said more than once, with the back and the point of support of the body on the piano stool. But the first to take care of all this is our reason or rather our discernment.[1]

[1] Even this has to be said. I had a pupil once, a very practical and smart young man in everyday life, who always managed to get his way but who was rough and clumsy at the piano. I often asked him: How is it that you manage so well in your life and so badly at the piano? Then followed, of course, advice. But as far as "life" is concerned, it was he who gave me advice . . . which I did not follow.

Strange as it may seem, pupils sometimes mistake the concept of "favourable position", "convenience", for the concept "inertia". These are not only two entirely different things, they are also contradictory. The attention required for ensuring well-ordered, organized playing, that same "reasoned playing" of which I keep on speaking, excludes both physical and spiritual inertia; this inertia is all the more inadmissible when practising technically difficult bits, for instance very fast leaps (such as in Scriabin's Sonata No. 5 or No. 8, the Second or Seventh of the Transcendental Studies by Liszt, etc.).

By "favourable position" I mean a dialectical concept which can also include, as one of the cases it covers, the concept of "extreme tension".

I derived great benefit in my youth from listening to my teacher, Leopold Godowsky, and watching him as he played at home, while I would sit not far from the piano. He was fond of playing at home his own most difficult arrangements of the Chopin études, Strauss waltzes, etc., which he seldom played in public. It was a delight to watch those small hands (he himself was short) that seemed chiselled out of marble and were incredibly beautiful (as a good thoroughbred racehorse is beautiful, or the body of a magnificent athlete) and see with what simplicity, lightness, ease, logic and, I would say, wisdom, they performed their super-acrobatic task. The main impression was that everything is terribly simple, natural, beautiful and completely effortless. But turn your gaze from his hands to his face, and you see the incredible concentration: eyes with lids lowered, the shape of the eyebrows, the forehead, reflect thought, enormous concentration—and nothing else! Then you see immediately what this apparent lightness, this ease, costs; what enormous spiritual energy is required to create it. This is where real technique comes from!

I confess that the delight and reverence which Godowsky's playing aroused in me was shared in equal measure by my ears and by my eyes.

To strive for the most favourable position of the fingers at every single moment is impossible without complete flexibility, and is achieved only through foresight. Teachers are aware how frequently their pupils' faults are due solely to the fact that they are incapable of looking ahead, of anticipating, and are caught napping by events. When the mistake has occurred the teacher must show the pupil that he was wise after the event and teach him to overcome this weakness. (Which of us has not had pupils who during their playing constantly—almost systematically— make mistakes and correct them, again make mistakes and again correct them. I used to tell them: Remember, a mistake not made is gold, a mistake made and corrected is copper, a mistake made and not corrected. . . . I leave it to you. Of course I also gave them more serious advice, the main purpose of which was to ease the work, to divide it.)

Here is a simple example of how to develop foresight; I suggest to play a scale thus:

Ex. 39

The aim is clear; since the difficulty of the scale lies mainly in the thumb (with inexperienced players it is wont to thump and destroy evenness) it is suggested that it be placed beforehand (gracenote) very lightly over the spot (key) which it must occupy in the near future, in other words that it be ready in good time (in actual fact this exercise, too, is more of an analytical than of a locomotor character).

So long as a pupil's playing is marked by "bursts" where smoothness is required, and angularity instead of flexibility, I am fond of inflicting on him exercises of the slow-motion film type. An excellent subject for such experiments is Chopin's Third Prelude in G major op. 28 (but of course there are endless such possibilities).

Ex. 40

Many pupils find it difficult to play this complicated figure fast and evenly. Then I make the pupil play it very slowly, step by step, as it were, watching to ensure that the necessary movements of hand, wrist and forearm are carried out completely smoothly, gradually, without a single hitch, without the slightest jolt. But the main thing here is to prepare with foresight, i.e. with an accurate estimation (with "previously determined intent") the position of each finger on the key it next requires. The critical point of this figure is:

Ex. 41

The "improvident" pianist will, after the notes:

Ex. 42a

leave his hand turned slightly to the left (outwards) since that was the previous position he needed and then, in a sudden spurt (there he goes, wise after the event!) change his position in order to send his thumb, which had just been busy with G, to the E it requires, and so you get your unevenness, angularity, instead of a well-rounded line—a zigzag, and instead of a curve—a sharp corner. The "provident" pianist will while playing the notes:

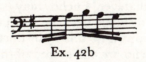

Ex. 42b

gradually turn his hand to the right (inwards), and will prepare the thumb in advance (he will space his thumb and fourth finger for the interval of the sixth) and quietly, supply and smoothly the thumb will take the required E.

When practising this exercise, which is again more useful from the analytical than the locomotor point of view (incidentally, I insist that this should be done many times and for a long time), attention is given mainly, as will be easily seen, to the work and movement of the hand (also the wrist and forearm, etc.),[1] in short to the "hinterland" near the "firing line" ("front"). In such playing the fingers are very quiet, they "lay" themselves on the keys without superfluous activity.

This is one of two main methods of mastering legato in passages. Another method, equally important but essentially contradictory, consists of playing the same figure from the Chopin G major Prelude with the hand (wrist and forearm) as still as possible, reducing movement to a minimum, in other words, trying as much as possible to do the whole work with the fingers which, in this case, must show maximum activity, liveliness and energy. A sequence of these two contrasting methods will guarantee the solution of the problem. And if you play this Prelude for a sufficiently long time ("repetition is the mother of learning") with these two (in principle contradictory) methods, bringing the tempo gradually to the speed required by Chopin and by the meaning of the work, you will yourself notice that what "comes out" is yet a third method which is a synthesis of two antagonistic principles, the unity of contrasts. It is at that precise moment that the problem is solved.

I dwelt at length on this question and went into the minutiae of all the stages of the work involved in this technical problem because I wanted to show that properly organized piano teaching which gives good results is inevitably based on the principles of materialistic dialectics.

A few words still need to be said in this section on flexibility about mastering large intervals, quick transfers of the hand, leaps and jumps. This is truly the realm of non-Euclidian geometry since, whatever Euclid may say, our first axiom states: the shortest distance between two points is a curve. The technically gifted pianists do this by instinct, but the less skilled, particularly those who are still scared of the keyboard, are apt,

over large distances, let us say: 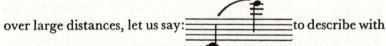 to describe with

the hand a broken line in the air instead of the natural curve: ⌒. In the first case the hand carries out three movements: ⌐ which is complicated and inconvenient. In the second case only one movement: ⌒. But in the second case attention,

----

[1] They can even be reasonably exaggerated.

intelligence, self-control are exercised much more intensely than in the first; it is not superfluous to repeat here this simple truth since it brings us to one of the fundamental formulae which determine good, skilful piano playing, as distinct from bad and unskilled. This formula is applicable to any psycho-physical work: mental tension is in inverse proportion to physical tension. (This formula—forgive the pompous expression—could already be deduced from my description of Godowsky's playing, but I nevertheless state it here because experience has taught me that, for some reason or other, the simplest, most lasting truths are particularly liable to be forgotten. This "formula" is as old as the hills, yet to this day many pianists are incapable of applying it in practice.)

The problem of flexibility is particularly important (because more difficult to solve) for pianists with small and hard hands. Large, supple hands, provided, of course, that they are governed by a well-organized head, find it much easier to acquire flexibility, freedom, *souplesse*.[1]

Small hands with a small stretch have quite obviously to make much greater use of wrist, forearm and shoulder, in fact the whole of the "hinterland", than large hands, particularly large hands with a large stretch. It's an ill wind . . .; sometimes this is just why gifted people with small and difficult hands have a better understanding of the nature of the piano and of their "pianistic" body, than the large-handed and broad-boned.

But the most difficult for small hands with a small stretch is to achieve freedom (and accuracy!) in heavy chord technique. I consider it a personal achievement, or rather not my own achievement but that of my hands, that they can easily perform such works as, for instance, Reger's "Variations on a Theme by Bach" and many others of that kind.[2] When a small hand which

---

[1] In this respect I know of no better hands than those of Sviatoslav Richter. He can easily take a twelfth, he can take in one go such chords as **a)** or **b)** , he has a tremendous stretch between the fingers, and as for the head, well this hardly needs commenting upon.

[2] At the same time such compositions as, for instance, the Chopin concertos hold no physical difficulties for my hand.

can just about take four-part chords with a minor third between thumb and index finger, for instance ♫ in the right hand and ♫ in the left, to say nothing of the practically unmanageable five-part chords such as ♫ in the right hand and ♫ in the left, when such a hand has to play such chords with great force and in quick alternation, it is almost precluded from doing a free drop of the hand from a great height (*h*!),[1] first of all because only extreme closeness to the keyboard will guarantee accuracy, and secondly because the extreme tension of the muscles (extensor) which stretch the fingers to the utmost limit almost inevitably deprives the whole system, from shoulder to wrist, of the greater part of its freedom and natural weight.

I must confess that with the hands I have, I was obliged to put in a great amount of work to acquire decent chord technique. In chords which are convenient for my hands, as for instance:

frequently (if this happens to be necessary and the music is full of enthusiasm and climax), without premeditation or qualms I raise my hands above my head (in general *quantum satis*, as much as I feel like). But when I have to take very difficult chords which require maximum extensor tension and where a milli- metre is literally decisive as far as "clean" and "smudge" are concerned, "*h*" is partially replaced by "*v*" because the hand is forced to remain close to the keyboard. But not altogether. I have at times painstakingly worked in order to force the forearm and upper arm, in spite of the sensation of extreme tension in stretch- ing, in spite of the great expenditure of strength caused by that stretch, to feel nevertheless detached from that stretch which is mainly the concern of the extensor and *interbone* muscles, in

---

[1] That same fall which, as I said earlier, produces a great volume of tone without any physical effort.

other words, to be independent and free as far as this is possible. As you see, it is again just a matter of discerning practically the difference between the work of various muscles and their groups.

Of course a very small hand will never achieve that feeling of freedom (and of might!), I would say of "mightiness' and "power" which is inherent in large hands able without discomfort or effort to grasp the biggest multipart chords and which is, so to say, their birthright. (Imagine, for instance, Anton Rubinstein's lion's paws, or the enormous soft and powerful hands of Rachmaninov). Small hands in such cases will not be able to forego the subterfuges, the ability to manage in a difficult situation which they acquired over the years by dint of hard work and not without the help of the intellect. In short, they turn their drawbacks into advantages and that is, of course, victory of the spirit over the flesh and consequently particularly precious. But, nevertheless, they will never be able to compare fully with hands which do not need any subterfuge and which, acting by instinct, at once, like nature itself, subjugate the piano and reign over it unchallenged. I know I shall be damned for this discouraging statement, "all wrong from the psychological point of view". But in fact there is nothing discouraging in this. One must reason soberly and not dodge reality. I often preach to my pupils that one plays the piano first of all with the head and ear and only then with the hands, and that it is possible to play very well with "bad" hands and very badly with "good" hands. This is already a great consolation for those who need it. But then I add that exceptional, unique pianistic achievement is possible only when there is full harmony between the pianist's spiritual and bodily faculties (i.e. when both his talent and his hands are exceptional). You have seen casts made of the hands of Liszt, Anton Rubinstein and others. Look at the hands of our contemporary, most powerful virtuoso pianists: Richter, Gilels, Horowitz . . . You will see immediately, at a glance, that these are hands that are particularly and exceptionally adapted to great piano playing. The origin of such hands is twofold: first, a person is born with talent and with excellent hands (and this, as we know, does not depend on us); secondly, being talented, that is, loving and wanting to play (and talent is, I repeat, a passion), the owner of such hands plays much, plays correctly, plays well and consequently develops in the best possible manner the wonderful hands Nature has given him (and that does not depend on us). Thus the real pianist becomes what he is: if pianists with inconvenient hands cannot imitate him as far as the first point is concerned, let them imitate him in the second—good results will not be long in coming.

5. *Elements of Piano Technique*

Now a few words about the various aspects of piano technique. From the point of view of statistics or, if you will, of phenomenology, there are exactly as many technical problems as there is piano music. Not only each composer, but also the various periods of his work present entirely different pianistic problems arising not only out of their content, but also their form and pianistic writing (compare Beethoven's "Pathétique", op. 13 with the "Hammerklavier" op. 106, or Scriabin's Preludes out of op. 11 with his Tenth Sonata op. 70, or Chopin's Rondo in E flat major op. 16 with the Sonata in B minor op. 58, or with many of the études, etc.). But this observation which is, in substance, appropriate for the musician who carries in his head an enormous amount of music—sometimes almost the whole of the history of music, gradually collected—is of little concern to us in this specific case since it has hardly any bearing on the problem of a pianist's development, his growth, maturity and mastery. It is merely the result of his development as a whole. The gradual development of the musical and pianistic potential of a young pianist should, according to the overwhelming majority of teachers, be based on the gradually increasing musical and technical difficulties of pianoforte literature. Some teachers even consider that this gradualness is a decisive factor in a pupil's progress and should be strictly observed. For the musically average pupils who fill our numerous schools this is probably true. But in our conservatoires, and specially the Moscow Conservatoire and even in the Central School of Music attached to the Conservatoire and attended mainly by very gifted children, this rule of strict gradualness is, for obvious reasons, subject to considerable variations and is sometimes completely done away with. Or let us say: the laws of development and consequently of a certain accumulation of knowledge remain in force but are implemented quite differently from what teachers believe, who deal mainly with the average pupil. What will you make of the following fact: one of my pupils, in the ninth class of the Central Musical School (Yuri Gutman, son of the well-known pianist, T. Gutman) played perfectly beautifully eight of Liszt's Transcendental Studies which are rightly considered as the summit of piano virtuosity and, incidentally, such extremely difficult ones as No. 2 in A minor, *Irrlichter*, *Wilde Jagd*, *Eroica*, he played in a manner that none of my finalists could equal. Yuri Muraviev, when he was sixteen played Scriabin's Fourth Sonata in a way which only a mature pianist, close to Scriabin's style and creative spirit could equal. It may be objected that these are exceptions, great gifts! Yes, they are exceptions as far as the great mass of pianists inhabiting the USSR is concerned, but within the precincts of the Moscow Conservatoire they are far from being as rare as all that.

Why do I say such well-known things? Only in order once more to dispute this time-worn teaching tendency to put all pupils in the same bag and lay down extremely rigid rules concerning the development of the pianist. If someone like Gutman were to be offered some special technical training, such training could embrace every aspect of technique that has evolved during the lifespan of pianoforte music, whereas an average pupil can be given only a limited and narrow selection.

And so, on the one hand, there are as many problems as there is music, and on the other hand—you can find in the most varied problems something common to all; the boundless wealth of form in the pianistic language can be reduced to its simplest elements till you get to the "fundamental nucleus", the "centre" of the whole phenomenon. And that is precisely the "nucleus" (from the point of view of the physical mechanical process) that I had in mind when speaking of the symbols "*m*", "*v*", "*h*", "*F*" or of Chopin's First Exercise.[1]

[1] The natural and justified desire to find a common denominator, the "original cell" of a complex phenomenon sometimes leads to amusing misunderstandings. Thus I sometimes heard teachers not unacquainted with questions of methodology say that "one should somehow be able to play a single note well, and then one can play everything well". If this isn't black magic, may I drop dead! This is a case where an observation which is fundamentally correct

And so, for the sake of being systematic—which is by no means so important for the talented or even the technically skilful—or those gifted from the locomotor point of view—for the sake of the system, let us consider that on the way between that "original cell" of which I spoke earlier and the universal piano technique which all truly great pianists possess, there is, as one of the useful means of organizing pianistic work, that same system (or table) of various aspects of technique which is what I now intend to discuss.

These "aspects" of technique I frequently call, in class, "raw material", "preparations", "prefabricated parts"[1] of which in the long run the great edifice of piano playing as a whole is made up. These fundamental aspects—let us call them elements —are not so numerous and one is tempted to draw a comparison between Mendeleyev's periodic tables which contain only 102 elements in our infinite, unbelievably wealthy and varied material world and that small table of fundamental elements which make up the whole of the limitless variety and wealth of

---

led to completely erroneous conclusions. The converse statement is true: if a pianist is able to play everything very well, he will also be able to play a single note very well. This expresses the conviction that one single note is sufficient to distinguish a very good pianist from a bad one. Logically this is of course true; a block of marble differs from a mound of quicklime as a whole and in each of its molecules, but I doubt whether we need go deeper into such questions. I cannot help thinking of the mediaeval disputation concerning whether or not ten thousand angels could hold on the point of a needle. I took this erroneous thinking as an example of the sort of thing I came up against in my travels through the Soviet Union and in my frequent meetings with teachers and pupils.

These are some of the questions put to me after my talks and public lessons in some schools: How should one work at technique? How should one work at tone? In what class should one allow the pupil to use the pedal? Is it good when practising to sing everything one plays, specially melodic pieces? What should one work at more: heavy technique or light technique? How should one use the pedal? etc., etc. I can't go through the whole lot. But these are exceptions and oddities. I was often asked sensible and interesting questions which led to fruitful discussions.

[1] For instance while you are learning the E flat major scale it is a prefabricated part; when you play it, let us say, at the end of Beethoven's Fifth Piano Concerto, it is the finished article, because it is music.

piano music, here considered from the technical point of view. Have no fear—it is not my intention to treat you to a "periodic table" of the technical elements of piano playing; suffice it that I have already dished up mechanical formulae for your benefit. But since a knowledge of the elements of technique is of very ancient and venerable origin and since here too, as indeed practically anywhere else, I do not intend to say anything new but only remind readers of what should not be forgotten, I shall take the liberty of giving this small "table".

As the *first element* I suggest we take the playing of one note. A pianist with an inquiring mind and a true thirst for knowledge cannot fail to be interested even in this amoeba of the piano-playing kingdom. As a proof that I am not alone to hold such views, I will tell you about an actor who in his early youth managed to have an audition with some very great actor. The young actor recited Hamlet's "To be or not to be", some poems by Pushkin, and some other pieces. The veteran actor said: "Yes. Very good, and now try to say 'Ah' seventeen times: an admiring 'Ah!', a questioning 'Ah', a threatening 'Ah', an astonished 'Ah', 'Ah' as a cry of pain, a joyful 'Ah', etc., etc." (Probably there are more than seventeen different "Ah's" in nature.) This is what I mean when I say that the playing on the piano of one single note with one finger is already a problem, and an interesting and an important problem from the point of view of knowledge and experience.[1]

Of course the interjection "Ah" has that advantage over a single musical sound, that it is already some sort of complete expression, it is already speech, whereas a single note is not yet music, musical language; music begins with at least two tones. The famous single G flat of the night watchman in the second act of *The Mastersingers* is music, and even the music of genius, but only because of what comes before and after it. If you were to imagine this G flat without "past" or "future", as a tone by itself, it would not be music. But on the piano it is possible to play a single note in so many different ways that this in itself is already an interesting technical problem.

---

[1] It need not at all be the same note (key); one could for instance alternate black keys with white, change the register, use the pedal or not, but the note should, in my opinion, be isolated from any context.

Earlier, in the chapter on tone, I said that even on one single note it is possible to experiment the whole of the tremendous dynamic range of the piano. Moreover, it is possible to take that one note with different fingers, with and without the pedal. And in addition it can be played as a very long note and held until its complete extinction, then as a short note, and so on, to the very shortest note possible.

If the player has imagination, then in that one note he can (as Wagner did) express a variety of shades of feeling: tenderness, and daring, and anger, and Scriabin's *estatico* and loneliness, emptiness and much more, of course, by imagining that that sound had a "past" and has a "future". If you are a musician, and a pianist, and that means that you love the sound of the piano, then this messing about with a single sound, a beautiful piano sound, this listening to the wonderful trembling of the "silver" string, is already a great delight, you are already on the threshold of Art.[1] Even a child can become interested in this at first sight mechanical and unmusical problem, if you awaken in him—as I already said—the love of experiments, knowledge, setting him for the first time on the path to artistic technique.

The second element. After one note (key) come, naturally, two, three, four and then all five (all that the hand is blessed with!) and here we come to the Chopin formula, from which it is but a step to learning the extremely useful first two studies in Clementi's "Gradus ad Parnassum". A manifold repetition of two notes produces a trill. I advise practising trills mainly by two contrasting methods (remember what I wrote on p. 108). The first method: play the trill with the fingers *only*, raising them from the hand, the arm remaining absolutely quiet and relaxed (no cramping, no hardening, no stiffening!). Play from *pp* to the *f* possible under the circumstances (without participation of arm, wrist, etc.) first slowly, and increasing speed to the

[1] Some may object: "Yes, that may be so, but only if you have a wonderful instrument. But where will the 'wonderful tone of the piano' come from, when one has so frequently to play on ghastly old upright pianos?" Those who say this don't know the piano. However horrible the original sound may be at first—the moment when the hammer hits the string, the rasping, jangling of loosened keys and other similar delights—what follows—the vibration of the string after it is hit—is good even on the most revolting instruments. Try it and see!

maximum possible. Play with all the fingers (1-2, 2-3, 3-4, 4-5 and also 1-3, 2-4, 3-5, 1-4, 3-1, 4-1, also 1-4, 3-2, etc.), play on white notes only, on black notes only, and on white and black. Play both slowly and fast. In non-legato raise the fingers over the keys—feeling their free but light swing. Play also (and that is perhaps the most difficult since it requires exceptional experience) without at all raising the fingers over the keys so that not even a cigarette paper or razor blade could be slipped between the fingertip and the key surface. Such a trill in some pieces (for instance Chopin Nocturnes, and a host of compositions by Debussy, Scriabin, Ravel, Szymanowski, etc.) sounds exceptionally beautiful (of course with the pedal!) and almost recalls the violin vibrato on one string. You will yourself understand the tremendous benefit—apart from learning to play the trill—of this type of work for the highly important sensory technique, for which it is so essential to master the minimum "h" which I mentioned above. The second method is the opposite of the one just described. It is the maximum use of rapid vibration of the wrist and forearm, possible thanks to our excellent bones—the radius and elbow—and their muscles. This method is particularly convenient when the trill must be loud, but also in other cases since it is always more natural and convenient than the first, which excludes participation of the arm and wrist and thus implies, from the natural point of view, a certain artificial "switching-off". (But the first method is still an irreplaceable means of developing the independence of the fingers; however, more about this later.) In actual playing, pianists will, of course, find the second method, or more accurately a synthesis of the first and second (with a certain hegemony of the second), the most convenient.

And here I draw your attention to the fundamental principle of solving a technical problem: thesis, antithesis, and synthesis.

The combinations of three and four notes[1] which have been used *ad nauseam* in classical piano methods (Lebert, Czerny, Schmidt, etc., etc.), I suggest we consider (and practise) on the one hand as a preparation for the five finger exercise and on the other as a component of the diatonic scale. I will not dwell on them specially since everything that can be said about them is

[1] Of course we are so far dealing only with conjunct motion, degrees of a scale, not with chords (arpeggios).

better said with reference to the "complete formula", i.e. the five-finger formula.[1]

About evenness—and that, after all, is the main purpose of all five-finger exercises—I have already spoken and shall not repeat myself. The problem of developing finger independence, which is closely connected with that of evenness, is solved all the more successfully, the more attention the player will pay to ensuring that the arm, quiet, loose and practically motionless, is supported by the fingers acting as props: with such playing the knuckles are naturally raised (specially where the fourth— the weakest finger—begins). The arc formed by the finger from its point of support on the key to its beginning on the hand, supports, just like in architecture, the whole load, the natural, free weight of the arm.[2] Such playing develops the muscles between the bones situated between hand and wrist and that is what gives the fingers maximum independence. If, however, finger figurations are played with a hard, contracted hand, the fingers derive no benefit whatsoever, the muscles between the bones cannot develop and as a result the hand and all its muscles will become tired and weak.

But all this is so old and well known that I shall draw the line here. Of course in many of our peripheral musical schools, children still stiffen and strain their wretched hands and painfully squeeze unpleasant sounds out of the instrument. Remember, friends, teachers and pupils, and take it from me: playing the piano is easy.

The third element I consider to be all manner of scales. The new factor in scales, compared with the previous element, consists of the fact that here the hand does not remain in one position as was the case up to now, but is carried to any distance up and down the keyboard (that is to the right and left). Of this carrying of the hand (turning under and turning over) as well as of studying scales I have already spoken and will not repeat what I said. To the exercise mentioned earlier (see Ex. 39) I would add the following:

[1] I recommend that each exercise be played every conceivable way: from *pp* to *ff*, from largo to presto, from legatissimo to staccato, etc.

[2] Of course in leaps and jumps the finger has quite a different task: that of grasping the right key in "mid-air" as it were.

Ex. 43

Here the problem of turning the thumb under or passing the whole hand over the thumb (or rather both together) is taken out of the general context of the practising of scales, the scale is differentiated and decomposed into two elements: on the one hand, "incomplete" five-finger positions:

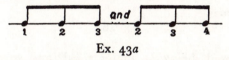

Ex. 43*a*

on the other—the passing under or over (change of position), change from one position to another. This exercise is also a transition from the scale to the arpeggio in its easiest form, since the positions:

Ex. 44

are simpler than the more difficult:

Ex. 45

which demand a greater capacity of wrist rotation.

And so, quite naturally, we have come to the *fourth element*, the arpeggio (broken chord) in all its forms (triads and every possible chord of the seventh). So much has already been written about this and so many études composed on this theme that I shall hold my peace. I would only mention once more (and probably not for the last time) flexibility and foresight and also complete evenness of movement if the arpeggio is in notes of equal value. I can just mention, as an oddity, that some

twenty-five or thirty times in my life, when I was young, I
played every conceivable chord of the seventh built on one and
the same note (let us say C): the result was the following
pattern:[1]

diminished second   second

minor third

Ex. 46

Then followed, below, a major third, and so on until all
possible chords of the seventh built on the same note were
exhausted. The awesome number of chords of the seventh (33!)
(and I naturally omitted the enharmonically identical ones)
cools the inventive ardour, but one can, if one so wants, play
passages which do not correspond to chord combinations but
which constantly occur in music.

One should not be too enthusiastic over this catalogue of
chords of the seventh, but the proof of the pudding is in the
eating; to play them evenly at a fast tempo, up and down over
three or four octaves is by no means easy, but a good pianist
does not shirk difficult problems and gives them his attention
when the occasion arises.

It is also necessary to work at other forms of chord passages,
for the study of which an immeasurable number of studies and
exercises has been written. One should not forget that, having
begun the study of arpeggios, for instance, with the Czerny
étude from the *School of Velocity*

Ex. 47

[1] This is a corrective to the usual arpeggio pattern on a triad.

or the *Art of Finger Dexterity*

Ex. 48

it should be completed with Chopin's Etudes op. 10 (No. 1 in
C major), or op. 25 (No. 24 in C minor), the F minor Etude by
Liszt, from the Transcendental Studies—for the left hand—and
other similar works including Scriabin, Rachmaninov, Debussy,
Stravinsky (once more, I repeat, the beginning and the end!).

Equally natural and indispensable is the progression of the
scale from the simplest study to such compositions as the Chopin
Prelude in B flat minor (No. 16) and a host of other similar
works. A talented and dedicated pianist does not shirk or shelve
such problems but tries to solve them in his early years.

The fifth element of technique I consider every kind of double
note (as I already said, from the second to the octave, and for
those who can manage—up to and including ninths and tenths).
The most essential things concerning them I said already on
pp. 77-79. But since the difference between double notes of
different intervals is rather great and the ways of playing them
differ considerably, I shall have to add a few words.

We are frequently faced, for instance in Liszt, with octave
technique which holds considerable difficulties for many,
particularly for pupils with very small hands. Apart from the
danger mentioned earlier—the "sympathetic" fingers, and
consequently inevitably smudged playing in a fast tempo or
f or *ff*—small hands are particularly liable to stiffness of the
wrist (as a result of the strain on the extensor muscles which
easily turns into stiffness of the muscles of the forearm). What
can one advise in such a case? First of all, be cunning as the fox,
crafty as Ulysses, and try with small accurate movements, with
the minimum of effort and strain and with maximum economy,
which is the result of reasoning, to achieve the desired aim, and
in particularly difficult cases at the beginning depart considerably from the required (assumed) degree of force and speed;
think first of all only of accuracy and that everything should be

done without any strain. Thus I advised several girls with small
hands who wanted at all costs to play the B minor Sonata by
Liszt, to play the most difficult octave passages—particularly
the passage after the exposition, which comes before the pedal
on A (in the bass), before the second subject in D major—to
play this for a long time not faster than "andante-andantino"
and not louder than *mf*, but absolutely accurately and freely.
This helped, a certain basis was laid upon which one could
build further. Afterwards I would allow them to play one bit of
this difficult fragment faster and louder, then two bits and more,
until they reached approximately the desired result (from the
virtuoso point of view) for the whole of the passage.

I can give an example from my personal experience: my
hands are not large and are fairly thin. Their only advantage is
their good build, strong bone structure and a harmonious shape:
when the fingers are stretched out and spread wide apart they
form a semi-circle thanks to a fairly long fifth finger and the
considerable stretch between thumb and index finger—which is
useful for octaves. The stretch between the other fingers is
far from sufficient; for instance I cannot take the chord
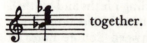 together.

For a pianist who is a "materialist" this is sufficient reason
not to seek "to apply his efforts" to a pianistic career; I myself
frequently thought so. And chords such as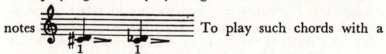
I can play together only by using the thumb for the two lower
notes 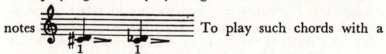 To play such chords with a
normal fingering (i.e. using all five fingers) is out of the question
as far as I'm concerned. Because of my thin hands and narrow
bones I do not have the springiness of pianists with larger, more
extended, supple and more fleshy arms (forearm and upper
arm)—whom I never cease envying—and consequently such
pieces as Rubinstein's C major Etude, many passages in Liszt
(for instance, in the "Fantasia quasi una sonata" *After a reading
of Dante*, or the quaver triplets in the Spanish Rhapsody—it is

impossible to mention them all) are, for me, of very considerable difficulty. Yet I studied all of them in my youth, including the "Campanella", the end of which:

Ex. 49

I found particularly difficult, and achieved a fully accomplished rendering of this bit only because I held my hand as near as possible to the keyboard, vibrating it but with mechanical accuracy, with a minimum "*h*", and listening with utmost care for accuracy, evenness and quality of tone.[1]

On such examples I mastered fully the rules of economy and proved to myself the truth of the adage that "necessity is the mother of invention". I need hardly say that this entailed protracted and stubborn labour (if a problem cannot be solved immediately it always requires lengthy training: this is well known), but I overcame the difficulty. I overcame it for three reasons: the principle of economy taken to its extreme limit, i.e. heightened imagination, a stubborn wish to get results regardless of any obstacles, and dogged patience.

This, I believe, is the picture of any and every successful labour if a man is possessed of a true passion, of wish multiplied

[1] Of course I sometimes also played this bit extremely slowly with the hand hanging freely down from the wrist (more "*h*"), in other words in a diametrically opposed manner.

by will. And for the sake of truth I must add that by no means have I always worked that way. I was frequently dull and indolent (I didn't feel like working—I was drawn to very different shores) and the result was what could be expected. There were times in my life when I worked simply stupidly and without will and alas, that would happen precisely when I consciously and deliberately turned away from music and music-making (luckily that happened fairly seldom) and set myself only technical virtuoso tasks (while my head was busy with entirely different and more interesting thoughts). Deliberately to turn oneself into a dullard without being one by nature cannot go unpunished.[1]

I must once more apologize for this excessively long story about myself; that is always somewhat indecent. But what can one do? I have already said that for a thinking man the pronoun "I" is one of the most interesting and reliable objects in his probing of the world of reality—and consequently needs to be reported on. Of course the description of my work on the "Campanella" cannot replace even ten minutes' demonstration on the piano, but I think the reader will understand me.

A few words more about octaves. The most important (this is already mentioned earlier) is to create a certain strong "hoop" or "semi-circle" from the tip of the little finger across the palm to the tip of the thumb, the wrist being maintained *absolutely essentially* in a dome-shaped position lower than the palm. This is far from easy for small hands and not at all difficult for large hands.

People with small hands—specially women—tend, when playing octaves—particularly *f*, involuntarily to raise their wrist higher than the palm and use it, instead of the "hoop" described earlier, as a support for the fingers playing the octaves. But then the middle fingers come too close to the keyboard with the resultant danger of "sympathetics" while the thumb and little finger (or if need be, the fourth) lose to a considerable extent their independence, their individuality, the "two-part" character of octaves becomes unattainable and the fingers become mere "pokers". It is not difficult to test the truth of this: I

[1] Incidentally this proves what actually does not require proof; that I am not a virtuoso pianist but simply a musician who knows the piano and can express himself on it.

stubbornly insist that all female pupils with small hands should hold their wrist lower than the palm and that they should concentrate all support in the "hoop" and not in a raised wrist. Sometimes it takes a long time until they master this position, but it can be mastered by anyone; this has been proved. The difference in tone—and that does matter!—between octaves played these two ways is also something anyone can hear.

In the correct position for playing octaves the palm and fingers form a rounded hollow. I repeat; a dome not too high, the highest point of which is not the wrist but the hand.[1]

Another observation which, as a matter of fact, refers not only to working at octaves but to any kind of technical work. As a rule difficulties are overcome by splitting up the work to be done, in other words by making the problem easier. This has been mentioned more than once already—if so-called intuition is not enough, then you have to use analysis and master the whole, one part at a time. With a certain amount of thought everything "difficult", complicated, unfamiliar, inaccessible, can be reduced to something much more easy, simple, familiar, attainable. This is the fundamental method. But, I repeat, not the only one. Dialectic requires of us an anti-thesis to this thesis. And consequently it will be right if the player, having understood that by facilitating his task he is gradually approaching its solution, will also understand that by increasing the difficulties, so to speak, to the limits of "theoretical maximum power", by making the problem more complex, he will acquire the skills and the experience which will enable him to solve his problem completely.[2] But the first method is the rule, the standard; the second is the exception which confirms the rule. To use a metaphor from everyday life, the relationship between these two methods is more or less the same as that between a working day and days off.

How then does this theory appear as applied to the practice of octaves? Very simple. I suggest that a difficult octave be studied with the fifth finger alone, holding the thumb at the distance of an octave, above the keyboard, "in the air" (see Ex. 29).

[1] For more detail on this see Preface to this edition.

[2] I repeat my advice: dig the tunnel from both ends, never lose sight of the beginnings and the ends.

If the player learns the octaves well with the fifth finger alone (if necessary, alternating with the fourth) and also plays them sufficiently often with the thumb alone (which is considerably easier) the execution of whole octaves will become infinitely easier for him. Let the reader think out his own variants of such work with respect to different technical difficulties.

The variety of ways in which octaves can be executed, as indeed any other of the aspects of technique, is very great and is governed by the musical content. I am, of course, speaking of musical literature as such, and not of exercises or études. Depending on the need, octaves are executed almost entirely with the fingers, only with the wrist, from the elbow (forearm only) and finally, with a very great ff martellato with the whole arm, which from fingertip to shoulder joint forms a strong, resilient but unbending pivot (excluding all movement of finger, wrist and elbow joint). This is so simple and well known that there is no point wasting more words on it. However, I often noticed that legato octaves (representing two parts comparable to an orchestral score where octaves are scored for 1st and 2nd violins), pupils play almost the same way as staccato octaves (but with the pedal), in other words by raising the whole hand over the keyboard and using excessive "h" (for the sake of force) which, precisely in this case, is unnecessary. The simple weight "m" plus some pressure, if needed, with minimum "h" and full finger movement—that is the proper way of playing legato, melodic octaves. A pianist who knows what he wants to hear and is capable of listening to himself will easily find the proper physical actions.

If anyone were to ask me which of the schools of octaves (ghastly word!) I consider to be the best, I would say—all or none.

In my youth, if I did decide to tackle octaves, I would sometimes play Bach's Two-part Inventions doubled, i.e. in octaves. This was both difficult and interesting. But mainly I would play all the octave passages of all the pieces I knew (and there were many) and thus learned octaves "in general". For some reason this method, which has been practised by all the pianists who have achieved something, is looked down upon by some teachers. I don't understand why. Am I really going to "forget", to "lose sight of" Liszt's sonata "as a whole" if, on certain occasions, I practise only its octave passages, together with octave passages from other pieces which I am just as incapable of "forgetting" as a whole, as the Liszt sonata? Will this really make me stupid, whereas I shall not become stupid from learning dozens of boring octave études which I shall never need, either on the concert platform or for my private delectation, while the octave passages from these beautiful compositions I need desperately? But I shall come back to this question at the end of the chapter.

As for the other more usual double notes—thirds, fourths, sixths, sevenths, ninths—I need only say that so much has been written about them and so much composed for their sake that I am reluctant even to start a conversation on the subject. To play scales in thirds or sixths (diatonic and chromatic scales, in major and minor thirds and sixths, taking into account the Godowsky exercises mentioned above) is, of course, an excellent thing.[1]

But if a pianist is interested in the problem of double notes not only as a performer but also as a teacher, he is bound to know the best examples of this type and learn them. Here is a short list of such examples (I refer only to artistic literature, ignoring this time the educational), Chopin, Etudes op. 10 Nos. 3, 7, 10 and op. 25 Nos. 6, 8, Posthumous Etude in D flat major, and a multitude of separate bits from such works (don't be shocked, dear friends and fellow teachers!) as the Second Ballade—from the following bit:

Ex. 50

---

[1] The main thing in double notes is precision of sound, the proven simultaneous sounding of both notes. Then, as in all passages— evenness, smoothness, mastery of nuances, bringing out where necessary the upper or lower parts, etc.

to the end, such as the Coda from the Fourth Ballade; Schumann
—Toccata op. 7 and a lot of places from all sorts of different
compositions (for instance: the Ninth Variation from the
"Etudes Symphoniques", No. 8 from *Kreisleriana*); Brahms—
the "Variations on a Theme by Paganini" (the first two
variations in the first volume and the first variation from the
second volume), etc.; Liszt—Etude *Irrlichter*; numberless bits
from various compositions, particularly arrangements and
fantasies; Scriabin—Etudes op. 8 Nos. 6 and 10 and a number of
Preludes as well as bits out of various compositions (for instance
in the Ninth Sonata the fourth and third pages from the end);
for those interested—three Etudes op. 65 (sevenths, fifths,
ninths); Rachmaninov—Prelude in E flat minor, from op. 23,
Etudes op. 39, Nos. 3, 4, 8, etc.; Debussy—Etudes Nos. 2, 3, 4
from the First Book, etc.

There I draw the line, probably to the great relief of the
reader. Why did I give this brief catalogue of double notes which
can easily cause bewilderment and even offence at the thought
of all the marvellous compositions which are here considered
from such a "prosaic", professional point of view? I do so in
order to show yet again that the performing pianist is not only a
musician, an artist, a poet, but also a workman at his lathe, a
100% professional, that his lathe is called a piano and that he
must not only know what articles he can produce on this lathe,
but must also be able to produce them and keep an account of
them. And it is such an account of a certain kind of article (in
this case, double notes) that I have given above. Take it from
me, the brain of any experienced professional pianist can at a
moment's notice produce such accounts referring to the whole of
pianistic literature no less accurately than a good book-keeper
in his own branch, and in so doing he does not lose a single
ounce of his dignity as a musician, artist, poet, but acquires
something else as a master-craftsman. And, anyway, what
would be the sense of the centuries-old and still not-outworn
division of the whole of our piano technique into elementary
aspects, if these aspects did not exist in actual piano literature?

Speaking of octaves I am reminded of a poem by Pushkin in
which the whole introduction is devoted to a discussion of the
octave[1] and its construction. This purely professional part of the

[1] Meaning the poetic form: AB, AB, AB, CE.

poem has lost none of its poetic quality through describing the technique of versification. Pushkin juggles with the octaves, setting himself the most difficult tasks and solving them as only a virtuoso can, to the utter delectation of the reader. I confess that no pianist yet has given me such delight with his octaves—not even Gilels in the Sixth Rhapsody—as Pushkin with his, in *The Little House in Kolomna*.

But let us look at the next aspect of technique.

The sixth element to be studied I consider to be the whole of the chord technique, in other words, three-, four- and five-note combinations played simultaneously with one hand. The most important thing in chords, as in thirds or sixths, is complete simultaneity, equality of all parts in some cases, and the ability in others to stress at will any one part by playing it with greater force. Here I would refer the reader to the basic exercises on p. 70. As always, success depends on complete freedom of the arm with complete concentration of the fingers (the soldiers at the front).

Pupils who are inclined to "labour" excessively at the piano should be reminded that the purely physical process of orderly and controlled piano playing consists of a constant alternation between effort and rest, tenseness and relaxation, more or less like the action of the heart (which beats without interruption from birth and even earlier, until death) or the action of the lungs in inspiration and expiration.

Diastole and systole—this is a very appropriate image for the piano. This is why experienced pianists can play ten hours a day or more without physical fatigue.

It is extremely important to observe this rule in playing chords since the tendency to overstrain—particularly for pianists with small hands—is here far greater than in passages of so-called "light technique" (the reason being obvious). So many times I have had to show and explain to pupils that to take a series of chords legato (of course with the help of the pedal) does not require any hard work if one can only rest—even for a brief instant—on each chord, sort of "sit on a chair", feeling relaxed, completely free, conscious of the natural weight of the arm from the shoulder to the fingertips and skilfully and quickly, keeping close to the keyboard pass from one chord to the next. A good example on which one can learn to do this and

understand once and for all what this is all about is the beginning of the exposition of Beethoven's Fifth Concerto (after the
tutti).

Ex. 51

Some pupils find this difficult and this is where a brief lecture on
rest, the full weight of the arm with concentrated, "intelligent"
fingers becomes appropriate, especially if supplemented by a
demonstration.

Since very frequently—or, rather, almost always, a series of
chords contains not only harmony but also a melody played by
the fifth finger (as in the example above) this should be given
special attention, the fifth finger should play clearly, it should
sing, *en dehors* as Debussy frequently indicates.

A good pianist has a special sense—a feeling which is born in
the ear and is transmitted to the hand—the "fifth-finger" sense.
Be it in *p* or in *f* it never abandons him when he plays
chords. Think of the Chopin Prelude in C minor, from op.
28, and hundreds, thousands of other cases. It is particularly

pupils with small hands who have to be reminded of the leading role of the fifth finger in chord playing. But actually, if the pupil is a musician and hears correctly, then not even the smallest hands can prevent him from producing the tones that are wanted. I have frequently noted this with great joy in class.

Chords that are neither legato nor staccato are relatively easier to play so long as the tempo is not too fast, for the hand can avail itself of a certain "h" which with a complete legato is reduced to a minimum (it is obvious that to take chords with the hand falling freely from above is easier than to take them practically crawling along the keyboard).

When first teaching chord sequences I would do the same as Chopin with his five-finger exercises. I would make my pupils play the chords slightly portamento but cantabile, in other words as they must be played in Chopin's marvellous Etude in A flat major (from the three posthumous études composed for the school of Moscheles and Fétis).[1]

Gradually one can tackle pieces (or exercises or études—but without getting carried away by them!) which require more f and greater velocity, for all this is more difficult and requires greater experience.[2]

Every time I try to give some "school advice" as I have just done, I cannot rid myself of a feeling of the futility of such an attempt—firstly, because our piano teaching has been codified into an excellent system (almost divided into courses); secondly, because the variety of learners and of their talents is so vast that however right all general statements may be, each case requires individual approach. In conclusion, I suggest that all those who are interested in the classification of the aspects of piano technique should draw up for themselves a brief catalogue, similar to the one I have given above, of the most characteristic (from the chord technique point of view) compositions or excerpts, in case they should be overcome by the sinful wish to

---

[1] Rimsky-Korsakov said of this composition: "here the very harmony sings".

[2] Anyway the best advice one can give someone who plays chords, is the advice of Liszt: Grab the chord, drawing the fingers slightly inwards towards the palm, and do not let them fall on the keys like lifeless pokers.

practise specially "the chord as such" but within the context of real music, that is, living piano literature.

As the seventh element one could consider the transfer of the hand over a large distance, so-called "jumps" and "leaps" (names which do not please me entirely). The main thing on the subject I have said already: the shortest path between two points on the keyboard is a curve. Accuracy depends on attention, watchfulness, will and training, and we can learn from the technique of sharpshooters. In both cases—shooting and "hitting" the right note—training and the whole psychological picture are very similar. Apart from attention, a feeling of complete freedom, a sensible economy of movement and the greatest demand on tone made by the ear, there is nothing one can advise. This last is particularly important since fast leaps of chords *f* are precisely that domain of piano playing where banging, thumping, and grating can easily occur. I have so many many times shown pupils, whenever these unpleasant complications occurred, that they can always be avoided; it is enough to make a small movement inwards with the fingers and sometimes the whole hand, towards oneself (only not outward, away from oneself!) and on no account to take the note—the key—sideways. However impetuous the leap, at the last moment the fingers come down on to the keyboard perpendicularly.

This perpendicular angle is so slight at a fast tempo that it is invisible to the naked eye, but it is there, it should be there and is achieved by precisely that slight grasping movement of the fingers to which I have just referred. When striking the key sideways, or away from you, the key hits the next key (or rather it touches the whole system of neighbouring keys).[1] That is precisely how you obtain a thump instead of a tone. It is easy to explain mechanically: part of the pianist's energy (force), instead of acting vertically on the key and the lever system it controls, is spent on a collision with the neighbouring key and not on raising the hammer which hits the string. Hence a brief formula. The more the thump, the less the tone. (Once, as a small boy, I saw a cat fall off the roof of our barn; she turned

[1] Forgive this metaphorical expression. In actual fact a physical collision is impossible. I merely wanted to stress the wrong relation of the fingers to the keyboard when the key is approached sideways.

over in mid-air and, accurately poised, landed on all four paws unhurt.)

Pianists please note.

It happens sometimes that the hand must descend rapidly on the keyboard and rise again, as an eagle dives for his prey, seizes it and soars away; if the hand were to fall lifelessly like a stone, it would get a painful blow, and the piano would howl with pain.

Believe it or not, these childish similes sometimes explained a great many things to the pupils, particularly since they were accompanied by illustrations on the piano.

Once, after a successful concert (it was in Saratov, I played the Scriabin concerto; I was in good form and was carried away, particularly since I knew the conductor needed a little help), a woman artist paid me a very nice compliment. She expressed admiration and added: "your hands hover over the piano like birds". I immediately remembered something Liszt used to say and which I had completely forgotten: *Die Hände müssen mehr schweben, als an den Tasten kleben* (The hands should hover over the keyboard, rather than stick to the keys). This excellent advice, delightfully expressed in rhyme, should be remembered when dealing with "leaps" and "jumps".

Why do I put them every time in inverted commas? I suggest we should speak of transferring, carrying, flying across, descending, etc., because leaping and jumping we do with our legs, and not with our arms,[1] or on horseback, but not astride the piano. Although we pianists cannot compete with singers as far as extravagance of language is concerned, yet even so we could do with some cleaning up of our terminology. Someone might object: "But you yourself keep using metaphors!". Yes, but they do not obscure the issue, but make it clearer. My pupils will confirm.

To conclude this point I would suggest that a list should be drawn up of particularly typical cases of "long-distance playing" (like a time-table of long-distance trains) and not just confined to the "Campanella". A must at the end of such a list is the famous passage from Liszt's *Don Juan* which, with the exception

[1] But birds, angels and other feathered creatures have wings growing from the same place as our arms, so I consider it justified to talk of flying.

of the Pianola, probably nobody but Ginzburg ever played
without a smudge. Here it is:

Ex. 52

The eighth element, the one dearest to my heart and the most
wonderful in piano music is polyphony. I have already
mentioned it previously, not only in the chapter on tone but also
here, in the chapter on technique, when I explained my scheme
of component "elements" in the section dealing with double
notes and chords. Luckily in this eighth section there is no need
to speak of exercises or études, since thanks to that great worker
and teacher Johann Sebastian Bach (and of course not only
him) they coincide with music itself in its best and purest form,
with the most noble of arts. For it would not occur to anyone to
attempt to master polyphony by playing Czerny's Fugue which,
when it appeared, caused Schumann to exclaim "Good heavens,
can it be that we can even expect an oratorio from Mr. Czerny?"

No. We will play Bach, Handel, fugues by Glazunov,
Taneyev, Reger and others, but we will manage without
Czerny's Fugue. We will begin the study of polyphony, as is
proper, with the "Anna Magdalena" Book, the two-part
Inventions[1]: then we will go on to the three-part Inventions, on
to the *Wohltemperiertes Klavier*, the Art of the Fugue and will
probably end with the preludes and fugues of Shostakovich with
which at the time of writing, far from everyone is acquainted,

[1] One of my teaching "peculiarities" is the advice to replace a
number of Czerny and Clementi études by a selection of "motor"
preludes from the *Wohltemperiertes Klavier*. Here is this selection:
Book I, Preludes Nos. 2, 3, 5, 6, 10, 11, 14, 15, 17, 19, 20, 21; Book II,
Nos. 2, 5, 6, 8, 10, 15, 18, 21, 23. Only twenty-one preludes in all!
Learn them—it will enable you to "save" yourself at least fifty
highly useful études. I know that this advice will arouse a certain
amount of displeasure in teaching circles; nevertheless I tender it.

but which have already caused excitement among all good musicians for obvious reasons: not only because "Shostakovich is Shostakovich", but because in his Quintet op. 57[1] (and also in other compositions) he gave us such a lofty example of the fugue that he is perhaps the only one to whom one might ascribe the slogan: "Catch up with Bach!".

A couple of considerations on polyphony on the pianoforte. As we know, Bach wrote his Inventions as a means of teaching singing tone. But, however hard you try, the piano does not sing as we would like it to sing; the piano is short of breath, the piano suffers from pulmonary emphysema. What can we do?

This is my advice: play the E major Fugue from Book II of the *Wohltemperiertes Klavier* some twenty times running. This is a choral fugue. It could serve as a conclusion to the second part of Goethe's *Faust* (chorus misticus). Suffer, yes, suffer anguish because the piano does not sound like a choir, because the fugue will sound dull, uninteresting, because the tones will die prematurely. Then try to play it faster than it should be played (belligerently, instead of mysteriously as is right) to prevent the tone from dying off; if you are a musician, the fugue will seem quite repulsive to you. Then get well and truly angry with old man Bach; say that this old wig-wearer did not know the first thing about the piano if he could write for that instrument a fugue that can only be performed on a harmonium or an organ, throw the music on the floor—then pick it up and start all over again.

Alas, this is no flight of the imagination. Something very similar happened to me (this was long ago) when I played on a dreadful upright one summer in the country not only this fugue but also many other very slow and cantabile preludes and fugues (for instance the very popular Prelude in G sharp minor from Book I). Now I no longer suffer or get angry, and not because I became less demanding of the piano (although of course we all get more tolerant with age), but because at that time I demanded the impossible, torturing both myself and the piano, and only *as a result of this* I achieved on it what is possible in terms of cantabile, enabling both myself and my hearers to delight in the piano works of Bach without any feeling of disappointment at the imperfections of the instrument. It was at

[1] Composed in 1940, ED.

that time that I thought of the following formula: "Only by
demanding of the piano the impossible will you achieve on it
what is possible". Thus, for instance, quartettists who have
learned Beethoven's *Grosse Fuge* op. 133—a work which is
practically impossible for the instruments—will play the
remaining Beethoven quartets and indeed any quartet infinitely
better. Perhaps it is this natural creative tendency of demanding
the maximum which is the reason for the three versions (and
particularly the second) of Liszt's famous *Douze Etudes d'Exécu-
tion transcendantale?*

But as a matter of fact this is a well-known phenomenon and
does not require further discussion. I just wanted yet again, and
on the strength of my personal experience, to repeat that well-
known truth that the study of polyphony is not only the best
method of developing the spiritual qualities of the pianist, but
also the purely instrumental, technical qualities, since nothing
can teach cantabile playing on the piano as thoroughly as the
multi-part texture of a slow work. Compare how much easier it
is to play cantabile Tchaikovsky's *Chanson d'automne* or let us
say, Chopin's Prelude in D flat major, than, for instance, the
following:

J. S. Bach, Fugue in E flat minor

Ex. 53*a*

Pianists who have not mastered their tone quality sometimes
produce a hideous effect with the two fifths:

Ex. 53*b*

Some might say: What is there to talk about? Everyone knows how much better, more beautiful, more cantabile is the effect of a one-part melody or a duet against the background of accompanying harmonies, particularly with the help of the pedal, than a strict polyphonic texture deprived of the support of a harmonic accompaniment or a pedal with its overtones. It is simply a case of different tonal problems. I am, of course, as aware of this as the next man. But what can I do if my stubborn desire, my "demand for the impossible" compel me, in the fugue referred to, to hear with my mind's ear a vocal part, a human voice just as in the *Chanson d'automne*, in spite of the completely different content of these compositions? I shall strive with all my might and in spite of all and every obstacle, to sing, sing, sing! Reaching for the impossible will achieve the possible!

I can imagine the ironic smile which this page would bring to the lips of Ferruccio Busoni who would not allow the vocal to mix with the purely instrumental. His idea to a certain extent was that when playing an instrument one should forget about singing since each instrument (and particularly the piano) has its own strictly defined characteristics, its own possibilities and demands which excellently match the music written for it and are entirely different from the characteristics and demands of the voice. Of course the proto-element of instrumental music is to be found in all the sounds of Nature, from the singing of the birds, the rustling of the forest, the gurgling of the brook, etc., to the fury of the stormy sea, the thundering of the avalanche and the howling of the hurricane and so on. But what can compare to the charm and expressivity of the human voice? To forget the voice of the human being, the proto-human sound, is impossible. It lives on in any and every music, like a hidden god, and everything stems from it and reverts to it.

I could add to this section hundreds of examples of the way polyphony is taught in our class, but I think it would be superfluous.[1] First, I have already said much (in the chapter on tone) about the many levels, perspective, and even about polyphony; secondly, so many good books have been written on the subject, well known to all musicians, that I can only refer

---

[1] I would only say that I have especially often to remind pupils that suspensions (usually discords) which are so important in Bach, must be clearly audible. Also syncopation.

back to them. I would still advise the reader to approach Kurt
and Schweitzer,[1] the most thorough and profound Bach scholars
along with our own Yavorsky, in a critical spirit. In spite of their
tremendous positive contribution and the great depth to which
they penetrated the subject, they are frequently guilty of
formalistic thinking (particularly Kurt in his *Musikpsychologie*).
But the reader will not find it difficult to sift the grain from the
chaff.

The best performance of Bach I have ever heard, or rather
the one I found most convincing and closest to my own
conception was by Sviatoslav Richter. Busoni made an unforgettable impression on me in my youth, but I only heard him
play his dazzling transcriptions. Unfortunately I never heard
him play any Bach in the original. I assume I need not explain
why I say this. I love what is truly authentic and not faked,
although many performers are naturally attracted by transcriptions.

If I were to attempt to say as briefly as possible why polyphony is so dear to me (as well as the greatest polyphonist of all
times—Bach) I would say: polyphony expresses in musical
language the highest union of the personal and the general, of
the individual and the masses, of Man and the Universe, and
it expresses in sound everything philosophical, ethical and
aesthetic that is contained in this union. It fortifies the heart and
the mind. When I play Bach I am in harmony with the world
and I bless it.

After this proto-element, or rather after my most beloved
element—polyphony, I have no wish to speak of any other
elements whatsoever. Besides, the fundamental, simplest types
of technique are exhausted. There is still a multitude of sub-
types, complex compound types, "hybrids", etc., which abound
in pianoforte music and which can be successfully classified,
joined or differentiated. But is it really so essential that I should
write a short report on the tremolo (of which Liszt was so fond
and which Chopin so completely neglected), or on "stretches"
or anything else, after all I have already said about economy,
firmness, sureness, flexibility, freedom, the "horrible" symbols
m, v, h, F? I think it would be unnecessary. Particularly since all

[1] Of Albert Schweitzer, another Albert, Einstein, said that he was
one of the outstanding figures of our century.

this is as old as the hills. If some "pedagogical prosecutor"—there are such!—were to catch me out in plagiarism I should be extremely glad.[1] I tried to speak only of things that really exist, and they have always been talked about by people who have searched for and found the truth. If, however, to spite the "prosecutor", "counsel for the defence" were to find in my notes traces of something new, all right then, I am game, let there be something new. I am not in the least bit worried as to whether this is old or new; I know as an old teacher who deals with the young daily and who has brought up hundreds of pianists, that this is *necessary*. Which is why I write.

In the near future such writings will probably be unnecessary. There will be tape recordings of actual lessons with "leading Masters" and of course all sorts of others too. These tapes will be duplicated and sent out to musical schools and conservatoires in various towns, as in the case of films. I hope that very soon someone will think of it. It would be tremendously useful. On the other hand it would be a great thing to make tape recordings of lessons in schools in various peripheral towns, including the smallest ones and play them to us who work at the centre, so that we should have a good idea not only of what they are doing there, but also of how they are doing it. Of course such lessons, both here at the centre, and on the periphery, must be entirely natural, unpremeditated, unprepared and unarranged, otherwise they would be without value. One could, of course, arrange an ideal lesson, a model of the highest level, worthy of being copied which would contain, compressed into portable form, hundredweights of wisdom and usefulness.

But, forgive my lack of modesty, I think that some of my colleagues, as well as yours truly could give such a lesson without any "arrangement" or, as Anton Rubinstein used to say, "as God willed it".

I may be accused of having failed to deal with many important questions of technique in my brief analysis of its component elements. But in passing, in the chapter on the artistic image and the chapter on tone I have constantly referred to technical problems; it cannot be done otherwise, for in art, as in life,

---

[1] It would mean that I am not the only one who says so, many others say so: one head is good, two heads are better than one, but a thousand heads—that is excellent!

everything is one, and all the aspects which we designate by different names are inextricably bound together. Moreover, I said from the start that it was not my intention to write a textbook on piano playing.[1] There are many textbooks, and very good ones too, from C. P. E. Bach to the *Notes on the Method of Teaching the Piano* published by the department for the theory and history of piano playing of the Moscow Conservatoire, (under the direction of A. A. Nikolayev). Unfortunately I am not very familiar with foreign publications on this subject. I merely wanted to pass on some thoughts and advice which occur to me daily in my work as teacher and performer, and to stress the more important aspects and principles. I repeat what I said earlier: the only exhaustive literary account of what goes on in class, in my personal work, at home and on the concert platform, would be a continuous diary, a daily record. But this I did not keep, for which I am truly sorry now, for every day brings something new and interesting in its own way. Man changes, much gets forgotten, including much that was valuable. The approach of old age and of that moment when one can say to oneself *finita la commedia* have prompted me to write these lines. On the other hand the legitimate requirement that all of us, professors in higher education establishments for the Arts, should study methodology, set out in some form or other our views on art and education and explain in words what we are doing, has served as a strong impetus.

[1] Although, alas, there is more than enough purely technical material in my book!

Addendum to Chapter IV

1. *On Fingering*

When thinking of fingering the first thing that comes to mind is the old Roman adage: *quot homines, tot sententiae* (so many men, so many minds).[1] But this fatalistic approach does not concern us; some men are nothing to write home about and their minds even less so (see the fingering suggested by some editors). What is important is to establish the supreme principle of an artistically correct fingering; all the rest will follow naturally. I think that in most general terms it can be formulated as follows: that fingering is best which allows the most accurate rendering of the music in question and which corresponds most closely to its meaning. That fingering will also be the most beautiful. By this I mean, that the principle of physical comfort, of the convenience of a particular hand is secondary and subordinate to the first, the main principle. The first principle considers only the convenience, the "arrangement" of the musical meaning which at times not only does not coincide with the physical convenience of the fingers, but may even be contrary to it. Here is an illustrative example from Beethoven's Thirty-two Variations—the last Variation before the Coda:

Ex. 54

[1] Actually this translation is not quite right, if only because there are, of course, many more men than minds. It should be: so many men, so many opinions.

It would be much more convenient, physically, to play this scale with the generally accepted fingering:

Ex. 55

But I must admit that even I, who have seen a thing or two in my time, have never met a simpleton who would attempt to play this bit with a "convenient" fingering. And the reason is obvious: with the "convenient" fingering it is dreadfully "inconvenient" to render Beethoven's phrasing (i.e. a definite musical meaning) of a series of two phrased semiquavers whereas with the physically less "convenient" fingers, 2-3, 2-3, 2-3, etc., it is extremely easy to render the phrasing and thus also the meaning. On the other hand, the fingering I have shown in Example 55 would be very good if the whole of this passage came under one slur.

Some may say: you have made things too easy for yourself, giving such an absurd example of "physical convenience"; didn't you say yourself that you never met anyone who would play it thus? I know thousands of editions and dozens of editors, and you can take it from me that I have come across fingerings almost as absurd as the one I suggested and sometimes, very seldom, it is true—just as absurd as the "convenient" example I invented.

After the first most important principle—finding the most suitable and useful fingering for rendering a given musical content, which will inevitably also be the most justified aesthetically, i.e. the most beautiful—we may take as our second principle the flexibility, "dialecticality", changeability ("variability") of the fingering, depending on the spirit, character and pianoforte style of the author concerned.[1] A small example from my personal experience: I never play a chromatic scale in Beethoven with all five fingers (going down

[1] This second principle is, in actual fact, merely a variant of the first, but I consider it so important that I prefer to stress it.

from B: five fingers, three fingers, four fingers, etc.) but in Liszt I constantly use this fingering. A similar case: nobody would probably think of playing even the quickest diatonic scales in the context of Mozart, Beethoven and up to Chopin, with all five fingers, in groups of five, as Liszt has indicated in the concluding part of the "Folia" from the *Spanish Rhapsody*—before the Jota:

Ex. 56

But it is quite unthinkable, quite wrong to play this bit with the usual scale fingering, without the little finger. And if one of my pupils evades this fingering because he is scared to play the thumb after the fifth finger (not used to it!) I torture him until he plays the passage quite dazzlingly and with Liszt's fingering. Why do I attach so much importance to this "trifle"? Because this fingering (with this music, of course) brings the whole of Liszt before me. I see his hands, his gestures, his eagle manner, I feel the breath of this demon in monk's habit. . . . There are no trifles in Art, everything is subordinate to the laws of Beauty, to the least detail. That is why I lay so much store on any fingering indicated by the composer himself, even if, because of the nature of my hand, I cannot avail myself of it. Look at all the fingering indicated by Rachmaninov in his compositions: why, it is a real lesson on how to perform them; "his own fingers" are an irreplaceable means of getting to know him as a pianist, of knowing his pianistic style.

A typical example of failure to understand the aesthetics of fingering, its inevitable correspondence to the aesthetics and character of the composer's own playing (which, again, is closely linked to his creative spirit) may be found in Karl Klindworth's edition of Chopin's First Ballade in G minor.

Here is his fingering in the arpeggio passage before the second subject of the subsidiary section:

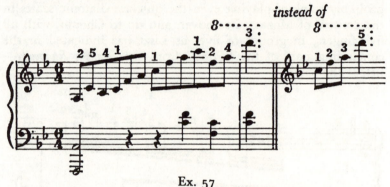

Ex. 57

Until the last (sixth) crotchet of this bar everything is perfect, and then suddenly, an unexpected gesture à la Prokofiev:

Ex. 58

Instead of the natural, logical fingering which corresponds to Chopin's idea of piano playing, which one meets at every step (see for instance the First Etude out of op. 10) in which broad intervals are performed in a complete legato.[1]

Ex. 59

Why did I mention Prokofiev? Well, because he was wont at times to use this insolently daring "football" flourish, so natural

[1] For those who doubt whether this fingering is suitable for very small hands, let me say: there is no hand so small that it cannot do this. The guarantee: flexibility, suppleness, freedom and accuracy.

for his temperament, but which Klindworth unexpectedly
adopted for the spiritually diametrically opposite nature of
Chopin. Here is an example of "evidence" from Prokofiev—the
Second Concerto in G minor, cadenza from the first movement
(all similar passages in that section are stubbornly marked with
the same fingering):

Ex. 60

Of course an experienced pianist can achieve the desired
effect with the most varied fingerings, but why, can you tell me,
use your right hand to scratch your left ear (and then over your
head) when it is so much simpler and more convenient to do it
with the left hand?[1]

A good artist can at all times and everywhere achieve
authenticity and harmony or, in other words, what we call
simplicity and we know that in Art there are no indifferent
trifles. And so don't scold me for having devoted so many lines
to two examples of fingering; for I think that for a pianist, the
performing problem I have raised is important and significant.

The third principle in the hierarchy is that the fingering should
be convenient for the hand in question taking into account
its peculiarities and the pianist's intentions. As for the pianist,
he is naturally bound by the two former principles. We all know
that a hand which finds it difficult to take a C minor tetrachord

Ex. A

[1] As we all know Mozart when a boy showed that it was possible
to play with the nose. Anton Rubinstein once said: "Play with
anything, even your nose, provided you play well!"

will manage the keyboard quite differently from a large hand like Richter's which can easily take a twelfth or such chords as the following from Rachmaninov's op. 39 No. 2:

Ex. B

The question is so clear that it is hardly worth dwelling on it. A pianist with even the smallest and most inconvenient hand can always observe the first and second principles of fingering if he understands music and has a sound pianistic culture; but he will observe them by using his personal, individual means and carrying out his own intentions and thus implementing the third principle.

If we study carefully the playing of great pianists we will see that their fingering differs as much as their pedal, their touch, their phrasing and, in general—their whole performance. For performance is also creative, that is, it is individual and unique.

I could, on the same lines as in the previous chapter, give a number of examples of discussions that took place in my class when we examined the fingering in compositions of various styles, or else give a critical survey of fingering in various editions. But that would again take me too far afield. The brief "theory of fingering" which I compressed into three principles seems to me entirely adequate to enable a player to come to his own conclusions in each case. But I would like to say something connected with myself personally and which, it seems to me, may be of certain interest.

Since I developed a pain in my right hand (as the result of serious polyneuritis following diphtheria in 1933-34) a radical change occurred in my "fingering administration". I not only began replacing certain movements by others (of course, entirely instinctively, for I have a great deal of experience, and I merely "registered" what went on) but I also changed the fingering ("If not with the cue, then with a stick" says the proverb). I used to be very fond of using Chopin's fingering (third, fourth and fifth fingers); nowadays I have to avoid it since after my illness these fingers have become "sluggish" (the fourth finger, particularly, has a tendency to lie permanently on the surface of the keyboard and it is only my intense watchfulness that prevents it from becoming a despicable "sympathetic" finger). I once had the following amusing and sad experience. I was playing for the pupils of a conservatoire in a fairly cold room (and that is really murder for my sick hand) Beethoven's Sonata in D minor No. 17 (op. 31, No. 2). The passage on the first page:

Ex. 61

did not come out quite clearly. The third and fourth fingers were "swallowed up". In repeating the exposition I quickly thought of a way out and played it with alternate hands, like this:

Ex. 62

The result was excellent. Then, in a talk I had with the pupils after the concert I begged the students for God's sake not to copy me in playing this bit and explained that I only resorted to this because of a certain weakness of my hand and the cold, but that a healthy pianist must play only as written by Beethoven.

All experienced pianists are able to replace one fingering by another if necessary, but in practising, one must, as a rule, learn one firmly established fingering, the best one of all those possible. For in actual fact we have also to use muscular memory,[1] which, as we well know, plays a tremendous part in all physical work (so-called automation). If I may so express myself ("scientifically") the pianist makes use of two memories, the musical (spiritual) and the muscular (bodily) memory. The first is, of course, much more important; it is the master and

[1] That is why "repetition is the mother of learning".

organizer. But the second also is indispensable; it is the faithful servant carrying out the work and making the master's task easier. It should be pointed out that when musically less developed pupils get confused or have accidents it is because they learn something mechanically, without the due participation of head and ear (the fingers remember better than the head), the "servant" does something but does not know what and the master is asleep. But accidents which occur to very good musicians (who have a strong master), occur because the servant is no good and does not carry out the master's commands. It is not always easy to make a clear distinction between the functions of the master and the servant, and to determine with accuracy who is responsible for the accident, but it is always possible; I know it from my own experience and from observing my pupils.

To come back to the question of my changed "fingering administration"; I will give one or two examples of what was before and what I do now. Before, I used to play the Second Prelude in C minor from Bach's *Wohltemperiertes Klavier* like everybody else:

Ex. 63

Now I play like this:

Ex. 64

Similar changes turned out to be necessary in many other bars. What caused these changes? In the second case, the hand has naturally more "swing" than in the first. Moreover the interval C—E flat (downwards sixth, see the beginning of the Prelude) if taken with the fifth finger and thumb requires a much smaller stretch than the same major sixth with the fifth and second finger.

And in view of the "sluggish" condition of my hand this is much more convenient. The presto from the Tenth Prelude in E minor out of Book II of the *Wohltemperiertes Klavier* I used to play with the normal fingering:

Ex. 65

not only without avoiding the "weak" fingers (third, fourth and fifth) but on the contrary, rejoicing that I could give them such good work to do.

Nowadays I am forced (I find it more convenient) to play it thus:

Ex. 66

In the Fugue in E minor (No. 10), which follows this Prelude, I used, of course, to play the subject thus:

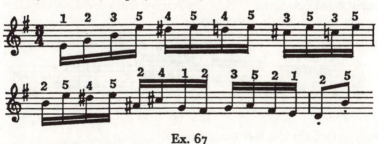

Ex. 67

But now I play it like this:

and so on

Ex. 68

I would point out in these three examples, how much more beautiful, economic and simple was the first fingering (the old) than the second (the new). But what can I do? At present the second fingering is more useful to me because it requires a greater swing in the rotating movements and a more frequent use of the thumb and second finger. One must make do with what one has.

Why, someone may ask, do I treat my readers to this "chirodactylopathology"? What is so interesting in it? I am interested in the pianist's ability to adapt himself to any given circumstances, to strive to achieve his aim by any means and not to feel bound by a strict dogmatic principle.[1] This principle is constantly applied by pianists with perfectly sound hands, but some dogmatists underestimate it, whereas my own trouble has convinced me afresh how effective and true it is. That is why I spent so many words and quoted so many examples.

The "undialectic" thinking of some young pianists, manifests itself for instance in such "trifles" as the preferred use of the same fingers in chromatic scales (not using the fourth, and even less the fifth finger), regardless of speed or force. Yet I am sure that they were taught that chromatic scales can be played, if and when necessary, with six different fingerings; I will not give these here as they are so well known, but I can add two more—mentioned previously—that are derived from dividing the chromatic minor thirds into parts:

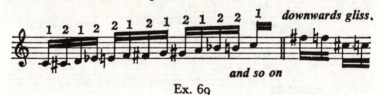

Ex. 69

and with only the last three fingers:

Ex. 70

[1] In this case, for instance, that fingering No. 1 in all three examples is better and more aesthetic than No. 2. If I were to reason this way, playing would be more difficult for me.

I greatly recommend practising these two fingerings. The first teaches an absolute legato by means of a glissando; the second strengthens the outer fingers and is a key to the mastery of Chopin's Etude in A minor, op. 10 No. 2, and of course op. 25 No. 6 in G sharp minor which, incidentally, I always suggest should be studied at the same time. I think that anyone who has a feeling for the keyboard and for his hand has derived pleasure from playing a complete chromatic scale with only "half" of his hand (the imaginary dividing line running between the index and middle finger).

In order to master glissando with all the fingers I sometimes suggested an exercise like the following:

Ex. 71

and also more spaced out:

Ex. 72

(but I do not suggest torturing oneself with it unduly).

Much more pleasant than this tedious stuff are the delightful exercises in glissando by Brahms with which he concludes his First Book of Exercises. These are no longer exercises, but almost intermezzi. They are full of delightful music, and are also most useful. Personally, I am so fond of glissando that I use it even for such passages as the following although it is by no means essential:

Ex. 73

I have dwelt on this particular type of fingering (glissando) at some length not only because it is so essential for chromatic thirds and many other instances, but also because practising it strengthens quite particularly the physical sensation of legato, that wonderful sensation which no pianist can do without. Sometimes when I am specially carried away and play with quite special love for music and for the piano, I am acutely aware of the pleasure I derive from the physical process of playing, the joy I feel not only in my "soul", my ear, but in my fingers from their contact with the keyboard. Chopin used to tell his pupils: "Believe that you play well and you will really be able to play well". In other words, feel pleasure, joy, happiness. This good feel of the keyboard is similar to the feel of a beautiful object that one holds in one's hand—a Greek statuette or something similar.

The understanding and sensation of individuality (of its own peculiarities) of each of the fingers, which I have already mentioned, is also one of the best counsellors for finding the appropriate fingering. I was overcome by a feeling of real "pianistic disgust" when I saw Ignaz Friedman's edition of Chopin's Fifth Nocturne in F sharp major with the following fingering:

Ex. 74

instead of the natural 4, 5, 3, 2, 1, 2. The thumb on B in Chopin! Surely anyone can see that the thumb on B would be right only if the phrase ran more or less as follows:

Ex. 75

After all, the thumb is used, obviously, when the hand has to be transferred from one position to another ("changing positions"), carried upwards or downwards along the keyboard, but it is senseless to use it when the hand, preparing itself for a non-existent "transfer", reverts to the previous position:

Ex. 76

I cannot understand how such a gifted and forceful pianist as Friedman with his tremendous experience both as a performer and as a teacher could perpetrate such nonsense. But as a matter of fact in his edition of Chopin, nonsense abounds! I will only give here the nauseating fingering of the passages before the subsidiary section of the first movement of the First Concerto in E minor:

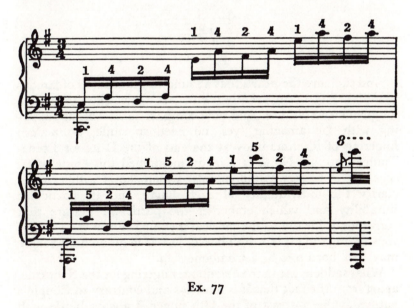

Ex. 77

(Particularly "lovely" is the addition of the non-existent grace note before the top E, which is added purely for reasons of fingering, and not for musical reasons. I find it difficult to refrain from bad language!)

Surely anyone can see that the proper Chopin fingering here is:

Ex. 78

i.e. the broad, first inversion (chord of the $^6_5$) of the chord of the seventh:

Ex. 78a

and not the cramped, anti-Chopin third inversion: (chord of $^6_4_2$)

Ex. 78b

And such are the pearls that abound in the editions of famous pianists! Pity![1] Apparently, with all their gifts they lack judgment and culture. And now compare this revolting fingering with the amazing (yes, no need to smile, a-ma-zing) fingering of Rachmaninov at the end of the D minor Etude-Tableau op. 39, No. 8 (I already mentioned this étude when speaking of fingers as individuals) which shows with extreme clarity the individuality of each finger and its particular suitability and which embodies the particular gesture that corresponds ideally to the musical meaning. From the point of view of fingering it is a thumb solo, just as in an orchestra there may be a horn solo or a trombone solo.

What saddens me in the Friedman fingering for the Nocturne, apart from the fact that it is senseless and contrary to Chopin's nature, is the mistrust of the fifth finger. I always battle with pupils who, because of their fear, replace the fifth finger in left

[1] My advice: never take on trust any editor's fingering. And study lovingly the fingering of great composer-pianists such as Liszt, Rachmaninov, Medtner and others.

hand accompaniments by the third or some other finger, particularly in *f* or *ff*. I tell them: do not forget that with the fifth finger you can even kill a man (although personally I have never had the urge to do so). There is nothing more anti-pianistic and unnatural than, for instance, the following fingering:

Ex. 79

Yet I have had to encounter even this particular delight (although, true, very long ago). Of course if you poke at a black key with the fifth finger you might miss, but if you take the key in a "prone position" with the fleshy finger-ball, you will not find anything more convenient or natural than the fifth finger, to say nothing of the logical side of the normal so-called "complex" or "five-finger" system.

Here is another example of "dialectic applied to fingering": in Chopin's Prelude in B flat minor, No. 16. op. 28 I play the passage given below with the following fingering:

Ex. 80

The second time, before the end, when the same passage occurs even faster, "sempre più animato", I prefer the "complex" "five-finger" approach.

Ex. 81

precisely on account of the more impetuous tempo (of course it is perfectly all right to play with the same fingering both times, but in that case the second fingering is better). When a passage has to be played very loud and not very fast I deliberately avoid the "five-finger method" and use the thumb as frequently as possible in order to take advantage to the full of rotatory, swinging movements—because this is the easiest way of giving force.

In conclusion I would say (but very confidentially): the fingering indications I prefer are the ones "marked" by Debussy for his Twelve Etudes: he did not indicate a single finger and in a short, witty preface explained the reason for it. How pleasant to see a clean musical text unburdened by arithmetic, and not dotted with figures! Almost as pleasant as looking at an autograph or original text of J. S. Bach where, apart from "bare notes" there is nothing.

A pianist who knows music, knows himself and knows the piano will readily come to the same conclusion as Debussy. This is the end of the road, the result of good schooling, experience and instinct.

2. *The Pedal*

To write of the pedal without constantly illustrating one's meaning on the piano is practically impossible if one is not to confine oneself to a few beautiful (and true) pronouncements such as: The soul of the piano is the pedal (Rubinstein) or: The pedal is the moonlight streaming down on a landscape (Busoni). But how can I write about piano playing without writing of the pedal, this original and wonderful property of our instrument, which for a master can be such a powerful means of achieving effect. It would be unforgivable; and so I shall make an effort and say a few words on the subject.

I think that one of the main tasks of the pedal is to remove from the piano's tone some of the dryness and impermanence which so adversely distinguishes it from all other instruments. That is why when playing a one-part melodic phrase in slow tempo (without any accompaniment) you are entitled to use pedal on each of the notes of the melody to make it sing more and give it a richer quality. Everyone knows how this comes about: when the right pedal is pressed down, the dampers on all strings are raised, each note played on the keyboard is enriched by over- and undertones. This, of course, does not happen without pedal.

I shall take the liberty of stating my heretical opinion about pedal in Bach. Bach must be played with the pedal, but with an intelligent, careful and extremely sparing pedal.[1] Of course there is a multitude of cases when the pedal is completely inappropriate. But if we were to play the whole of Bach totally without pedal (as some demand that we should) on our modern piano, how impoverished it would sound compared with the harpsichord. The harpsichord has a wonderful, silvery, rustling sound (*das silberne Rauschen*) which is only possible because it has no dampers like the piano, its strings vibrate considerably longer than those of the piano without pedal, and it is rich with overtones. It can be said without much exaggeration that the harpsichord is played with a constant pedal (which is absolutely impossible on the piano). The most gentle of instruments, the clavichord which Bach loved so much, had with all its impotence (it was already difficult to hear it ten feet away) one advantage over the piano; it was possible to vibrate the tone as on a string instrument. This wonderful means of expression, too, is denied to the piano. Must we then really deprive it also of the pedal, because of some grammatical, "professorial" considerations? "Professors", that is—teachers—suffer greatly from bad pedalling by bad pupils, but it does not mean that pedal should be done away with altogether. It must be improved; from unintelligent it must become intelligent. But to forego such a wonderful means of tone colour seems to me ridiculous. Do not take me for "a Knight of the pedal, wholeheartedly devoted to its cause". I assure you that I use it as much as I refrain from using it, that 80% of the music I perform (with the pedal) I play with a half-pedal (or quarter-pedal) and only 20% or less on a full pedal. (The whole of the Brahms Capriccio in B minor, op. 76, No. 2, for instance, I play absolutely without pedal, with the exception of the two concluding bars, which only then really sound like a conclusion.)

This is my pedal alibi. I could give thousands of such alibis: Bach, Mozart, Haydn and even Beethoven are my unbiased witnesses. But I am unable to name a single piece by Chopin or Tchaikovsky[2] (to say nothing of Liszt and Scriabin) in which

---

[1] Of course so as not to detract for an instant from the clarity of the polyphonic texture. If, in any of the parts we suddenly hear two notes, in my class this sad occurrence is termed ventriloquism.

[2] Not excluding his *Album d'enfants*.

my foot is not in constant contact with the pedal.[1] All this leads me to a conclusion: to refrain absolutely from using the pedal is the exception to the rule; to use it constantly but wisely is the rule. The pedal is an organic, integral and most important property of the piano, a part of its very nature, and to eliminate it altogether is tantamount to a merciless emasculation of our instrument.

Only the most primitive, general ways of using the pedal can be considered and defined without relating them directly to tone. The "sphere of activity" of the pedal separate from tone is very restricted. It is mainly the simultaneous pedal (when the pedal is taken exactly together with the note) or retarded pedal which is particularly necessary in cases when a series of legato chords cannot be played legato by the fingers alone. Then, as everyone knows, the pedal is released immediately after the next chord has been played which is then held by a new pedal, etc.

Sometimes there is an urge to open up all the piano's pores, so to speak, beforehand. For instance, when I begin playing Beethoven's Sonata in D minor (No. 17) my foot, without my wishing it, touches the pedal before my hands settle on the keyboard. The same thing happens in the beginning of the Sonata in B flat major, op. 106, when one would like the very air to be filled with the expectation of the B flat major chord before this shout of victory is actually heard. Such a pedal could be called "preliminary" but this is really a trifle (and without inverted commas).[2]

These three forms of pedal are of course only the alphabet with which we build the whole language of artistic pedalling, but even so it has to be mentioned and sometimes even in the advanced classes of conservatoires.

Questions of artistic pedalling are absolutely inseparable from questions of the tonal image. That is why any pedal indication in the music, however precise, is so imperfect. It is still but an equation with three unknowns. It may be argued

---

[1] I am, of course, leaving aside the beginner's pieces where shortness of legs as well as the shortness of the music require the piano to be "short of breath", i.e. entirely without pedal.

[2] We all of us constantly use this preliminary pedal, sometimes even without realizing it.

that the indication of the other two unknowns (tone and rhythm) is just as approximate as that of the pedal, but it is still sufficient and understandable. We know that it is possible to produce about one hundred dynamic gradations on the piano, yet we only have four indications for piano: *p*, *pp*, *ppp*, *pppp* and four for forte: *f*, *ff*, *fff*, *ffff* (very rare!) which makes eight, and if we take the intermediate *mp* and *mf* or *più pp*, as Debussy often puts it, that makes twelve, or about one-tenth of the real dynamic gradations used by any experienced pianist. And do the metro-rhythmical indications in Scriabin's Poem in F sharp major op. 32 correspond to the way the composer himself, and in fact all pianists able to play it, actually do play it?

Yes, this makes one think and I am often prepared to withdraw my invectives against pedal indications or else apply them equally to dynamic or rhythmic indications, which would be more appropriate. We should not forget that anyone who has a blind faith in the pedal indications of all sorts of editors will find himself in trouble. As a teacher I know this only too well.

I could give scores of examples of strange indications printed black on white but I do not want to turn this into a collection of sad curios. I shall only say that to these carefully placed, sometimes extremely doubtful and sometimes merely absurd pedal indications I much prefer Liszt's brief note to his transcription of the *Tannhäuser* Ouverture: "*Verständiger Pedalgebrauch wird vorausgesetzt*" (it is assumed that the pedal will be used with understanding) after which you will, of course, not see a single pedal indication in the text. This is similar to the absence of fingering in Debussy or any indications whatsoever in Bach. It is clear that in each of these cases the laconic use of indication, taken to its extreme, i.e. nil, is accessible and understandable only to those who know; it is the end of the road, the result of knowledge and experience. And it is equally clear that I do not suggest to begin studying the piano with the *Tannhäuser* Ouverture. I merely point out once more "the beginnings" and "the ends" (not for the last time). And the sooner we master them, the sooner will we acquire wisdom.

One of the most important characteristics of the pedal, and which is by no means mastered immediately by all, is the difference in the effect produced, depending on how far down you press it. To put it more simply, there is a full pedal, half-pedal, quarter-pedal, and you can even have gradations between these. By skilfully using half- or third-pedalling an experienced pianist can obtain almost the same results as those produced by the third pedal invented by Steinway; that is, some notes (usually the lower notes) will be sustained by the pedal while others, lighter and higher, do not come under its influence and remain perfectly transparent. Perhaps this is not only because of the different effects of the dampers depending on the extent to which the pedal is depressed, but because of its fundamental property—that of producing a different effect on sounds depending on their pitch. Even the most inexperienced pianist can hear that the bass notes continue to sound on the pedal while in the higher registers when the half-pedal is changed everything is clean and transparent; or, to put it more simply, for the upper registers the pedal is changed (in accordance with the change of harmony, the melody, etc.) while for the bass it remains unchanged and the note or notes continue to sound as if they were held down by the fingers and not the foot.

This excellent quality of the pedal enables us to give a perfectly accurate and clean performance of music which could otherwise only be played accurately with three hands. It is particularly useful to remember this when playing Glazunov whose piano music I term "three handed", since it is full of sustained tenuto basses in octaves while both hands are busy in the upper registers (the left with accompaniment figurations and the right with the melodic line; the reverse also occurs). Play, for instance, his First Sonata in B flat minor and you will see that this is so. The same is frequently found in Szymanowski and in fact in any piano music which recalls to a greater or lesser degree an excellent transcription of an orchestral score. This is in no way an implied criticism of Glazunov's music for the piano which is beautiful and perfect, but its very writing immediately reveals a composer who thinks mainly orchestrally. This can never be said of Chopin. (There are composers of whom it may be said—allegorically and paradoxically, of course,—that they create their music as much with their head as with their fingers, for instance Chopin, Debussy or Rachmaninov, which is why they are beloved of pianists.)

But very often the difference in the pianistic writing of

Glazunov and Chopin is more in the form than in the substance; if Glazunov had composed Chopin's Third Ballade he would have written the end probably like this:

Ex. 82

whereas Chopin, as everyone knows, wrote the bass octaves (E flat, A flat, etc.) as quavers, relying on the pedal. I should, however, point out that if I had seen in Chopin's notation the bass written in the way I have imagined Glazunov would have done, I should probably have had to play it somewhat more heavily, "più pesante", than one wants to do in Chopin. Hence a conclusion which is of tremendous importance for learners: composers write very accurately what they hear and want to hear from those who perform their works.

One of the best and tested examples[1] which I use to make my pupils study the properties of the pedal that I described above (its "multilevel" properties) is the Chopin Prelude in A flat major, op. 28 (the coda on a pedal A flat); here one can see and once and for all remember how inseparable pedal is from tone and how the slightest change in nuances calls for, must call for, changes in pedalling. This is the place:

[1] There is hardly any need to say again that one can find hundreds of such examples.

Ex. 83

The problem is clear: the lower bell-like A flat must sound for two bars, i.e. one has to hold the pedal, but during that time the harmony of the chords in the middle register changes togethei with the melody three times, consequently the pedal must be changed to avoid cacophony. Nothing is easier than solving this apparent contradiction: the bass is played *sfp* ("sforzato piano"), but gently, the melody tenderly but clearly stressed and with fine nuances, and the accompanying chords (harmony) are played softer than all the rest (*pp*); when the harmony changes the pedal is raised (changed) ever so slightly (this is what can be called quarter-pedalling) and the result is that there are no "false notes" and that the bass sounds as long as it is supposed to. The wolf is fed and the sheep are safe. But try to play the harmony chords a little louder or the melody less distinctly or take the bass note with insufficient depth (or all of this together) and cacophony is inevitable or else the bell must cease tolling. Either is inadmissible. I have more than once shown my class that this bit can be played so as to be artistically right, without confusing the harmonies and yet without even changing the pedal at all (many editors do not know this but all good performers are able to do this). In that case, the bass must be somewhat thicker, the chord accompaniment still somewhat softer and the melody is stressed just a little more, soaring over all the rest. But the first method is more reliable, the second requiring supersensitive fingers and ears. It goes without saying that the pedal, just as tone (and as indeed all music) is governed by the ear which is the only one to issue laws and the only one capable of correcting mistakes.

I am again overcome by a desire to continue listing examples and to give at least a brief summary of piano compositions from the origins of the piano to our day, with a detailed analysis

of the use in them of the pedal and an explanation of all the
possible mistakes and misunderstandings, together with advice
about overcoming them.[1] But this would again make for a huge
volume and therefore I won't.

There are still a few considerations about the pedal which I
must pass on. I shall try to set them down very briefly.

There is no correct pedal "in general"[2]; we know that in art
nothing is "in general". What is right for one composer is
completely wrong for another. (Go over the Twenty-Four
Preludes of Scriabin in your mind, and then the Twenty-
Four Preludes of Chopin.) In Beethoven the subject is frequently
constructed on the notes of a triad which sometimes gives
learners the wrong idea that since "there are no wrong notes"
the subject can be played on one pedal because "it sounds good".
One cannot imagine anything more mistaken. Melody (which
is individual) is turned into harmony (which is general).
Instead of a subject you get a sort of background on which a
theme no longer appears. The theme has been swallowed up. It
was drowned in the harmony. Strange as it may seem, I still
have to make remarks of this nature in class. Frequently, also, I
have to indicate that passages made up of arpeggios which
abound in Beethoven lose half their energy if they are played on
full, too thick pedal,[3] their shape is blurred, the "meander" is
effaced. Richter is so sensitive to such things that even the
following passage from the First Movement of the "Appassionata" he plays almost without pedal,[4] yet one would like to
take the pedal here as the passage requires maximum force:

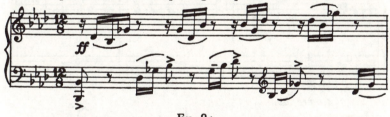

Ex. 84

[1] After all, I *am* a teacher.
[2] Or rather, general rules about how to take the pedal have the
same relation to artistic pedalling as some chapter on syntax to
poetic language.   [3] There only half-pedalling is possible.
[4] Which I believe every pianist plays on a full pedal, i.e. holding it
down the whole of the harmony.

One must admit, however, that this is better than taking an uninterrupted pedal for each harmony (that is, one bar) since the zigzag of the passage which resembles lightning, flares up more brightly and distinctly, whereas with a constant pedal it can become extinguished in the harmonic downpour.

Richter plays the introduction to the D minor Sonata op. 31, No. 2 like this:

Ex. 85

apparently in order to give the "slogan", so portentous, more weight and significance and, above all, in order not to turn it into harmony (first inversion of the dominant of D minor).

It goes without saying that Beethoven sometimes needs a very thick, full pedal (for instance, the first cadenza in the Fifth Concerto in E flat major and lots of other instances). After all it is well known that he loved the pedal and used it willingly. On the strength of these traditions Artur Schnabel plays the récitative from the same Sonata in D minor on literally such a pedal (and "espressivo cantabile"), that is, fairly loud and releases the pedal only after the F has finished sounding).

Ex. 86

This brings to mind Toscanini's aphorism: *tradizione è tradimento* (tradition is betrayal). For one cannot fail to see that the first inversion of the dominant should boom out, and over that boom, distant and mysterious, and dreadfully expressive, appears the voice of the récitative. But the boom stops somewhat earlier than the récitative and therefore the harmony, the D minor triad, the tonic, is not audible, it has melted away, it is lost, it is no more; only one, hardly perceptible voice is left which ends its sorrowful récitative on these two notes:

Ex. 87

But if the boom of harmony were to continue a little longer, if it did not get lost, the harmony would, of course, not remain a dominant but would become a "tonic", the D minor triad. How fortunate that this did not happen, that the tonic died unborn, but how sad that such a great pianist as Schnabel failed to understand this and showed his lack of understanding in his inappropriate pedalling:

Ex. 88

I have dwelt in detail on this case because everyone will see that it is the principle that is important (and not just the fact that a great pianist with a great name did not play it as it should be played).

Among the pedalling faults most frequently found in pupils I would note the insufficiently quick changes of pedal and the failure to use the imperceptible "smudges" of pedal so essential not only in Scriabin but also in Chopin, Liszt, Tchaikovsky, Rachmaninov, Debussy, Ravel—and indeed in a multitude of instances. I often tell my pupils: when you dance a quick, light dance, your feet, I am sure, can move very fast, gracefully and execute the tiniest movements. Why then, when you press the pedal, does your foot become a stump capable of only the simplest, most elementary movements? Then I show with special insistence, what irreplaceable services the pedal may render at times if one knows how to use it on sixteenths, thirty-seconds or just "in passing", in "mid-flight". One should be able to take the pedal as one takes a note or a chord, "in flight" as it were. It is closely linked to the general freedom and differentiation of movement as required by an extremely fine and demanding ear. If you hear well, it is not difficult to use a half- or quarter-pedal. Believe me, your foot is capable of performing much more complicated operations. Safonov[1] used to tell his pupils, when they looked at Scriabin's hands as he was playing: "What are you looking at his hands for? Look at his feet!"

Some teachers make the unreasonable demand that the pedal be changed on every note of the melody even when the harmony remains unchanged. This is due to their inability to understand the tonal picture and to create the necessary dynamic balance. This "grammatical" approach produces a hiccoughing pedal, or a "sanitary" pedal as the late Igumnov[2] used to say. Unfortunately, some of our editions of the classics and romantics are full of it. I can guarantee that no good pianist ever uses such a pedal.

The use of pedal in Scriabin's music should be extraordinarily rich, varied and sensitive. Unfortunately it is impossible to describe it here in detail. I will only say that perhaps nowhere else is such a variety of levels needed in pedalling, nowhere such rapid changes in half- and quarter-pedalling or the ability of the foot to keep up with sixteenths and thirty-seconds.

The Finale (presto) of Chopin's Sonata in B flat minor can, of course, be played entirely without the right pedal if played with exceptional evenness, velocity and sensitive shading. But the howl of the wind in the graveyard requires the pedal, the more so since this single-voiced unison conceals many marvellous harmonies buried under snowdrifts. Try to set down the harmonic skeleton of this wonderful Finale and you will immediately see what it is all about.

[1] Conductor and pianist (1859-1918); Director of Moscow Conservatoire 1889; appeared frequently in London and New York, ED.

[2] Famous piano teacher at the Moscow Central Music School, attached to the Moscow Conservatoire, founded in 1932, ED.

Ex. 89

As a matter of fact I always advise my pupils—and this refers
not only to the pedal, but to all music—to have a clear grasp of
the harmonic skeleton of any musical composition and to play it
more or less as indicated here. This greatly helps to understand
fully the harmonic structure of a piece and to avoid mistakes,
including the incorrect use of the pedal. (A great painter who
draws the naked human body sees with his "X-ray eyes" the
skeleton, covered in living flesh, and not only the skeleton, but
everything concealed by the skin: the muscles, ligaments,
nerves, various organs. Remember the drawings of Leonardo da
Vinci! The good musician acts likewise.)

In the Finale of the B flat minor Sonata one can show what a
magic tool the pedal is when in the hands (or more accurately,
under the feet) of one who is familiar with its secrets.

And a couple of words about the left pedal. There is a very
good rule which says: the left pedal should by no means be taken
for every *p* or *pp*, but only when a change of timbre is needed
(the deaf Beethoven had an extremely clear idea of the subject;
remember his very precise indications, *una corda, due corde,
tre corde*, which, alas, are impossible to follow since our pianos
allow us to play only *tre corde* or *due corde*!). Not all learners
know that the main charm of the left pedal lies not only in the
fact that the hammer is made to hit two strings instead of three
and that the resulting tone is less loud, but in fact that the first
of these strings, which does not get hit (since the left pedal
moves the action from left to right) vibrates together with the
other two strings without being hit, merely because the damper
over it is raised, and it vibrates purely in sympathy with its sister
strings tuned in unison to it. It is the least percussive sound that
it is possible to obtain on the piano and it is impossible not to
love it quite specially for this. And it is for this reason that

the fundamental rule which I fully approve admits so many exceptions.

When you have to play on very old and jangling pianos you have, of course, to use the left (and the right) pedal more frequently than when playing on good, new instruments in good condition.

Since the only rational supplement to this chapter would consist of a series of examples from various composers and of work with various pupils, and since it is not feasible to give such examples here, I shall now conclude these considerations on the pedal, "the soul of the piano".

occupation, that of performing. And even if this awareness does not have a negative effect on his teaching, it inevitably affects his morale. Even before he realizes it, dark minor tonalities creep into his heart. (Chopin referred to the lessons he gave as the labour of a hireling.) Happily these vague feelings do not disturb the heart of a pure teacher. A psychologist said that a real teacher assesses himself seriously only from the point of view of his pupils. For a performer this is unthinkable. I know from personal experience that as soon as my teaching workload is such that I have not sufficient time to practise myself, the quality of my teaching immediately suffers. I lack temperament and breadth of vision because of the bleak and nagging feeling in my heart. And the bleak and nagging feeling is there because I am marking time, I do not go forward, I do not improve, I am not being creative.

I have more than once observed the tremendous "material force" of purely psychological experience; for instance, you may be playing at home, you play, you get carried away, elated, excitement overcomes you and it may be that from sheer joy you break into some exotic dance between pieces or burst into song and then there is a knock on the door and a pupil comes in (and one who is below average, on top of it all) and you have to sit down and struggle with her and worm your way through the "Moonlight" Sonata or a Chopin Ballade already so much picked to bits as to have lost all meaning, and repeat the same thing for the thousandth time. . . . If the state I was in before the lesson was like a sunny day in May, after the lesson it was like a November puddle.

True, that sort of experience is a thing of the past; it is a long time now since I had any pupils who could affect me that way. But in general one can say: a talented teacher and an ungifted pupil are just as unproductive as an ungifted teacher and a talented pupil. Like unto like is one of the wisest principles in solving the teacher-pupil problem. The wise Latin saying *similis simili gaudet* stresses the fact that like rejoices in like, and its antithesis is that unlike do not rejoice in each other. The fullest possible understanding between teacher and pupil is one of the most important conditions for fruitful teaching. All this is well known and accepted. No one makes a prominent academician teach in a secondary school, just as secondary school teachers are not requested to lecture to the Academy sitting in plenary session. I have often sinned against the Latin saying in the past; that is why I mentioned it. But I said at the very beginning of these notes that I do not for an instant regret either the efforts, or the suffering, since they bring knowledge and also because the "road of perfect well-being and success" is not my road, and the people who constantly strive to obtain the best out of life for themselves, at any cost, leaving the work for others, are not my sort of people. I find them repulsive and doubly repulsive because I have seen so many of them.

One of the most depressing experiences for a teacher is to realize how little he can do, relatively, in spite of all his honest efforts, if his pupil is not gifted. The impresario-like enthusiasm, the conviction that he can achieve all he intends is gradually whittled away. It is soon replaced by the humiliating realization of how much more important it is for a good pianist to have good parents than good teachers. Am I describing childish feelings? Yes, of course, but which of us, overcome by the mania of teaching, education, "making" an artist, has not been tortured by them? For it is painful to see the sum of labour, knowledge and suffering yield such a tiny result, whereas sometimes a couple of words, a fleeting remark, give such a rich harvest. Man's age-old imperative urge to take nature into his own hands and fashion it according to his will plays a tremendous part even here, in our modest task. All these quixotic ups and downs between elation and dejection finally lead to an optimistic formula: one cannot create talent, but one can create culture, which is the soil on which talent prospers and flourishes.[1] The circle is closed; our labour is justified.[2]

[1] The greater, broader and more democratic the culture, the more frequent is the appearance of talent and genius. A learned man once referred to the paintings of the Italian Renaissance as an epidemic of genius.

[2] I cannot fail to remember my father who was a music teacher in the provincial town of Elizavetgrad (now Kirovograd) for sixty-five years. It sometimes happened that he taught three generations of the same family. Once, after giving a lesson to a "granddaughter" he said, not without satisfaction: "You know, granddaughters are usually much more musical than grandmothers". I think that my father must have been, unknown to himself, one of those convinced "forerunners" of academician Lysenko. [Soviet botanist and agriculturist, sponsored by Stalin as champion of "dialectical materialism", propagated the theory that acquired qualities could become hereditary, a theory refuted by international science in that field, ED.]

I consider that one of the main tasks of a teacher is to ensure as quickly and as thoroughly as possible that he is no longer necessary to the pupil; to eliminate himself, to leave the stage in time, in other words to inculcate in the pupil that independent thinking, that method of work, that knowledge of self and ability to reach his goal which we term maturity, the threshold beyond which begins mastery. While consciously striving to achieve this I do not wish to reduce to a minimum myself as a person, as an individual; I merely wish to cease being a police-man, a trainer, and want to remain one of the many vital forces of the pupil, one of the impressions in his existence, one among many, be they stronger or weaker. This awareness increased as I got to know the work of my colleagues (particularly those who were "pure" teachers and not performers), who simply could not admit that a pupil, however clever, could ever cease to need them; for them pupils were perpetually children.[1]

When Emil Gilels came to study with me at the Moscow State Conservatoire I was once forced to say to him: "You are already a grown man, you can eat steak and drink beer, but so far you have been fed with a baby's bottle". His teacher, B. M. Reingbald, an excellent teacher who had trained many talented youngsters, studied with him, at the lessons, the left hand separately from the right, etc., instead of making him do this himself at home, and did not develop his musical thinking sufficiently; nor did she acquaint him with music in general, in spite of his tremendous receptivity and talent. Yet the greater the talent, the more legitimate is the demand for early inde-pendence and responsibility. Busoni used to say that if a man is meant to be a pianist, he must be able to give a good perform-ance of a Liszt sonata at the age of seventeen or eighteen. This was said half a century ago, and we are, after all, moving forward.

Hofmann's recollections of his studies with Anton Rubinstein provide us with an example of the best teaching method and the way in which the most important problems are pinpointed, and

[1] This is a very touching, maternal but wrong, feeling. I remember that when Glazunov was about fifty his mother used to tell the washerwoman to be "careful with the child's linen". The funniest thing is that when he was seventeen, Glazunov wrote a symphony which was anything but childish.

show us the shortest road to the main task of performance. Hofmann relates how, after listening to a piece, Rubinstein would ask him: What is the nature of that music, is it lyrical, dramatic, sarcastic, solemn, joyful, sorrowful, etc.? It seems to me that the right answers to these questions, given not merely verbally but embodied in performance, are the highest achievement of pedagogical thinking and practice, and the most gratifying result of the joint efforts of teacher and pupil. Some might say: yes, but this was Hofmann! To which I could add: yes, but first of all it was Rubinstein! But does this change anything essential? The work of a teacher of genius with a wonderful pupil can always serve as the highest example and guidance in our work; the work of a bad teacher and a bad pupil can in the best of cases only serve as a proof to the contrary. However far from a truly artistic performance a pupil may be, because of his weakness or inability, however bogged down he may be in the morass of overcoming elementary handwork, he must still be aware of and remember the "stratosphere" into which he must penetrate some time or other; he must divine the remote guiding star—though it be still hidden by mist and cloud—which he will ceaselessly strive to reach. All the more must the teacher remember it.

Teachers who for years have been relentlessly working with very mediocre pupils frequently lose their faith in "stars" and "stratosphere"; they believe much more in the études of Czerny and Clementi, and you cannot really hold it against them. But even Clementi called his collection of études *Gradus ad Parnassum* and not *Parnassus*.

I already said that a teacher of any instrument (let us consider the human voice also as an instrument) must first and foremost be a teacher of music, in other words an expounder and interpreter of *music*. This is particularly necessary with pupils at the lowest level of development. In such a case it is absolutely essential to use the comprehensive method, i.e. the teacher must make the pupil grasp not only the so-called "content" of a composition, he must not only instil into him its poetic image, but also give him an extremely detailed analysis of the form, the structure—as a whole and in its every detail—harmony, melody, polyphony, pianistic texture; in short he must be at one and the same time a historian and theoretician of music, a

teacher of theory, harmony, counterpoint[1] and pianoforte
playing.

I think that the eternal troubles that plague schools of
singing, the insoluble problems of teaching singing are due
mainly to the fact that teachers will not (or cannot) use a
comprehensive method; they do not teach the art of music but
are concerned mainly with voice production. The advantage of
instrumentalists compared to singers is that they usually begin
their studies in childhood and by the time they come to the
conservatoire they have already a fair knowledge of music and
of their instrument. But vocalists frequently come to the
conservatoire as adults with merely a good voice (the rest being
tabula rasa), in other words as the possessors of a good instrument
without any knowledge of music, any musical culture, frequently
without any "musicality".[2] But it is clear that in their case
education and training must be comprehensive and should not
be split into component parts by the name of theory, harmony,
etc., including voice production, which a musically undeveloped
person simply cannot grasp as a single whole. I am not trying to
say, God forbid! that a student of singing should not take all
these subjects in a separate class, but a singing teacher must
merge all these into a whole *during the lesson*, and keep on
explaining and showing to the pupil until the latter has learned
to listen and think as a musician and an artist. For the simplest
Lied or operatic air can serve to give the pupil a multitude of
information concerning harmony, theory, part writing, musical
form. In the case of a vocalist who finds it difficult to master not
only the meaning of harmony or theory but also their terminology it is specially important to tell him what I so frequently
repeat at my public lectures for pupils and teachers. I tell them:
we humans do not twitter like birds or moo like cows; we use
words and concepts, in other words we name every phenomenon
of the inner or outer world that we perceive, we give them
names regardless of whether it is a distant star or a tiny insect, a

[1] But all this of course in a concentrated, compact, "portable"
form, and *ad hoc*!

[2] The possession of a good voice is frequently mistaken for natural
musicality and artistic talent. Yet we do not tend to consider a young
pianist musical mainly because he happens to have a good Bechstein
grand at home.

mood or a physical action. To name a thing is to begin to understand it. Is it then admissible that a professional musician should not know what to call, what name to give to what he hears, what he creates? The deeper this simple truth will sink into the minds of learners, the easier it will be to teach them music and art and to teach them the technique of a particular kind of art, for instance voice production.[1]

With very gifted pupils I hardly ever analyse the harmony or form of the composition we study; they understand and know all this themselves. But there have been pupils with whom during a year or two I constantly used the pieces we were studying for a brief course of harmony, melody construction, form analysis, etc., until they learned to think like musicians. With highly

Ex. 90

[1] Hence the conclusion: "compulsory piano" should be particularly compulsory for singers.

developed and gifted pupils I need only draw their attention
from time to time to some particularly significant place, some
"turning point" such as so frequently occurs in the piano works
of great composers. For instance, I cannot remember a single
occasion when we have not dwelt at length and amply discussed
the Fugato from Chopin's Fourth Ballade, when polyphony
gives way to the homophonic writing of the beginning.

While this amazing transition from polyphonic "reflection"
to the initial simple flow of song—the threshold of the recapitulation—is accomplished by means of a wonderful modulation
and as we seem to witness the birth of the melody the germ of
which was present in the polyphony:

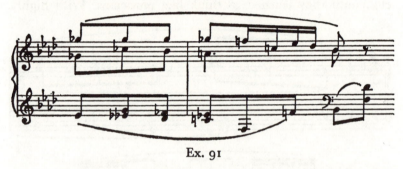

Ex. 91

one is so overcome with joy, with such emotion, that it is
impossible not to share it with a pupil, it is impossible not to
draw his attention to this marvel of musical art, and hence we
analyse the whole Fugato and try to understand why this is so
beautiful, why this passage is so moving. We attempt to find
in the very substance of which music is made a confirmation
and an explanation of our undoubted and intense musical
experience. This cannot fail to affect performance; when one
delves deep into one's perception of what is beautiful, and
attempts to understand its origin, how it arose and what was its
objective cause, only then does one grasp the infinite order of art
and one experiences a new joy because intellect throws its own
light on what was perceived directly by the senses. In justification of these lines I am prompted to recall Pushkin's laconic and
masterly definition: "Inspiration is a disposition of the soul
toward an acute perception of impressions and their reasoned
understanding". Anyone who merely feels art remains for ever

an amateur, anyone who only thinks about it will be a research musicologist; a performer needs the synthesis of the thesis and antithesis: he needs an acute perception and reasoning.

It goes without saying that such "specially beautiful" passages as the Fugato in the Fourth Ballade are to be found in music by the hundred, thousand and tens of thousands; they are as numerous as beautiful landscapes which captivate the wanderer and make him return again and again. Sometimes I am amazed at myself, and I expect those present in class must also have been amazed that, when studying with a pupil the Chopin Barcarolle, for instance (which I have taught hundreds of times), when going deeper into its incredible beauty (specially in the transition to the recapitulation—again the recapitulation!—after the second subject in A major beginning with the trill in the right hand and until the dominant of F sharp major—C sharp major) I frequently experience quite childish delight doing this purely analytical, explanatory work and find it hard to hold back my tears because of my joy that this marvel should exist. And there is nothing surprising here. One cannot get "uzed" to the beauty of art, just as one cannot become used to, or be indifferent to the beauty of a May morning, of a moonless summer night with myriads of stars and, even more, to the spiritual beauty of man which is the cause and the source of everything great in art.

In such conversations about music with talented and intellectually mature pupils the teacher ceases to be a teacher in the narrow sense of the word and becomes a senior colleague endowed with greater experience and knowledge, talking to his younger brothers-in-art of their favourite subject. It is precisely this aspect of teaching that is most attractive, most engrossing and satisfying. Not only because here professional teaching is gradually turning into real education, but mainly because this is a pure form of communication, of bringing people together on the basis of their common devotion to art and the ability to create something in the field of art. This latter is particularly important. Without this ability to strengthen and develop, which is the purpose of such talks, everything would boil down to conversations that are pleasant only for amateurs but useless and uninteresting for artists.

Anyone can see how far removed such teaching is from the

original, mainly dictatorial type based on obedience, on command and its execution, on discipline, the best example of which is the relationship between the army commander and the private. The usefulness of this dictatorial principle and its application is so well known that I shall not dwell on it. Every experienced teacher knows the extent to which it is possible to depart from "military" discipline depending on the pupil and his character. There are many cases when it really cannot be applied; even the strictest teacher would have hardly applied it to the child Mozart. With pupils devoid of artistry and initiative I naturally resorted to the original, imperative method. When the pupil fails to show any intentions or ideas, the teacher works for him and instead of him in the hope that he may show some personality in the future. With highly gifted pupils I was usually much more liberal. Emil Gilels later even reproached me; he claimed that I did not show him or tell him enough, that I did not impose my will as a teacher sufficiently, in fact that I did not pay sufficient attention to him.[1] True, later still he thanked me for having, by my teaching, helped him to become independent.

When Arthur Schnabel visited Moscow he said, in a conversation with teachers and pupils at the Conservatoire, something paradoxical. He said that for a man who was fated to become an artist it was almost immaterial whether he was taught well or badly at the beginning; whatever the case, when he reaches the age of fifteen to seventeen he will change everything according to his own lights, he will acquire his own habits, his own technique, he will go his own way which is the way of the true artist. I do not believe that for such a man the initial teaching is immaterial (good teaching is in all cases better than bad) but without a doubt there is a grain of truth in what Schnabel said. That is why, in the presence of a great talent, I have frequently refrained from the imperative attitude that I used with weaker

---

[1] In actual fact the reason was partly outside my control. I was, at that time, director of the conservatoire and led an extremely busy life. I had twenty-five pupils and naturally had to give more time and effort to the weaker than to the better ones (a truth of which many teachers, particularly ambitious ones, seem unaware; they work really seriously with only two or three of their most gifted pupils leaving the rest to drift in their wake).

pupils and which some other teachers might adopt even with exceptionally gifted pupils.

Sometimes, with pupils who lacked all creative initiative, I would try, by all means at my disposal, to show them all the hidden treasures of a composition, to tell them in every detail what I felt and thought in connection with the piece in question. The result would sometimes be a fairly good copy of my interpretation. My instinct made me shy away from this method with a very talented, creatively gifted pupil. I would say to myself: let Gilels (when he was still a student of the Moscow State Conservatoire) go on playing this piece (for instance, a Chopin Ballade or a Beethoven Sonata) with insufficient inspiration, his mind and heart have not yet perceived all its depth and beauty, but still I will refrain from meddling too much. What I can tell him now, he will be able to do himself, his own way, not my way, and for a real artist, as I already said, this is the decisive moment in work and in development.

The method of "cramming" is, in general, a fairly bad method, but to "cram" a talented person is plain sinful. An attempt to make a talented pupil produce a carbon copy of what the teacher thinks and does is worthy of neither of them. My teacher, Godowsky, said at my third lesson when, in a piece of Chopin, I simply could not (because I did not want to) achieve a certain nuance which I thought too precious: "All right, you have your own individual personality and I am not going to interfere with it". Wise words!

With such as Gilels the best method would be—in addition to learning the set repertoire—daily sight-reading, preferably four-hands, and getting to know the inexhaustible wealth of chamber and orchestral music, in fact all of the non-pianistic literature. With such an elemental virtuoso gift as that of Gilels, a broad knowledge of music is the surest and fastest way of developing talent, quite apart from the fact that it is the duty of every good musician, as well as his delight.

An endless chewing over of the same pieces, as some teachers and even some pupils are fond of doing, this endless repetition with the addition of new, small details of interpretation and even more, the repetitious drumming in of the same thing—this is the wrong approach with a truly talented person. When Menuhin as a young man (but already famous) began studying with Georges Enesco, his new teacher constantly played with him sonatas, trios, quartets, quintets, and did not inflict on him an endless repetition of the same few solo pieces, apparently leaving it to Menuhin to study them at home when necessary. I would also recall that Anton Rubinstein did not allow Josef Hofmann to play for the second time a piece they had already gone through together. And when, on one occasion, Hofmann asked somewhat timidly whether he would agree to hear him once more in order to see whether he had done everything the maestro had said, Rubinstein refused, saying that a second time he might tell him "something quite different". A memorable example! On the one hand it immediately brings to mind the infinitude of art (it is always possible to play better and also to play differently), on the other, it shows that Rubinstein was an amazing pedagogue and psychologist. He was obviously afraid of confusing the youth, however talented he might be, by his own excessively broad and rich musical conception; he deliberately restrained himself as a teacher; he did not give every advice possible, but only some advice—the most necessary.

These sincere words, that seem to be a confession of inconsistency, clearly show the immeasurable, even contradictory, nature of art thanks to which a performer can render the same composition in several different ways and cannot confine himself to one standard rendering; and this is so very understandable with such an elemental and inspired pianist as Rubinstein, who recognized the value of improvisation and the significance of the moment, so important for the performer.

I would also add that it is precisely here, in questions relating to the freedom and diversity of interpretation, that it is so important to observe the principle of "beginnings and endings" of which I have been constantly speaking. It is essential, so as to avoid falling into the trap of pernicious relativism—"there is no truth, everything is permitted". What Rubinstein did might perhaps be better expressed by the formula: "there is only one truth, but much is permitted to him who has the ability".

Some might say to me: you have only just told us that sometimes you bare your whole soul before a pupil, in an attempt to open for him all those innermost treasures of music that you have managed to perceive, yet you are full of admiration for Rubinstein and see his method of work as a deliberate limitation of communicable matter, as a strict selection from all the possible advice he could give, and see it as great wisdom. This is inconsistent!

No, friends, it is not inconsistent, but if you think it is, you did not understand what I wrote. May I, for the sake of clarity, use a rather primitive metaphor. Imagine that an ardent lover of flowers has a little plot of land consisting of sand and stones on which nothing can grow, specially since there is no water in the vicinity. But his passion for flowers is stronger than stone and sand and he will patiently carry earth from afar, plant flowers and carry water daily from a distant stream until he finally has his longed-for garden.

What I sometimes did with pupils who resembled that rocky plot of land was similar to the efforts of the garden lover. When I "poke around" in music ("look how the melody curves here", "listen to this marvellous modulation", when I use metaphors, allegory, quote poetry, etc.) I am merely trying to create fertile ground for the perception of music, that same topsoil on which, with good care beautiful flowers may perhaps be made to grow. But why carry topsoil and water when there is enough earth and moisture? Here the problem is quite different: weed the flower beds, prevent the weeds from choking the flowers, destroy parasites, if any. This is much easier!

But enough allegory! I need hardly add that these semi-conversations, semi-instructions which take place between a teacher and such talented and comprehending pupils as those I have just mentioned, are not a bit like what I have been trying to describe in my oversimple simile, because their motivations are entirely different.

By way of criticism and self-criticism I could add that music-making, playing four hands, etc., which I considered the best way of developing the talent of such a pianist as Gilels (and of course other young pianists too), is something I did with him very seldom, mainly when we were evacuated to Sverdlovsk during the war, and even then not for long, since very soon we parted. In so-called "musical life" there is absolutely no time for this essential work at home; the generally excessive load of work, the excessive curriculum, preclude any possibility of finding time for this very important work. I hope that the time will come when those bodies which draw up our curricula and plan our work will understand how much bureaucratic thoughtlessness there is in their work and will amend the mistakes that cause so much harm to our young musicians.

I have already said that in working with Richter I mostly followed the policy of "friendly (but by no means passive) neutrality". From his early youth he showed such an excellent understanding of music, he could carry so much of it in his head and was endowed with such marvellous natural pianistic gifts, that I had to follow the proverb which says: "to teach the learned is to spoil him".[1] I have probably helped him a little in his development, but most of all he helped himself, and first and foremost he was helped by music, to which he devoted himself with passion. I will merely recall that he was one of the moving spirits behind the Music Circle set up in the Moscow Conservatoire and which held ninety-nine meetings. All the best pupils of the Conservatoire took part in the work of the Circle[2] which only stopped on account of the war. That was precisely the kind of music-making (the performances were always of a very high standard and carefully prepared) of which I dream and speak and which is stubbornly ignored by those who ought to encourage it.

I shall now describe very briefly two lessons which show with particular clarity how different is the work of a teacher, depending on the person he is teaching. Two pupils followed each other with the same work, the Liszt B minor Sonata. The first to play was Richter, the second was a young girl with excellent pianistic gifts, musical, but with very moderate artistic gifts and initiative. Richter knew the sonata perfectly and both technically and musically his playing of it was excellent. Obviously I did not interrupt him a single time before he finished. The discussion that followed took thirty to forty minutes. I gave him some advice on a few minor points, some passages were repeated, I argued with him about the interpretation of a certain episode which, as I tried to convince him, did not appear to me sufficiently dramatic after what preceded it,

[1] Here is an example from the "higher spheres". Liszt who had recognized at once how outstandingly gifted the young Rubinstein was, refused to teach him, yet he willingly took on much less gifted pianists.

[2] The Circle performed all the Mahler symphonies, the Miaskowski symphonies, several Wagner operas, works by Richard Strauss, Debussy and several new works by Soviet composers.

and that was all. When the girl who came after Richter sat down to play the same sonata, discussions, corrections, examples, repetitions, began with the very first note. Literally every bar had to be examined, "edited" so to speak; sometimes we dwelt at length on one note, one chord, a small bit of a phrase. To say nothing of a brief "lecture" I gave her on the meaning and content of the sonata. We worked for over three hours and only managed to get through one-third of the Sonata. Thus this sonata, which held no technical difficulties for her turned out to be that "chink" or "pipe" through which I tried to drag her into awareness of the realm of music, of art and of spiritual culture in general, without for an instant ceasing—in so doing—to deal with piano playing. Subsequently she played this sonata at an examination and gave an excellent performance of it, getting top marks.

Had an ardent partisan of a "single method" of teaching been present, he would probably have begun to doubt his theory.

And now a few "intimate" thoughts. Am I not guilty of the error so well expressed in the French saying: *fais ce que je dis et non ce que je fais?* (do as I say and not as I do). When Gilels studied Liszt's "Spanish Rhapsody" with me it always occurred to me that I could not play octaves as fast, as brilliantly and with such strength as he could and, consequently, wondered whether he should really be studying with me and not with a pianist who could play such things even better than he could (alas, not so easy to find!)? My professional integrity, the sober thinking of a performer and not only of a teacher, prompted these thoughts. But since apart from octaves and a great deal else[1] there was much that I wanted to tell Gilels about the interpretation and content of this rhapsody, my desire resulted in real musical and pianistic advice, and I found sufficient justification for continuing to work with him.

I mention this with a purpose in mind.

The ideal teacher is one who, in every case, from all points of view, knows and can do more than the pupil, even if the pupil is a genius. But even with such an exceptional combination as Rubinstein-Hofmann the teacher's superiority over the pupil was not absolute, since it is well known that, as Rubinstein

---

[1] Everyone knows what this "else" is: temperament, rhythm, tremendous willpower, purposeful rendering, "penetrating" and virtuoso brilliance, beautiful tone, etc.

himself put it, "half his recital would fall under the piano", whereas it was extremely rare for Hofmann to hit a wrong note.[1] If the requirement that the teacher should always and in every respect be superior to any of his pupils were to be applied, all teaching would go by the board. I would recall what I said earlier about the great contribution of "pure" teachers who do not appear in public as soloists. As the pupil grows stronger and more mature the influence of such a "pure" teacher diminishes whereas the influence of a teacher who is a performing artist usually lasts much longer. The critic-counsellor and the performing artist are usually entirely different people in real life; when these conflicting qualities are present in the person of a true performer-teacher, they represent a combination which is not only rare but also particularly valuable. (I know a number of excellent performers who could not force themselves to be good teachers although life seemed to impose this occupation upon them. Teaching they found irksome and boring while performing was interesting and a source of joy. On the other hand, how many good teachers are there in the world, who are of no interest whatsoever as performers—but we have said enough on the subject.)

Even a brief description of the basic teaching methods, or rather let us call them "themes", used in my class would make this small book too bulky. But I have to say a few words at least about two of these "themes".

One of my favourite ways of teaching I described fairly accurately in the first chapter when I related how I went through the second movement of the "Moonlight" Sonata (C sharp minor, op. 27) with a pupil. What I described is perhaps one of the main, fundamental themes of my talks with pupils: from the image to its embodiment, from poetry (poetry as the innermost essence of all art)—through music—to artistic pianoforte playing.

But here is another "theme". I visualize music, the sum total of all music created through the ages, as some gigantic "genealogical tree" with its numberless ramifications, ruled by the

---

[1] Incidentally, if Godowsky had four to five wrong notes in a recital, they stuck in one's memory like so many nails hammered into the brain, whereas with Rubinstein the audience frequently failed to notice wrong notes.

laws of heredity, somewhat inaccurately termed "tradition",
as well as the laws of struggle against these traditions. The
evolutionary and the revolutionary principle impregnate all
music and are in complete harmony with life. And that is why
during a lesson when, for instance, we are studying Scriabin and
his harmonic language I cannot fail to recall the genealogical
tree of his harmony and give examples from the harmonic usage
of his predecessors, which clearly show the origins of Scriabin's
harmony. Here are a few examples at random.

Chopin's Third Ballade:

Ex. 92

The combination of three intervals of a fourth with a seventh
—that is almost Scriabin. This find of Chopin's genius Scriabin
"inherited"; he inherited it lawfully, developed it and enriched it.

And here is another, no less striking, example of heredity, or
rather of inheritance (in Liszt's "Mephisto" Waltz):

Ex. 93

The harmonic combination (altered chord of the ninth):

Ex. 93*a*

is one of the fundamental chords in Scriabin's work.

When a pupil plays Scriabin's Fourth Sonata (seventh bar from the beginning):

Ex. 94

one is compelled to remind him of *Tristan*:

Ex. 95

Scriabin was particularly fond of Beethoven's Sonata in D major op. 28 ("Pastorale") and the reason is obvious: the opening bars with their gently discordant harmonies on the strong beat:

Ex. 96

have something in common with Scriabin's harmonic thinking.

Beethoven's work contains a particular wealth of such
"prophecies" of future music. I always show my pupils the bits
(and not only those "bits") where he foretells Schumann,
Brahms, Wagner, Chopin, Tchaikovsky (and there are lots of
them!). The Twenty-first Variation (from the "Diabelli" Variations op. 120) is almost Prokofiev, while the scherzo from the last
Quartet in F major op. 135 has something of Shostakovich in it.

And in this same connection we also discuss the phenomenon
of "genetics" in other arts, for instance the descriptions of the
Caucasus in Pushkin, Lermontov, the Georgian poets.

One may find in the work of composers who are completely
different in spirit, melodic and harmonic expressions of remarkable similarity, inspired by the spirit of the time and the historic
evolution of music. The phrase from *Tristan* quoted above can
be found in almost identical form in Chopin (end of the Largo
from the Sonata in B minor):

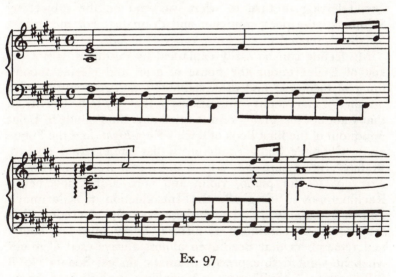

Ex. 97

Such "coincidence" between great composers of completely
different temperament (it is difficult to imagine two personalities more diametrically opposed than Chopin and Wagner)
remind us of what frequently happens in the field of science. It

is well known, for instance, that Newton and Leibnitz both discovered integral and differential calculus at the same time, though entirely unaware of each other.

Of course I know that I need not have mentioned any of this in class, since it is dealt with in much greater detail by good teachers of history and theory of music. But the whole point is that such considerations acquire an entirely different meaning when they are directly related to performance, and put into practice. That is why I cannot abandon my "complex method" and use it frequently.

To the considerations which follow from my conception of a musical genealogical tree I should add the following: I believe that the key in which a composition is written is far from accidental; I believe that it has a historic basis, that it is the result of a natural development, obeying secret aesthetic laws, that each key has its symbolism, its meaning, its expression, its significance, and its intent. Schumann wrote (in *Charakteristik der Tonarten*) of the definite expressive meaning of each key, referring in turn to what was said on the subject by Schubart,[1] the poet, musician and dramatist. For me, too, a tonality is related to a definite range of moods.

My feeling can be easily explained by examples: is not the key of E flat minor the house of grief and elegiac moods, funereal memories and utter sadness? One need only recall a number of marvellous compositions in that key to be convinced that I am not just giving rein to my fancy: the Prelude in E flat minor out of the First Book of Bach's *Forty-Eight* (and the Fugue also), Chopin's Sixth Etude in E flat minor from op. 10, Brahms' Intermezzo No. 6 in E flat minor from op. 118, his Trio op. 40 (for piano, violin and horn, third movement), Rachmaninov's "Elegies", the Introduction to Glazunov's Fourth Symphony. . . . I took these examples at random, but they could be continued *ad libitum*. Every musician knows and remembers that Beethoven almost always used C minor when he wanted to express a dramatic image: Sonata No. 8 ("Pathétique"), the Thirty-two Variations, the Fifth Symphony, Sonata No. 32 op. 111, etc. It is not by accident that Brahms' First Symphony is written in C minor, just as it is no

[1] 1739-1791, ED.

accident that Chopin's Twelfth and Twenty-Fourth Etudes are also in C minor. They are all of them children of the same country, they have the same fatherland. F minor I would call the tonality of passion, and not only because it is the key in which Beethoven wrote the "Appassionata". Bach used the key of F minor to express intense religious fervour: think of the Three-part Invention in F minor, for instance, the F minor Prelude and Fugue out of the First Book, the first movement of the F minor Sonata for violin and piano, the last aria *Oh, zerfliess* from the *Passion according to St. John.* Subsequently F minor became the best vehicle for expressing more earthly, human passion. To name but a few examples: Beethoven: Sonata No. 1, *Egmont* Overture, "Appassionata"; Brahms: first and third movements from the Third Sonata op. 5; Chopin: Etude No. 9, op. 10 in F minor, the whole of the Fantaisie in F minor, Prelude No. 18 op. 28, everything, from the recapitulation to the end, in the Fourth Ballade in F minor, including the Coda which could be called "passion as a catastrophe"; Liszt: Etude in F minor from the Transcendental Studies; a great deal in his symphonic poems; Rachmaninov: Prelude in F minor from op. 32 (even marked: "appassionato") etc., etc.

I know that some may object, saying: "in each of the keys you have mentioned numerous compositions have been written which do not fit into the narrow content you have attributed to the key in question. Is your theory not far-fetched?"

There is no need to argue. Of course there are many passionate compositions in other keys than F minor, many of an elegiac character in other keys than E flat minor (but very often in related keys: B flat minor, A flat minor; remember Bach and Beethoven, to name but these two). On the other hand, numerous compositions have been written in F minor which cannot be considered as mainly passionate; for instance Chopin's Nocturne in F minor and Etude op. 25 No. 2 etc., etc. Yet, in spite of this, it must be admitted that certain emotions and moods have a certain "selective right" with respect to the key and that it is not by chance that a composition is born in the composer's mind in one key rather than another. To my mind there is absolutely nothing accidental in the fact that the

Twenty-Fourth Prelude and Fugue from the First Book of Bach's *Forty-Eight*, Chopin's Sixth Prelude and Tchaikovsky's Sixth Symphony were all written in B minor.

The more passion there is in a man, the more purity, too, and chastity. Depravity and cynicism are born of weakness and impassivity. At the risk of being taken for a sentimental school-marm I admit that I am happy to feel that so many compositions, the innermost meaning of which is perfect chastity, were written in the relative major of the "passionate" F minor—in A flat major. I hear it in the subject of the A flat major Fugue from the Second Book of the *Forty-Eight*, in the first subject and indeed in the whole of the first movement of Beethoven's Sonata op. 110, in Chopin's Seventeenth Prelude, in his Third Mazurka from op. 59, the second of the Three Etudes written for the School of Moscheles; in the first subject of Medtner's Sonata in A flat major (from the triad); and especially strongly do I feel it in the Allegretto in A flat major from Brahms' First Symphony ("an innocent girl at the dawn of life")[1]. . . . I think that as Venus arose from the foam, the sea greeted her birth by murmuring a song in A flat major.

Sometimes there can be a certain similarity between compositions written by a composer in the same key, and that similarity is not so much a matter of poetic feeling or of meaning, but is simply textual. I have in mind a certain resemblance in theme, melody, figurations, etc. In this connection it is interesting to compare both Books of Bach's *Wohltemperiertes Klavier*. Busoni already referred to it when he compared the two Preludes and Fugues in A major (from both Books). For this same reason he takes the liberty on two occasions of "pairing off" preludes and fugues from different books (E flat major and G major) as if indicating their "elective affinity". This transposition seems to me far from essential,[2] but the observation that inspired him is perfectly correct.

When we study Brahms' Second Concerto in B flat major in class I feel I must draw the pupils' attention to the amazing strength and expressiveness in the simple modulation from A

---

[1] This does not mean that I do not imagine with this music sometimes something entirely different: for instance, a walk along the banks of the Rhine on a spring morning . . . etc.

[2] It is markedly individual, as everything Busoni did.

major to B flat major in the transition to the recapitulation in
the first movement. This is the plan of the modulation minus
piano part:

Ex. 98

Smoothly, majestically, the first subject glides like a swan into
recapitulation. This miracle is achieved with the simplest, the
most "permitted", classically proved harmonies[1]—A major,
then A minor, then the first inversion of F major, then the
syncopated appearance of the seventh of the dominant of B flat
major, followed by its root position with F in the bass, then in
the upper part the first subject (in sixths) with a slightly
retarded bass which at first gives a second inversion and only
later goes on to the tonic B flat: that is all there is to it. I have
already mentioned Chopin's marvellous recapitulations. This
recapitulation, too, is a marvel of the composer's art. The
impression of something natural, majestic, I would say un-
obtrusive and unpremeditated, given by the appearance of the
long expected first subject is mainly due not only to the beautiful
and simple modulation from A major to B flat major, but also to
that lazily noble retarded appearance of the root position of the
B flat major triad, because the bass, giving the indefinite
flexible chord of the $^6_4$ does not immediately move from the fifth
to the tonic. Of course one should, when speaking of this, also
say that the transition from A major to B flat major (recapitulation) is superb because it was preceded by superb moments in
the development. These harmonic progressions (orchestra):

[1] The feeling of well-being, of affinity and at the same time of an
individual person (if one may so express oneself) is present here in
every harmony.

Ex. 99

foretell the appearance of the first subject and already imply the dominant of the recapitulation.[1] But in the bars that follow the music evades it (apparently these are not yet the doors through which we may enter the parental home), modulating still to A major, and only after resting on the A major triad it gradually moves on to its own key of B flat major. And it is precisely through this gradual, this unhurried, uncanonical, unscholastic transition, this "homecoming", that I am made particularly aware of the genius of Brahms. I cannot refrain from drawing a parallel between two such different composers—Chopin and Brahms, recalling how on other occasions they solved problems of composition, creative problems, in an identical manner. I mentioned earlier the transition to the recapitulation in Chopin's Barcarolle, one of the most marvellous moments of revelation in music. Is it not obvious how similar the writing of these two composers is in this case? The recapitulation has long been expected and sensed, the modulations are coming closer and closer to it, but now they once more lead the music away from the goal (in epos this is called "retardation"; this is constantly used in drama, generally in the fourth act). In Chopin's Barcarolle it takes place here (and earlier):

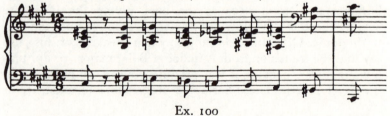

Ex. 100

[1] For me every good recapitulation is like a return to the homeland after a long journey.

in Brahms it occurs in the modulation mentioned earlier, the dominant of the recapitulation (from A major to B flat major).

I have dwelt at length on these two approaches to the recapitulation by two such different, such profoundly dissimilar composers, because I am fond of finding in the most different, even in the contradictory, something in common. It brings one closer to understanding the laws of music. Moreover, I wanted to give an example of the manner in which I sometimes try to analyse a composition with my pupils. It is useful not only for a composer but also for a performer—an obvious truth.

Very frequently when analysing some passage or other, some fragment of a great composition, one finds it impossible not to go back to what went before, what led to this place (and so one usually comes back to the very beginning) and also to think ahead, where this fragment leads to (and so one usually gets to the end of the composition).

In such cases it becomes particularly clear that musical composition is a single indivisible process, and the clearer this conviction, the more understandable music becomes (I would bring to mind Mozart's story of how he composed, which I gave in the chapter on rhythm).

The reader will remember: I said earlier that I frequently use my considerations on tonality and my analyses of such harmonic and form-moulding marvels as the ones just described for polemical purposes. With the help of such examples I polemicize about the musical currents that led to such harmonic phenomena as tonal, polytonal, atonal and "mono"-tonal music. I understand perfectly the historic and aesthetic laws which gave rise to these phenomena, as well as the stylistic finds related to them, but I must frankly confess that my sympathies lie with what went before them and not with what came after them. Polytonality and atonality destroyed the structural order of harmony and its forces with their attractions and repulsions; they turned harmony into a diffuse, porridge-like mass, while monotonality, because of the excessive enthusiasm it aroused, was inevitably transformed into monotony which is so clearly detectable even in the later works of Scriabin.

In spite of his undoubted genius Scriabin obviously got into a blind alley. The vertical triumphed over the horizontal, the instant over the process, the particular over the general. Music of that kind was reduced to a state of petrification. The great historic merit of Prokofiev and Shostakovich is, in my opinion, that while continuing always to innovate,[1] looking always ahead, they (not only they, of course, but mainly they) helped music to get out of the morass into which it had been driven by atonality and monotonality; they gave back to harmony its structural force and wealth, to melody its breath, to form its dimension and shape, and to the whole musical process its significance: continuity and unity.

Talks on this and similar subjects play a great part in my relations with my pupils; they broaden the outlook of the young musician, increasing his awareness, and develop in him the true professional artist.

Now about something quite different.

One of the things that most grieve me in my present teaching work is this:

I cannot require of my pupils what I am entitled to demand of them as a musician and a pianist, because of their excessive workload and the appalling lack of time for the most important work of all, work at home. I am well aware that this is also one of the things that most upset pupils during their time at the conservatoire. Can we never get out of this dead-end? It is absolutely no exaggeration to say that even the most talented pupils in all their time at the conservatoire only get through one-third of the repertoire they ought to have mastered by the time they graduate. I shall never depart from my firm conviction that a pupil must have at least six hours a day to work alone at his instrument: about four hours for working at the repertoire and technique, and two hours for getting acquainted with music in general (and that too is work). It is on the basis of this minimum professional work that the study timetable should be drawn up.

But with us it is just the opposite: the work which helps a

---

[1] I stress this deliberately: there are composers who do not "fall into error" for the simple reason that they do not dare, they are retrograde. (In other words they are themselves an error.) Whoever does not create anything new cannot create a great work of art. [This remark clearly alludes to the attacks on Shostakovich in 1936 and in 1948 and the following years, ED.]

pupil to acquire most of his knowledge and skill is considered the least important. Twice a year all instrumental teachers witness the same phenomenon: pupils cease to attend their classes, they are embarrassed to come to their lessons unprepared and they cannot prepare themselves because all their time is taken up in preparation for their examinations, and once again the student's profession, his speciality, is left to trail behind. When will there be an end to this disgraceful state of affairs? Of course in some relatively rare cases it is the fault of the pupils themselves because they are incapable of organizing their time rationally but, in general, it is our fault, and by "us" I mean the authorities in charge of teaching establishments, the administration of the conservatoire, and the teachers.

Previously, when I had to cope frequently with very difficult pupils, I would sometimes lose patience; I would shout, throw the score on the floor, and, in general, lose my temper. I knew that it was quite wrong and reproached myself, but I found it very difficult to keep myself in check. For instance, I once had a pupil who was gifted musically and technically but was so completely devoid of any inner fire, so indolent and indifferent to things that I bore with her as long as I could and then would have a real row, rebuking her, screaming, etc. After this she would show much more interest in and love of music for a couple of weeks, the lessons would be calm and pleasant until her vitality would once again sink to normal, i.e. to a state of utter and disgraceful indifference; then there would be the usual row and so on at intervals of a month or six weeks. I despised myself for these rows, but what could I do when they were quite obviously good for her and I had no other means at my disposal to get anything worth while out of her?

In that fairly distant time—for nowadays I have an excellent class all of whom can bear witness to the fact that I hardly ever raise my voice—I soon managed to detect in my teaching make-up a certain "scale of irritability". It then transpired that the ones who most annoyed and irritated me were not the least-gifted pupils ("you can't get blood out of a stone") but pupils like the girl I mentioned earlier, who were endowed with quite good gifts but did not bother to use them; in other words, that I was irritated by flippancy, indifference, and weakness of will and temperament. I sometimes had pupils with very average gifts, for whom piano playing meant a great deal of effort, who were devoid of what is known as the divine spark, but who thought, reasoned and strove with assiduity; with such pupils I never once in my life raised my voice or became irritated; on the contrary, I respected them most sincerely, as one respects honest striving and the achievements of sheer will-power, and I found lessons with them pleasant and even interesting.[1]

My many years of work with pupils convinced me that sometimes there is a very sharp predominance of one particular aspect of musical talent over all the others and that in general a musical artistic gift is an extremely complex "conglomerate" and that only in very rare cases all the elements and components of this conglomerate are equally perfect, whole and un-impaired.

One excellent pupil was the cause of much grief and I sometimes found myself at a dead-end when pondering over the problem of his talent. He was endowed with amazing physio-logical musicality (hearing, pitch, etc.), he could sight-read perfectly, his memory was almost photographic, he had "golden" hands and could perform without any effort the most bafflingly difficult virtuoso compositions; one might think that everything was perfect, his was a gift of the highest order. But it required incredible effort to make his playing "contagious", to give it impetus, artistic subtlety, depth and unity, and make it convincing. If we did sometimes achieve it such achievements were surprisingly short-lived and with the very next piece we had once more to tackle the same Sisyphean labour; and so it went on. I felt like a cook faced with a mountain of magnificent foods and quite incapable of producing a tasty dinner. The playing of this pupil could be described as follows: when he played solo, he seemed to be accompanying magnificently a non-existent soloist. The main thing was lacking, namely, creative will, artistic imagination, fire and understanding. All the rest, all the component parts of piano playing were present in perfect form. Sometimes the heart of a pedagogue is parti-cularly grieved at seeing such a first-class gift, deprived of the most important element (creative will), slip out of his grasp like an eel and elude all efforts to refine it.

[1] Usually such pupils subsequently became very good teachers and methodologists.

A few more words about some of my disagreements with certain teachers.

I. One well-known professor—a piano teacher—used to say sometimes, not without modest pride, but apparently bestowing on his words the significance of a thesis: "I do not teach music; I teach piano playing". I recall this case for the second time because this attitude is still to be found among teachers.

I cannot imagine anything more mistaken. Even if he were a teacher of percussion instruments, he should at the same time also teach *music*. The more so in the case of the piano, which, as I have more than once pointed out and as everyone knows, is a unique and irreplaceable instrument for teaching music, for the simple reason that it is possible to play and hear on the piano absolutely everything. If the piano teacher and piano pupil study together, not music but only piano playing (how that is done I don't quite see), then they both ought to study music with a third person and namely with a music teacher. Unfortunately such a need really does arise in some classes. Perhaps such a teacher—a "pure piano teacher"—relies on the musical education which the pupil acquires in the harmony class, polyphony class, form analysis class, etc., but surely each practician of piano teaching realizes that questions arise in his class that are never referred to by a teacher of harmony, or form analysis, questions connected with the particular work, the particular moment, the particular pupil, questions which arise out of a factual situation. I have already said that in the case of performers any teaching of music comes to life and becomes action only when we play, and particularly if we play very well (obviously the better we play, the more clearly will we make apparent the inner structure of music and the order which govern it).

I recall Goethe's words: "I hate all knowledge which does not immediately prompt me to action and does not enrich my activity". A piano lesson with a good teacher, i.e. with a pianist who is an artist, is the junction at which knowledge leads to action and action is supported by knowledge. But how can this be achieved if the teacher declares in all seriousness that he teaches only piano and not music?

II. Some very honest and very keen piano teachers, anxious that the pupils should derive the utmost benefit from their lessons, are sometimes inclined, without being aware of the fact, to turn the sum total of artistic piano literature into training material. They look at the "Appassionata" only from the point of view: is it "useful" to the pupil at that particular moment or not. Such a relegation of the "Appassionata" to the status of a mere teaching aid prompts me to protest and ask: and is the pupil in question useful to the "Appassionata"? (It also happens that a pupil who has been working at the "Appassionata" for a long time, and is still not "ready", finally declares—as a justification of his imperfection—"I am fed up with the 'Appassionata'!" In such a case I reply mercilessly: "You are mistaken, it is not you who are fed up with the 'Appassionata', but the 'Appassionata' that is fed up with you".)

As I study some beautiful musical composition with my pupils, I mentally draw up a work graph in accordance with their abilities; in one case the pupil needs merely stretch out his hand, in the other—he would have to walk a hundred miles. But this does not alter my attitude to the music (a distant star does not cease to shine brightly for me). I merely change my teaching method. Teachers who are too preoccupied with "usefulness" ("the use of usefulness is not clear" I sometimes say), inevitably develop performance criteria to which I playfully refer as: "school-Beethoven", "third-year Beethoven", "graduate Beethoven". . . . In other words they adapt the composer to the pupil instead of raising the pupil to the composer. But the truth is somewhere in between: the inter-reaction between composer and pupil through the influence of a good teacher striving to help the pupil penetrate as far as possible the composer's intention, makes for the best possible solution of the problem.

III. But this is an objection not to the teachers but to their way of life, for which they are not really to blame. I consider it a great mistake, a serious failure, extremely damaging to the whole teaching profession, that the great majority of teachers in our schools and teaching establishments do not even attempt to become acceptable performers. I know full well how many talented people there are among them who, without pretending to be concert pianists could still give their pupils good, convincing samples of performance, if only of those pieces which they teach in class. How wonderful it would be if this ardent wish of mine could become a law for all schools and teaching establishments! There is hardly any need to say how much higher the general standard of teaching would be. Yet this is a rewarding task for a performer, to say nothing of its usefulness for the pupils: to play in an accomplished manner such compositions as Tchaikovsky's *Album d'Enfants*, Schumann's *Album für die Jugend*, the easier sonatas of Mozart and Haydn, the Beethoven sonatas, Tchaikovsky's *Seasons*, etc., up to and including our own Soviet children's literature.

But as a matter of fact, the situation has improved slightly recently: teachers in schools and teaching establishments have been performing in public more and more frequently.

I consider it a great failing of our conservatoire system that owing to the multiplicity of subjects they have to study and their overloaded schedule, pupils can only rarely listen to each other and hear the teacher's comments in class. After all, work in class can be compared to work in any laboratory: if one student is engaged in a chemical experiment, twenty of his fellow students who carefully watch him and listen to the instructions of their teacher will derive just as much advantage and gain as much knowledge as he himself.

I remember a successful experiment concerned with the organization of study in my class—an experiment which completely answered my requirements—when I was working in the Sverdlovsk Conservatoire during the Second World War. This is what we did: those who were interested in my lessons came to an agreement with the director and the teachers of other subjects that during the times I taught in class they should be free, so as to be able to attend my lessons. Those present included not only my pupils but also pupils from other classes and even other departments: in this way work which in essence was individual, became collective. This naturally encouraged me to generalize and comment on theoretical subjects much more than during strictly individual lessons, and the practical lesson acquired a profoundly methodical character. And anybody will understand how much more interesting it is for a teacher when what he wants to communicate is not limited to just one pupil but reaches immediately some twenty or thirty listeners. It is astounding that in spite of the efforts of the administration and the professional staff to improve the quality of teaching, this simple and most useful measure cannot be implemented. Yet this is a well-tried method, known of old. When I was studying with Godowsky in the *Meisterklasse* of the Vienna Academy of Music, there were some ten of us who played, and about twenty to twenty-five who attended as listeners (*Hospitanten*), who never played but listened to everything. At the end of each lesson Godowsky would draw up a precise programme of the next lesson, deciding on the performers and the works to be performed; the pupils and the listeners came to the lesson with the scores, on which they followed attentively the playing of the pupil and the comments of the teacher. The advantage of this for all concerned was obviously very great. Then why cannot we have this? Of course, we, too, have in our classes non-playing pupils who listen to their friends as far as possible, but it is done in a highly unorganized manner; it often happens that when we are studying some particularly beautiful composition in which everyone is interested and which is performed by an advanced and interesting pupil, the others— just when they should be sitting and listening—suddenly all take off like so many sparrows and rush headlong to some other class for their next lesson which may be athletics or a foreign language. We must insist and ensure that this serious error in our teaching system be eradicated.

I try, just as many other teachers, to instill into my pupils a love of and a yearning for simplicity and truth (I have already mentioned this). Tolstoy used to say that an artist should have three qualities: sincerity, sincerity and again sincerity. It is much easier to say such things than to instill them into others. I have had pupils who tried at all costs to play in an "interesting" manner, somehow "specially", and it was very difficult to make them feel and render the simplicity and truth of the music. Sincerity meant for them something ordinary and "everyday". They were as if ashamed of their sincerity and perhaps they even had some reason to be. And it followed from this that all should be artificial. I most urgently advised such pupils, apart from becoming familiar with folklore, to come closer to Mozart, Schubert, Tchaikovsky, Tolstoy, Chekhov, Gorky, Stanislavsky. I strained (an aristocrat would say: I stooped) to show them how a simple phrase of Tchaikovsky or Chopin could be played in an "interesting", "amusing" and "original" manner and

how—giving free rein to conscience, yes, precisely to *conscience*[1]
—it can be played truthfully, that is with feeling, simply,
sincerely, unobtrusively and well. In the case of a few pupils my
efforts remained fruitless; they were too much in the devil's
thrall and continued on their tortuous way; with others truth
and simplicity finally prevailed over the "interesting" and they
found the path of sincerity.

Simplicity, according to Pasternak, is what men most need,
but complexity they understand better. We ought to be quite
clear about the meaning of "simplicity" and "complexity".
Every artist knows that to achieve an impression of simplicity
requires much more effort, labour (if it is not a heaven-sent gift)
and serious intent than is necessary to create a work of art that is
"interesting", "striking", "unusual". The public, audience and
readers, have an impression of "simplicity" mainly when the
artist expresses himself with unusual force, conviction, sincerity
and passion; the listener feels it, he is carried away, he believes
in what happens, he feels in art "reality", "life", something
familiar, something he has himself experienced and lived
through. It is then that he speaks of "simplicity" and how
necessary it is to art. He is pleased that he, too, turns out to be an
artist because he feels and understands art. And precisely that
which we call "simplicity" because it reminds us of nature, is in
actual fact most complex, just as any work of nature is much
more complex than anything invented by man. The famous
physicist, Rutherford, used to say that the structure of the atom
was much more complex than that of a Bechstein grand.

All this is well known; I only wanted to recall that the notions
of "simplicity" and "complexity" are not absolute and are
subject, as all on earth—to the laws of materialistic dialectic. I
can explain this dialectic with the help of an example from my
own life. I love simple lyricism in music, as expressed, for
instance, in the Chopin Mazurkas, the melodies of Tchaikovsky,
the Schubert Lieder, etc. Sometimes it seemed to me that I
would give up half of the sum total of music just for the second
theme in Tchaikovsky's Overture to *Romeo and Juliet*.[2] And

[1] I could say a great deal about this conscience which is also good
taste.
[2] An amusing detail. I used to weep buckets over it when I was
six years old and I can still not listen to it without tears.

while enjoying that music, for which the word "simplicity" is quite particularly apt, at the same time I experience a quite special joy, that I can compare to nothing else, from the last quartets of Beethoven, his Fugue from the Sonata op. 106, etc., in other words, the most "un-simple", the most complex, most intellectual, most "inaccessible" music, almost entirely deprived of what we call "lyricism"[1] in music. I ask myself: is there no contradiction in the fact that I am equally drawn to the Chopin Mazurka and the driest of all Bach fugues, to *Eugene Onegin* and to the Quartet op. 133, etc., etc. Yes, there is, if you will, a contradiction, but of the type that permeates all of life, all existence and from which mankind is not exempt; on the contrary, we are in the very thick, the very centre of these contradictions. Indeed, we are dealing here with the different facets of a single phenomenon which we call life.

Why do I write of this, some may ask? Has it anything to do with our business? Yes, it has, because such thoughts and feelings occur every day during our work and particularly when such contrasting compositions as, for instance, Tchaikovsky's *Seasons* and Beethoven's op. 106 follow each other practically without a break, causing a certain emotional shock that prompts such considerations. It often happens that I have hardly finished going through Prokofiev's Fourth Sonata with a pupil, having both of us put a lot of temperament and enthusiasm into our work, and we are carried away by the music and then the very next pupil plays Scriabin's Fourth Sonata. I noticed that until about half way through I wholeheartedly hated the Scriabin; the shock had been too great, the plunge from one musical *Weltanschauung* to an entirely contradictory one was too sudden and unnatural. But all the same I would honestly go through it with my pupil, tell him what is necessary, i.e., what I know, stress its beauties with which I am so familiar and then, gradually, a metamorphosis would take place, I would begin to forget Prokofiev and the emotions he aroused in me, I would begin to be carried away by Scriabin and when we have finished the sonata I am in love with it, just

[1] The Fugue from op. 106 or the Fugue for the String Quartet op. 133, I sometimes call *in petto* "a banquet of the mind, an intellectual orgy" and it is precisely this that gives them their emotional and musical foundation.

as sincerely as I hated it before. "How unstable you are", some will say, "at your age it is time to be a little more objective and balanced." Yes, of course, I can also be objective and balanced, but then I teach my pupils less well. And again I write about this because these are facts, and facts out of my teaching career, and facts are stubborn. And I repeat, these facts prompt many very far-reaching considerations that are of interest not only to the teacher but also to the pupil who, after all, will also be a teacher one day.

It may be that I say too little about the pupil "as such". Of course in order to review the whole multitude of pupils one could divide them into groups or types just as, for instance, people are divided according to temperament into the choleric, melancholic, etc. I think that every experienced teacher considers his pupil first and foremost as a personality in spite of the many characteristics he may have in common with others. And the clearer the individual element, the clearer the general whole. And what is general in our task and from which all particular aspects and details flow, is the need to create a high level of musical culture worthy of our people and of the great times in which we live.

Since I have discussed teaching problems in all the chapters of this book, I think I shall leave off here in spite of the fact that there is still a great deal that I should like to relate from my personal experience and practice.

In conclusion, I shall add that if I have given something to my pupils, they gave me no less, if not more, and that I am infinitely grateful to them for this, for our joint striving to know and master art was the foundation of our friendship, intimacy and mutual respect, and these sentiments are among the best that one can experience on this planet.

CHAPTER VI

Concert Activity

In our times it is clearer than ever that a concert pianist can and must be a propagandist, like any other artist. After all we, too, are to some extent "engineers of the soul". It is with a feeling of deep satisfaction that I watch the manner in which the best Soviet pianists carry out this commendable task. I would mention, in particular, Sviatoslav Richter who may serve as an example worth following. Richter does not confine himself to playing Soviet, Russian and Western classical music, but he repeatedly performs in various cities of the USSR the whole of Bach's *Wohltemperiertes Klavier* (apart from other Bach compositions). He has literally brought back to life the marvellous Schubert sonatas and some Weber sonatas that for some reason had been forgotten, and has played a multitude of seldom heard pieces by Liszt, Schumann, Beethoven; in short his concerts not only give pleasure to a wide audience but also open before it new horizons and bring before it excellent little-known compositions, thus constantly broadening and raising the level of artistic culture and musical experience. But as a matter of fact many of our pianists do this; I need only name Sofronitsky, Gilels, Zak, Oborin and there are others.

Vladimir Horowitz once told me (I had advised him to play some excellent but not yet very popular compositions) that he plays in public only what the public likes most, the rest he can play at home. The concert activity of Richter and Horowitz betrays a certain difference of approach (I am here speaking of the youthful Horowitz; later he changed considerably). It amounts to this: one of them is led by the public, while the other leads the public, taking into account its possibilities and character. The slogan of the youthful Horowitz was: "Success above all". Richter's slogan: "Above all, art!". The second slogan implies the idea of serving the people, while the first implies the action of pleasing the public.

For many pianists and (even more) learners, a public performance is far from a simple matter. It is well known that there were excellent virtuosi who suffered from stage fright and whose performances in public were usually much below their real standard. They obviously did not have the fervour of the prophets of old, or of the Roman tribunes, the gift to "come before the people". But this fervour, or instinct, is a most important condition for concentration. In our age much is done to accustom young persons to all types of social activity and this is also extremely useful for our young pianists: I have noticed that in the last twenty to twenty-five years stage fright has been definitely on the decline.[1]

The question of how to prepare for a public performance is obviously of interest to many learners and teachers. Considering the vast variety of characters, gifts, and circumstances in which pupils live, it is very difficult, even impossible, to give a general prescription. Joseph Hofmann gave this advice: learn a new composition three times and put it away three times before playing it in public. This is very good advice but presupposes a highly organized way of life aimed constantly at achieving the best possible "concert form". In our circumstances only a very few can do this in view of the numerous pursuits and studies that have nothing to do with the best possible concert form.[2] Yet

[1] For the sake of accuracy, however, I must say that in the last few years cases of amnesia during auditions and examinations have become more frequent even among good pupils; I attribute these cases solely to the excessive work-load and fatigue during examination periods. I once had an excellent pupil who did not once play in public without forgetting and losing her place. The reason was that she was absolutely overworked and was in a constant state of fatigue.

[2] Here is a small example: One morning I had to adjudicate at a conservatoire competition in which nine pianists played nine sonatas by Soviet composers, after which, of course, I had to discuss their performance at length, and in the evening I played a most

excellent recitals can be given even if their preparation is completely contrary to Hofmann's recommendations. Here is an example: several years ago Sviatoslav Richter played three Russian concertos with orchestra. One of them (Rachmaninov's First in the new version) he had already played, but a long time ago; the other two—Glazunov's First Concerto and the Concerto by Rimsky-Korsakov—he learned in exactly a week (he took the score on the 2nd and the performance took place on the 9th) having never played them before. Nevertheless the concert was excellent. Of course it is not only a question of having a tremendous talent but also an amazing capacity and ability to work, to learn. I would call this the "emergency method". But as a matter of fact Richter mostly does prepare his concert appearances this way, the "emergency" way. The reason is not that he does not have sufficient free time, as is the case of some others (for instance Oborin, Oistrakh, or myself, poor sinner, who carries a constant load of thirty-five pupils). Richter does not teach, he hardly takes part in any committees or adjudicates at competitions, but he is moved by a tremendous artistic ambition (an excellent ambition) which forces him at every public appearance to play something he has never played before.

I spoke earlier of Tausig who, coming home from a concert, was fond of playing the whole of his programme through, most carefully, attentively, in order to clear it from all the hazards of a concert performance. Richter, because of circumstances, sometimes immediately after a concert seeks out some quiet corner with a piano and plays until 5 or 6 a.m. learning a new programme for his next recital. Is this not an "emergency" method? I think that nowadays it is very important (although for entirely different reasons) that everyone should . aster this "emergency" method which was by no means so necessary before, when there was more time. But on the other hand the concert activity of this same Richter confirms the truth of Hofmann's advice: Richter himself told me that it was only at his fourth public performance of Mozart's Sonata in A minor

---

difficult Scriabin programme which included, *inter alia*, the Sixth, Eighth and Tenth Sonatas. From the point of view of concert discipline this is a crime.

that he achieved what he considered a satisfactory interpretation.

From my personal experience I could give the following example: the general public as well as musicians usually react very favourably to my performance of Chopin's First Concerto in E minor; and it may well be that the rendering of this work is less liable to be affected by the inevitable vicissitudes of mood, concert form, the influence of the moment, than the performance of some other compositions (the "standard" of performance being so to speak more constant).

To me the reason is clear: not only did I put in a great amount of thorough work into this concerto in my youth, but for some reason I have performed it specially frequently (in various cities of the USSR), and before each performance I would work at it again, if only two or three days or even one day or a few hours; what is important is that I worked at it again and again and consolidated yet again what had been achieved previously. (Here you have it, the Hofmann method. This also explains the high standard of performance of pianists who give many recitals in many cities, usually performing not more than two or three programmes). To say nothing of the fact that I love this concerto quite particularly and perhaps this is one of the main reasons for the approval of the audience.

This most useful method, the method of acquiring mastery by repeated performances, by routine (in the best sense of the word) is to all intents and purposes not available to learners since what they need above all is to acquire a repertoire, and after playing in public one or two compositions they immediately begin learning something new. Sometimes a learner has the possibility of testing in public his performance of a composition twice or at the very most, three times, whereas the concert pianist plays a composition dozens and hundreds of times.

I refer to this fact, of which everyone is well aware, only in order to stress once more the inequality that exists between the position of the learner and the concert pianist. In order to remedy this situation even slightly, pupils should not only be made to appear as often as possible at all kinds of private concerts (in schools, conservatoires) but they should also go through some of the more important works with their teacher again, after a lapse of time, repeating them, perhaps "doing them" three times during their years at the conservatoire and each time again play them in public. I sometimes deliberately use this method although it meets with opposition on the part of some of the members of the piano faculty who consider that "the rule" (which incidentally is nowhere to be found in writing) is that a pupil should never play the same things in public twice, to say nothing of three times. After all, what I recommend is just as natural as reading Pushkin at the age of ten, twenty, forty and even a hundred if one can only live that long. Of course at the same time I also struggle against the attempts of some pupils to perform at every public performance pieces they have played again and again, using as an argument against them the well-known saying of Kuzma Prutkov:[1] "You can't hatch the same egg twice". Such is the simple dialectic of life.

May I be forgiven for describing now a few facts and observations from my personal experience as a concert performer. One can always draw some conclusions from the experience of others that are useful to oneself.

Just as other pianists I have in my time given concerts, the quality of which differed: good, medium, bad. Perhaps I should honestly confess that in my case the fluctuations between the best and the worst were greater than "usual" and that perhaps it might have been better in some cases to cancel the concert than to play "in spite of everything". But it is not this that interests me at present, but something else. When, after a concert or a number of concerts, I sometimes considered why the concert was as it was and not different, I could very easily establish a connection between the quality of the concert and the mode of life that preceded it and the way I worked. It almost always appeared that for me the most important condition for a good concert was preliminary rest, good health and vitality, freshness of spirit and body. I always found it especially easy and pleasant to play after a holiday; there were no small mishaps, no feeling of weariness from which I sometimes suffer in Moscow where I am snowed under by my teaching work. In spite of the minimum of preparation (sometimes for only a day or two before the first concert, and of course I never worked while on holiday) the technical level

[1] An imaginary poet, reputed for his aphorisms, invented by Count A. Tolstoy and the brothers Zhemchuzhnikovy, ED.

was high. Of course I did not learn new compositions but played works which I had played many times before and since I have a large repertoire I sometimes gave eight or nine recitals with different programmes quite easily.

None of this would perhaps be worth mentioning were it not for the fact that three-quarters of my life are lived in conditions that are entirely wrong for concert work and I always recall with gratitude that "island of happiness" on which from time to time I find myself when, after a complete rest (and first of all a complete rest from the playing of others to which I frequently have to listen for days on end), there is nothing which physically prevents me from being what I am.

(Cortot used to say that for a concert pianist on tour the most important thing is sound sleep and a good digestion. All great artists have always required on their tours every kind of comfort, thoroughly planned in advance. This is understandable: it is the first and most essential condition for a performer's activity. That is why in the first place I mentioned rest and health.)

It would frequently happen in Moscow, that in the middle of my work with pupils, meetings, and sometimes even competitions, I would, in spite of my tiredness, have to prepare a concert. I prepared it honestly, trying to make use of all my spare time, but because of excessive fatigue the concert would not come up to the desired standard, a certain amount of spiritual wear and tear would, on the concert platform, sometimes turn into highly strung tenseness (for this reason some musicians consider me a "nervous" pianist, but they are completely mistaken; what to a superficial or unfriendly observer appears to be "nervousness" is in actual fact the healthy protest of spirit and body against an enforced, irrational way of life which hampers the free manifestation of the artistic will). What sometimes particularly hampered my spiritual freedom on the concert platform was the mere feeling (not even always justified) that I had not managed to work as much or in the way I had wanted and considered necessary, while the amount of work actually done was sometimes twice or even three times greater than the amount I put in when I was in perfect health, completely free of other duties and spiritually rested.

I also noticed that it is much more difficult to give a single recital in the space of one or two months—because the recital then becomes an exception to the rule, this rule being, as I already said, usually entirely incompatible with concert work—than to give a series of concerts on a tour, since in this case the whole way of life is aimed at one thing only: public appearance, and nothing or practically nothing interferes with it. And then, as the saying is, one gets the knack, one gets used to doing it and since concert playing (why not say it?) is infinitely more pleasant and a hundred times less tiring than teaching, particularly if you see that you are giving pleasure to your audience, your whole vitality increases and it sometimes even seems that life has more roses than thorns (and this is immediately reflected in one's playing).

I am describing the most ordinary things, well known to all. But what can I do if our life is made up of precisely these most ordinary things? We all know perfectly well how we should organize our lives in order to achieve the maximum development of our abilities yet we are frequently completely unable to put this knowledge into practice. I became very sad, once, when David Oistrakh, this amazing artist and magnificent virtuoso, admitted to me that it had not been easy for him to play even the Rachmaninov Trio at the memorial ceremony for Antonina Vassilievna Nezhdanova because he had not held a violin in his hands for almost a month; at that time examinations had coincided with endless competitions, and like all of us he had had to sit and listen, and judge and prepare his pupils.

Such an admission, made in passing, ought to get to the ears of the officials of the Ministry of Culture; it should worry them as it worried and grieved me. Perhaps I am making a tragedy out of a trifle? I don't think so. We all of us want to be Stakhanovites in our work but Stakhanov would never have allowed his pick-axe to lie idle while he attended meetings.

About stage fright, from which so many people suffer, Rimsky-Korsakov said very accurately that it was in inverse proportion to the degree of preparation. This formula is true in spite of the fact that it does not exhaust all cases and kinds of stage fright. I remember, for instance, the first recital given by Leopold Godowsky at the beginning of the 1906 Berlin winter season. He was, of course, perfectly prepared, yet the feeling of special responsibility connected with the first concert of the season was apparently so strong that the first part of the recital was marked by nervousness and stiffness. I saw him the next day. He was very displeased with his recital. Anton Rubinstein, as everyone knows, was very nervous and once even broke a mirror in the artists' room with his fist before walking on to the platform (this seemed to have calmed him). The nervousness of such artists as Rubinstein can hardly be confused with the feeling of fear and timidity which frequently overcomes the fledgeling pianist. Such nervousness as that of Rubinstein is, I think, due partly to the fact that every public performance is subject to "the power of the moment" and the highly artistic personality capable of inspiration is more liable to be affected by it than the standard, balanced artists who experience neither great flights nor great falls; secondly, since a reputation already acquired and the high regard of the public imply special obligations, there is, here too, a certain element of fear—fear of losing the goodwill of the listener. But the main reason is the great spiritual tension without which a man called upon "to come before the people" is unthinkable: awareness that he must communicate to the people who have come to hear him something important, significant, deep, different from the daily humdrum experiences, thoughts and feelings. This type of nervousness is a good and necessary feeling and anyone incapable of it, who walks on to the platform as a good official walks into his office certain that today, too, he will perform the tasks required of him, such a person cannot be a true artist.

One of the main mistakes in preparing for a concert (and in work in general) which I noted in some pupils and pianists, is the complete divorce between their work at home and the performance in the concert hall. For them the notion of learning is identical with that of practising; they are prepared to play by the hour some beautiful composition, thumping out every note, to practise each hand separately, and to repeat the same passage endlessly, in short to learn music without music. It does not occur to them to play the composition in its entirety thinking first of all of music; for them the notion of "music making" is incompatible with the notion of "work". It is understandable that with such an exceptive method the best musical compositions are turned into exercises or études. The logical and practical mistake made by pianists who adopt this method, is that they consider it as an intermediate stage on the way to reaching some other, higher goal, but since they stop at this stage for too long (some remain there for good) it becomes an end in itself beyond which nothing can be achieved. I repeat: in striving to reach the goal, that is, an artistically accomplished performance, one should proceed in a straight line (there is bound to be some meandering anyway). This helps to organize the purely technical work rationally and if at times, when trying to solve particularly difficult virtuoso problems, that work prevails, it will still not lead the pianist down a mistaken path, but will be precisely that stage which enables him to reach his goal. Here I must again recall Tausig's method: the temporary exclusion of all expression and artistic quality of performance; a method I frequently use. But I do so when working on compositions that I have already played, already used, that have been verified artistically and musically accomplished. Before the composition is allowed to see the light of day (or rather the lights of the concert platform) I play it many times at home, by myself, in the same way in which I would play it for an audience. (True this is not the aim I set myself, but as I get carried away by the composition, I "perform" it for myself and for others though these others are not present.) It is obvious that works that have been played in public frequently are the ones that least require this treatment; in their case the "dry" workmanlike playing through of the composition is more suitable.

But, in general, one may say that both the method recommended by Hofmann and the emergency method and many others too are good and proper according to the circumstances. Personally I have more faith in the method of Hofmann, or a similar method, but I, too, have had occasion to prepare a recital by the emergency method. For instance, I had to play the Second Sonata by Szymanowski at a concert of his works in Vienna in 1913 exactly nineteen days after receiving the music and I played it quite well though this composer is very difficult and complex.

It may perhaps be worth while relating an instance which I consider interesting since it was the most intensive and strenuous work I have had to do in all my life.

When I was seventeen to eighteen (this was in summer in the lovely village of Manuilovka, in the region of Poltava which subsequently became famous because Gorky used to go there frequently for a rest) I tackled for the first time that most difficult of Beethoven sonatas, op. 106 (the "Hammerklavier") with fugue. I tackled it with enthusiasm, and thought of it constantly away from the piano, when walking, bathing, dining. On going to bed I used to put the music on the chair near a candle (there was no electricity in Manuilovka then) and read it until I fell asleep. I dreamt of it in my sleep and it sometimes happened that in my dream I would get "stuck" in the fugue and couldn't remember how it went on. Apparently this worried me so much that I would wake up, light the candle, take the music and start reading the fugue from the place where I had got stuck. Then I would fall asleep again. This happened more than once. As a result of this kind of "work" I learnt the whole sonata from memory in exactly six days and for that kind of composition this is really a very short time. Sometimes I took much longer to learn much easier pieces because I did not have that tremendous will, I was not "possessed" as I had been when learning the "Hammerklavier". (The reason I was so possessed is clear; I knew beforehand that this is one of the greatest and most difficult of Beethoven's works; so naturally there was the challenge: "let's see if you can cope with such a task!".)

This factual example shows the tremendous importance of intensive will-power, passion, determination to forge ahead in order to reach the goal one has set oneself. (I forgot to say that during those six days I did nothing else, I did not even read a book.) This experience brought me to a strange conclusion, namely that in addition to the four ways of learning a piece recommended by Hofmann (the first, to learn a piece at the piano, with the music; the second, at the piano without the music; the third, with the music but without the piano; and the fourth, without the piano and without the music, i.e. walking in town or in a wood and just thinking the composition through) there is yet a fifth way, to learn a piece in one's sleep. This is not the product of a feverish brain; it is the truth. I need hardly say that subsequently, before every performance of this sonata, I studied it again and again and only rarely did I manage to play it as I would have liked. Busoni used to say that life was too short to learn Op. 106, which is perhaps why he played it as no one else.

The example of Godowsky is memorable for me. I sometimes

happened to be at his home when he was preparing for a recital. Pieces that he had played dozens and perhaps hundreds of times he would again and again check against the score, he compared the different versions of various editions (of Chopin alone he had seventeen editions at the time!); in other words in the shortest possible time he again went through the work he had done long ago. An example of artistic honesty worthy of being followed.

Zadora, a well-known pupil of Busoni, told me that on the day of a recital Busoni frequently played his whole programme from beginning to end slowly and without "expression" which is what Tausig used to do after a recital (but as a matter of fact he probably did it before the recital too). It is very important to save one's emotional energy on the day of a recital, to say nothing of the usefulness of playing the work through carefully, accurately and attentively (only with the fingers and with the help of cold reason). I know this from bitter experience. Once when I was due to play in the evening (for the first time) the Twenty-four Preludes of Debussy, I began rehearsing them in the morning on a concert grand. The piano was good, I got carried away and instead of doing "cold" work, I played the whole programme with excitement, completely involved spiritually and emotionally and derived tremendous pleasure. In the evening I played twice as badly as I should have and could have done. Of course, the reverse can also happen, but such cases are exceptions and not the rule.

I think that a typical great virtuoso pianist who has from childhood or youth been accustomed to the concert platform, who has devoted his whole life to it exclusively, and achieved perfection and consequently great fame, could write much better and more convincingly than I about concert work and its requirements. To name but a few of our contemporaries: Gieseking, Horowitz, Artur Rubinstein, Casadesus, Petri, Claudio Arrau, and others; and of the younger generation: Gilels, Richter, Benedetti Michelangeli, Gulda.

It occurs to me that it would be very interesting for young pianists to have more detailed information about the way in which prominent pianists prepare for recitals and about their concert work in general. A musical journal (why not our *Sovetskaya Muzyka?*) could send a brief questionnaire on the subject to our own and to foreign pianists. I imagine that many great pianists might wave it aside with a joke or some brief aphorism. But there would probably be some who would reply seriously and in detail. After all, we do publish a series of books in which painters write about themselves and which are extremely interesting. Why not have some about pianists? I think that all professionals and lovers of the piano would be most interested in such books.

The trouble is that the very great virtuosi who are constantly engaged in playing at home or on tours, and now also in making records, hardly ever write or tell anything of the behind-the-scenes aspect of their work which is of such interest to young pianists; the fact that they do not write is due not only to a lack of time but also, apparently, to the "sound commonsense" reason that the whole of their performing work speaks for itself so convincingly that it needs no comment and anyone with the least bit of intelligence, especially a professional, can draw his own conclusions.

My own "concert biography" is rather an example of an argument to the contrary than an example to be followed. After finishing the *Meisterklasse* of the Vienna Musical Academy with Godowsky, because of war conditions (the First World War had then broken out), I immediately plunged into the very thick of teaching work, and at the beginning had extremely poor pupils. Elizavetgrad, Tiflis, Kiev, Moscow (in 1922)—this was the thorny path unsuitable for a concert pianist and one which I continue to tread even now that I am grey and wrinkled.

I mention all this in order to warn young pianists who are sufficiently gifted to become concert pianists not to allow themselves to be prematurely submerged in teaching. Just as it is useful and even essential for a true teacher, so it is harmful for a true performer.[1] Of course, working with a few talented pupils ("homeopathic teaching") is useful and fruitful for any performer; it is only a question of quantity and selection.

The ideal would be for a great concert pianist not to begin teaching before he is forty or forty-five years old. He himself would then be happy and his public would be grateful to him.

[1] I remember that Szigeti, the violinist, once asked me how many pupils I had and when I told him "about thirty" he cried out, aghast, "But this is suicide!".

In Conclusion

There is a lot (a tremendous lot!) that I have left unsaid in this book. My experience is much richer and my thoughts much more numerous than can be set down in a few printed pages. Moreover, I am an inexperienced writer, I find it very difficult to be laconic and concise. Since I intended this book mainly for the average piano teachers and their pupils, I have inevitably had to show, on frequent occasions, that "the Volga flows into the Caspian Sea". I think that the average teacher will hardly hold it against me, for he knows as well as I do that, as far as pupils are concerned, the Volga sometimes flows into the White Sea and occasionally even into the Indian Ocean. I have consequently had to dwell at length on some of the typical mistakes made by pupils (mainly in the chapters on tone and rhythm) which, strictly speaking, are rather cases of ignorance than absence of culture or artistic sense.

I can imagine the yawns of some prominent musician who may come across my book and read these lines. But I repeat, I had no other way, partly because of the average learner for whom this book is meant, and partly because in art, and all the more in learning art, there are no "trifles" and it would be fundamentally wrong—"unpedagogic"—to pass over in silence the beginners' difficulties and misunderstandings.

There is something else I regret: that in these pages I could not give full rein to my imagination and that they are rather descriptions of "what actually happened", "reliable accounts" supplemented by a fair amount of heuristic, than the fruits of freely soaring thought.

I would add in conclusion a few thoughts on music, the

composer, the performer and the musicologist—more by way of thinking aloud than preaching, though the latter may at times creep in. Preaching, I must honestly confess, sometimes makes me a little sick. Alas! I love pupils (specially if they are talented) and music, but teaching. . .? Perhaps I am simply not a teacher in spite of having "on my books" fifteen prize-winners and hundreds of pupils successfully working *urbi et orbi*.

On music. *"De la musique avant toute chose!"* This call which the poet Verlaine addressed to the poets' camp brings an echo from the musicians' camp: "Poetry above all!" That Poetry with a capital P which is the primary foundation of art and with which all great art is permeated: Tolstoy's *War and Peace*, Chekhov's *The Lady with the Little Dog*, Balzac's *Le Père Goriot*, Thomas Mann's *The Magic Mountain*, Giotto's Campanile. I purposely take these examples at random.

Music has been the subject of thinking, writing and discussion since time immemorial. A historian of the time of Nero noted with a sigh that among all the panic, disorder, and the flames of burning Rome, the foreboding of the imminent fall of the empire, at every street corner people sang and strummed and argued heatedly about music. And what of the "revolution" of a Terpander?[1] Opinions about music change, as everything changes, for everything in the world is subject to the swing of history's pendulum. Yesterday's law is tomorrow's taboo. At the close of the Middle Ages it was considered that the greatest impediments to creating music were feeling and passion. But barely five centuries passed before the music of Wagner and Tchaikovsky was born. The musical trend abroad which preceded the appearance of Shostakovich and is known as "modern" or *neue Sachlichkeit*, attempted to span the gap between our times and the past by a bridge across the whole of the romantic and partly also the classical era, which would come to rest on the stable foundations of pre-Bach professionalism. After an excessive poetization of music, its "literization" (when programme music flourished), there appeared people who maintained that music is only music and was not to be confused with other arts (a protest against Wagner's idea of a

[1] Greek musician and poet who lived in Lesbos in the VIIth century B.C. and is believed to have been the first to introduce the heptachord, ED.

Gesammtkunstwerk). Anyone who is thoroughly acquainted with the history of music and is able to follow lovingly its meanders, will find his way through them without much difficulty. May I use a somewhat artless metaphor: just as anyone flying over great rivers such as the Yenisei, the Kama, the Volga, looks down with pleasure at their majestic and clear flow, their broad expanse, and their sparkling sheets of water (while the smaller rivers, winding busily in and out, almost hidden by shrubs, flow one knows not whence or whither)—so, too, from the summit of a loving knowledge of history lie clearly visible the main channels through which the mighty flood of music rushes into the unexplored ocean of the future. Such knowledge leads to some simple conclusions: there is no "old" and "new" music; but there is good and bad music, lofty and low music (with all the intermediate degrees).

"Old-fashioned" and "contemporary" music are only the thesis and antithesis; their synthesis is mediocre music. If we consider a great work of the past as out of date, then we simply lack historic perspective (in other words, culture)—that is a fact out of our own unfortunate biography and not out of the biography of the work in question.[1] Anyone who loves literature, poetry and philosophy can (almost in the same breath) read with the utmost delight Sophocles' *Oedipus*, Tolstoy's *Polikushka*, the *Odyssey* and *Quiet Flows the Don*, become engrossed in Aristotle and immediately after take Karl Marx, and listen with equal joy to a mass by Palestrina and a mass by Janáček. . . .

It seems to me that this is possible, because for a truly cultured person three or four thousand years is a ridiculously short span of life.

I say this as one who knows and loves not only music, but art in general; as a servant of art. But the voices of the indifferent or the inexperienced would probably sound a different note. Yet that is why we exist—we teachers and educators—to tune the voice of the inexperienced, the unknowing, to unison with us. Experienced teachers know what means to use to reduce indifference and increase knowledge, to awaken love and inspire reverence.

[1] The same may be said of the failure to appreciate a great contemporary work (to mention but Shostakovich's Eighth Symphony).

A few words about the composer. Volumes and volumes have been written about composers; one might say, tons of books, articles, pamphlets. Many of them are extremely interesting and are invaluable in enabling the performer to study and get to know the author.

But Pushkin was right when he said that a poet's words are almost his deeds. That is probably why no biography, not even the private correspondence or memoirs, or even profound psychological research can give such a clear impression of an author as can "his deeds", in other words his work (let us recall once more Rachmaninov: 85% musician and only 15% man). Can one compare the "impression of Wagner" one gets from his music with the impression of him one may get from his numerous articles and autobiography (*Mein Leben*)? Or the impression of Rimsky-Korsakov as composer of operas, with that of him as the author of *My Musical Life*.

With all my respect for Romain Rolland and his noble humanitarian aspirations, I must (at the cost of arousing someone's indignation) say that in spite of his love and adulation of Beethoven and his vast knowledge, everything that he wrote about that great composer seems to me inaccurate and distorted, I would even say somehow unpleasant. He overdoes his picture of Beethoven as "a bundle of misfortunes" and his life as unrelieved suffering (incidentally he writes of Berlioz with the same tedious insistence on the tragic and the gloomy). The author's worthy and wise desire to show the reader that a great man has a greater ability to endure suffering than an ordinary man, that the abyss which separates him from the rest of the world is deep, if not bottomless, and that this tragedy is inevitable and that the path of genius is thorny, all this forces Romain Rolland deliberately to belittle the consolations and joys which an artist derives from the act of creation, from his daily work on his compositions, frequently making him forget all else. Artists themselves have often said so. Suffice it to recall Beethoven's own *Heiligenstadt Testament*. Or the wonderful words which Blok addresses to the artist, words that seem chiselled in marble: "Efface the accidental features and you will see the world is beautiful!"

Only a true artist has the strength to efface the "accidental features" and this is all the more difficult because, clearer than anyone else, he sees and realizes all the evil of the world, and suffers from it so that his suffering is almost equal to his awareness.[1] And that is precisely why his joys are so great that an ordinary man has difficulty in visualizing them.

The "15% man" of whom Rachmaninov speaks should not be inflated to the full 100%. One should not exaggerate everything "human" or "too human" in him. And that is just what Romain Rolland has done. For an artist to be a man means above all to be an artist, that is: all his life to create works of art and to do so to the best of his ability. But those who write about a great man and study his life and work are not the only ones guilty of a tendentious and one-sided approach. On the one hand there are performers with a confident and domineering personality who adapt the composer to fit their own image; such was Busoni in his rendering of the Romantics, specially Schumann and Chopin. On the other hand (and this is much worse) there are performers with a narrow spiritual horizon, unable to grasp all the wealth and diversity of music as it developed through the centuries and who resemble those mediocre actors who, instead of acting a part, can only act their own selves.

Let us come back to the composer. I want to refer to what I consider one of the most important problems for a performer, the solution of which will at the same time help to solve the highest aesthetic and cultural task facing him.

We are all acquainted with examples of extreme intolerance on the part of some of the great composers towards their fellow composers whose creative path ran counter to theirs. We know that Chopin could not stand the Finale of Beethoven's Fifth Symphony and did not approve of Schubert, accusing him of what we would now call "naturalism"; that Tchaikovsky said some very harsh things about Brahms; that Prokofiev and Shostakovich do not like (to put it mildly) Scriabin; that Scriabin himself, in the last years of his life, reached a state of almost musical solipsism (only approving of some of Chopin and Wagner as being an approach to his own music); that when Wagner was given Brahms' *Requiem* which had only just

[1] Of course the same may be said of any great man, in any case of a learned man.

appeared, he threw it on the floor in anger; that Rachmaninov, in a conversation with Artur Rubinstein,[1] said "Music finished with Schumann and Tchaikovsky"; that Debussy, or was it Stravinsky (I don't remember which, perhaps both) said that Beethoven was undoubtedly a great man but hardly a musician, etc., etc., *ad infinitum*.

This picture is very familiar. Every powerful personality tries to spread, like an elemental force, over the whole world, but happily it encounters other personalities, just as strong, and this gives rise to conflicts just as in Heraclitus: struggle is the father and master of everything on earth. I hope that the great but unliveable-with will forgive me if I say that they reminded me of dandelions and rabbits: if there were no other plants and animals on earth, in two or three months' time dandelions and rabbits would have filled the earth.

To attempt to convince, to instil a sense of fairness, to soften the dislike of these "fighters" (the great creative artists) is senseless and useless. What if we tried to convince Schopenhauer that Hegel was a great and profound philosopher!

Tolstoy's hatred of Shakespeare, so unequivocally expressed in his article on *King Lear*, or his version of Wagner's *Ring der Nibelungen* told in his book *What is Art?* for some reason always bring me to a state of irrepressible mirth. If there were no such brawls between the "masters of our thoughts", if we did not have this enjoyable spectacle, so much more fun than boxing or football, life would become dull indeed.

Quarrel to your heart's content, dear "masters", but remember that we, performers, and even more so teachers, will not follow you in any circumstances. It behoves us to be spectators and not actors in the show you put on.

I do not preach either omnivorousness or absolute tolerance, both of which are signs of a lack of personality or of indifference. But it seems to me—and I have said so earlier—that there can be a degree of historic awareness (plus experience) which allows one not to take part in the disputes or quarrels of composers, but to see in them the component parts of a great, wonderful and profound process governed by laws. The morals

[1] I have it from Artur Rubinstein himself. They met in a train and travelled in the same compartment.

of a composer are entirely different from the morals of a performer. The performer must have that sense of objectivity and fairness which the composer cannot have. Yet fairness can be a feeling loftier and more passionate than any love or hate. That, perhaps, is the only advantage of a performer: his ethico-aesthetic predominance over the composer; a very rare phenomenon since it is impossible without a very great talent.

Very frequently instead of Justice (with a capital J) we see merely a readiness to give in.

In actual fact, of course, it happens all the time that a performer prefers one kind of music to another (one may feel more kinship with Brahms, another with Scriabin, etc.). Performers often consciously favour one trend, one style, but not all of them and not different ones. This is a natural phenomenon, it is life itself.

But justice, "universality" are still concepts of a higher order.

When Vladimir Horowitz was twenty-two, he told me with great emphasis how much he loved Mozart and Schumann and how alien Beethoven was to him. Beethoven did not move him in the slightest, he was no Mozart, and certainly no Schumann, but something half-way between the two. You can imagine what I felt listening to this, as my love for Mozart and Schumann did not detract from my love of Beethoven, but on the contrary, enhanced it. However, I suppose that Horowitz's views must have changed very considerably since that time.

In their youth, very great virtuosi like Gilels and that same Horowitz usually prefer Liszt and Rachmaninov to many other composers who deserve no less, if not more, attention, probably because these composers (who were also pianists of genius) give special scope for their amazing pianistic gifts. But the youthful Gilels only needed a few years' thorough work on music and on himself before he told me that he considered Schumann's Piano Concerto the best in the world. And that was when he had already played the concertos of Liszt, Tchaikovsky and Rachmaninov. We all know how excellently he later played the Second Brahms Concerto and in the 1955/56 season all five Beethoven concertos.

The demand (or rather wish) for "universality"[1] which I

[1] Obviously by "universality" I do not mean a mastery of the entire piano literature quantitatively speaking, but qualitatively.

require of a pianist—particularly of a pianist, since the music written for the pianoforte, in its scope, variety, wealth and beauty does not yield to symphonic, chamber, operatic or choral music—this demand or wish may perhaps bring an ironic smile: after all, you cannot encompass immensity. Yes, you can. This was proved by Liszt, Rubinstein and practically to the same extent by Josef Hofmann and some others; in our time it is being proved by Richter, Gilels, Sofronitsky and, probably several foreign pianists whom unfortunately I know only from some of their records. One of the foremost, it seems to me, is Benedetti Michelangeli, and not only as far as repertoire is concerned. The enormous and varied repertoire of Sofronitsky, Yakov Zak and several other of our pianists is a joy not only to myself but to all our musical public.

A certain "resultant" acting between the life and personality of a pianist determines the nature and scope of his activity. One man, having brilliantly finished the conservatoire becomes a professional accompanist to an operatic choir, another devotes himself entirely to teaching, leaving himself hardly any time for practising and improving his playing, while a third begins playing in public at an early age, captures public interest and devotes himself entirely to concert work. But all of them need "universality", i.e. culture, without which in our time nobody can play a useful or welcome part. This truism, too, has to be repeated. Pushkin was once reckless enough to say: "Poetry, God forgive me, should always be a little silly". Some musicians —and they include composers and performers—come to a somewhat erroneous conclusion: "If that is so, then music should be completely stupid".

We teachers are sometimes amazed that, in spite of their superlative gifts, in spite of an understanding of music and of their instrument—the result of good schooling—so very few pianists become performers of interest who carry you away and are able to captivate their audience. The reason, I think, is that with all their other gifts the majority lack the "conductor principle", the creative will, or personality; that they play what they have been taught and not what they themselves have experienced, thought and worked out. And for a pianist, in view of the fact that he is at once the legislative and the executive, "master and servant", this absence of a creative will is fatal. In opera a singer is helped by the conductor and the stage director, in chamber music by the accompanist (remember the marvellous combination Dorliac-Richter), but who shall help the solo pianist if he does not help himself? There is scarcely a more saddening experience than listening to the performance of a "good", "senior", "musical" pianist with an "accomplished technique" who plays as if he were accompanying a non-existent soloist. Alas, the voice behind the scenes is not heard, the disconsolate "headless horseman", after wandering aimlessly among the musical expanse, disappears without leaving even the impression of a ghost.

At the opposite pole is the performance of a great pianist with a vivid personality, a passionate will, particularly if he is, at the same time, a composer (Rachmaninov is a striking example). Since we are again speaking of Rachmaninov let me put down some of my thoughts about him because to me they seem to be of fundamental importance.

Perhaps some may find paradoxical my assertion (or rather my personal feeling) that on the one hand Rachmaninov's performance of his own work or, for instance, of Tchaikovsky's *Troika* (and much, much else) and, on the other hand, his performance of Chopin's Sonata in B flat minor (as we know it from records) belong to two entirely different categories of the performer's art. In the first case there is complete fusion of the performance with the work performed; there is authenticity, truth, truer than which nothing can even be imagined; in the second case, a Rachmaninized Chopin, an emigrant who has received such a hefty injection of Russian blood, of daring from "beyond the Moscow River", that he is hard to recognize after this treatment. Yet in both cases the performer is the same unique pianist of genius. I know that many will disagree with me and will even be offended on Rachmaninov's behalf. What can I do if this is my insuperable feeling or, if you will, my conviction? One witty writer said that in any philosophy one may find a place where the author states his convictions or, using the words of the old mystery: *adventavit asinus, pulcher et fortissimus* (here comes the ass, handsome and strong). I shall not be in the least offended if the reader remembers that ass in connection with my conviction, especially since I shall defend it with the stubbornness of an ass.

What I called two entirely different categories of the performer's art inevitably touches on "questions of style". I shall state my opinion on the subject lightly, without due gravity.

In my opinion there are four types of "performance style". The first—no style at all! Bach is performed "with feeling" à la Chopin or Field; Beethoven—dry and businesslike à la Clementi; Brahms—impetuously and with eroticism à la Scriabin or with Lisztian pathos; Scriabin—drawing-room fashion à la Rebikov or Arensky; Mozart—à la old maid, etc., etc. This is not fancy; all this I have heard with my own ears.

The second—is the "mortuary" style. The performer is so hampered by the "code of laws" (frequently imaginary), he tries so hard to "keep to the style", and is so pedantically convinced that one should play thus and not otherwise and tries so hard to show that the music is "period" (if, God forbid, it happens to be Haydn or Mozart), that in the end the poor composer dies in front of the sorrowing audience and nothing is left of him except a smell of death.[1]

The third type, which I beg the reader on no account to confuse with the second, is the "museum" performance, based on the most accurate and reverent knowledge of how music was performed and how it sounded at the time it was composed; for instance, the performance of the "Brandenburg" Concertos by a small orchestra and a harpsichord as in Bach's time, observing strictly all the rules governing performances at that time (Stross ensemble, Wanda Landowska with her harpsichord; for the impression to be complete the audience should be in period dress and the hall should be lit by wax tapers instead of electricity).

The fourth type, finally, is the performance illumined by the penetrating rays of intuition and inspiration; a contemporary, vivid performance, backed by unostentatious erudition, imbued with love for the composer that prompts the wealth and diversity of technical methods; a performance, the slogan of which is: "The composer is dead, but his music lives on!" or, if the

---

[1] That is why I call this the "mortuary" style. Sometimes this style is mistakenly referred to as the "cerebral" style. This is a regrettable misunderstanding. I have the utmost respect for the brain, and the utmost distaste for the mortuary.

composer is still alive: "And he shall go on living in the distant future too!"

Obviously, styles no. 1 and no. 2 fall by the wayside; the first because of its stupidity, immaturity and youth; the second because it is old, overripe and stupid.

There remain: no. 4, without contest the best, and no. 3, as a valuable, extremely valuable, addition to it.

But enough of this analysis. It cannot cover all the variety and wealth of trend and personality in the art of performance. To my mind one thing remains true: style, good style, is truth, authenticity. Buffon's famous saying: *Le style c'est l'homme* (the style is the man) should be supplemented by the no-less famous saying of Boileau: *Il n'y a que le vrai qui est bon* (only truth is good). Not everyone can find this truth easily, but to one who seeks, who desires it passionately and works tirelessly to find it, it will be revealed.

The more talented, the more musical[1] the pianist, the less worried he is about questions of style as they usually appear to teachers and methodologists, the more vividly will he portray truth in his performance. The musical material gives birth to the form—truth, which can explain so much in art. Rachmaninov, playing Chopin as a genius but not à la Chopin, arouses admiration, in spite of his obvious departure from the composer's spirit, because his powerful personality together with unprecedented mastery will always carry away the listener and also because this is an elemental phenomenon which is not the result of a process of thought, of striving or of reasoned preparation. "For him it is permitted" is what we feel. This is the reign of force, of power, of might. The words of Beethoven come to mind: *Kraft ist die Moral derer, die sich von den anderen auszeichnen— sie ist auch die meinige* (Force is the moral of those who stand out from the others; it is also mine).

But take away the genius and leave the strength and what will be the result? In the best of cases—arbitrariness, in the worst, rowdyism.

I repeat once more, there is no falser premise than the famous: *Nichts ist wahr, alles ist erlaubt* (Nothing is true; everything is permitted).

[1] A word which Busoni hated. He considered that it could be applied to an instrument but not to a person.

The performer in search of truth will be guided by the opposite formula: there is a truth, not everything is permitted. When a pupil falls into the arbitrary, tries to be original and becomes wild, I remind him of that excellent rule of strategy: one must have artillery but not show it. If the word "artillery" is replaced by the word "individuality", "temperament", "personality" and many others, the artilleryman's rule will also apply to the pianist.

The almost infinite possibility of playing *differently* (for truth, too, is infinite) while playing well and beautifully (but variety, too, has its hierarchy!) is a phenomenon that has always filled me with admiration; the same happens in other arts also, the same thing happens in nature with its infinite variety of forms of life.[1]

Imagine, for example, that you are listening to a three-hour concert at an average-good music school or conservatoire at which some dozen pupils perform—even if they play their pieces faultlessly; and then imagine that in the same three hours you hear six or seven excellent pianists—artists. In the first case everything merges into a uniform grey mass, you feel as if you were always listening to the same thing. In the second case, what variety, how many unexpected wonders, how many contradictions and conflicting qualities; every time it is a different instrument (although in actual fact it is the same), different music, everything is different as in infinite Nature where there can only not be two noses alike, but not even two small leaves. Or imagine that the PERSIMFANS[2] is playing three different symphonies after which these same symphonies are given under three great conductors. . . . These artless impressions and considerations (in spite of being very elementary their significance is difficult to refute) lead to the optimistic conclusion that the good is much more prevalent than the bad! Here, quality really turns into quantity.

If I write about these very well-known commonplace things it is, as in so many other cases, only because observing the most

[1] This awareness considerably softens my own personal requirements as a teacher, but, of course, in cases when it is already possible to engage in discussion with a pupil and not merely give him instructions.

[2] See footnote on p. 64.

ordinary manifestations in life and pondering over them will provide the key to the solution of many problems and help correct many mistakes. If the founders of the PERSIMFANS had been as clearly conscious of the phenomenon of the "headless horseman" as I am, the PERSIMFANS would exist (and with every good reason) only as a method of work but in no case as a concert organization called upon to perform before tens of thousands of people. I referred to two impressions: that of a concert by good pupils, and the other of performances by several excellent pianists; these are impressions that anyone can easily experience, or else imagine, and I referred to them because even the recording of this simple fact can set thoughts in motion and lead to most useful conclusions. It is to these conclusions that to a large extent this book is devoted. I repeat again that the readers for whom this book is meant are the average piano teacher and his pupils.

Albrecht Dürer, in his reflections on painting, said that there were canons of beauty, truths capable of proof, which rejected the approach based on taste ("I like", "I do not like") by which the crowd is usually guided. The experienced, knowing man will more than once say to himself: "I do not like this, but *it is good*". The inexperienced, non-understanding man says: "I do not like (or do not understand) this, which means that it is bad", or "I like it, therefore it is good", (even if in actual fact it is bad). Oh, if we could only attain such a "passionate objectivity" as that of Dürer or Leonardo, how much better we could decide the lesser as well as the greater questions of art!

I feel bound to quote here a judgment that is particularly dear to me: Haydn was asked whom he considered the best composer. He replied: "I swear before God and as an honest man that I consider the best composer to be Mozart, for he has a perfect mastery of the laws of composition and has the best taste!" And that was that.

This seemingly chary sentence is in actual fact full of profound significance; analyse it carefully and you will see the importance of what it says.

On musicology. Questions related to the appreciation of our art obviously lead to thinking about the scholar, the musicologist, the musician and writer. I know that some great composers and

performers take a very cool view (to put it mildly) of this
category of people whose activities are connected with music.
Everyone knows of the numerous witticisms at their expense—
for instance that writing about music is like speaking about food
which for the hungry is quite inadequate, etc., etc.

I personally value and love expressions of thought and
research in this field, provided, of course, they emanate from
truly authoritative persons.

For instance, in our own field, the pianoforte, the work of
C. P. E. Bach *Versuch über die wahre Art das Klavier zu spielen* was
and remains a most reliable and excellent guide, primarily
because the old music, for the understanding and mastery of
which that work was written, was and continues to be superb
music to this day.

And how many excellent books on music have been written
by great musicians and musicologists! Think of those in our own
country: the writings of Glinka, the wonderful articles of
Tchaikovsky, Serov,[1] a great many writings by Stassov,[2] etc.,
etc.; and in our own times, the writings of Asafiev (Glebov)[3],
Sollertinsky[4] (he, unfortunately, wrote very little; with his
tremendous talent and erudition he could have written many
outstanding books); the interesting books of Professor Mazel[5]
and much more. (I have cited only a small part of all the
valuable work done in our country in the field of musicology.)

I would also include in the field of musicology everything
written by Schumann, Wagner, Liszt, Berlioz and many of their
predecessors. True, the works of Wagner were aimed mainly at

---

[1] 1820-1871; composer and critic; opponent of Russian nationalist
school and hence of Stassov, ED.

[2] 1824-1906; scholar and art critic, champion of the "Mighty
Five", ED.

[3] In spite of a certain persistency in his opinions, his "trinity" as a
magnificent musician, writer and scientist remains a unique event (I
need only recall the *Symphonic Studies*).

[4] 1903-1944; brilliant lecturer and art critic; member of the
Leningrad Conservatoire; friend of Shostakovich; wrote a study
of Schoenberg in 1934; was violently attacked in the late 1930s,
ED.

[5] At that time member of the Moscow Conservatoire, ED.

furthering and proving his own rightness as the creator of the music drama. Even in his excellent book on Beethoven he plainly states that the Finale of the Ninth Symphony is a forerunner of his musical drama and that therein lies its main significance. Such a passionate and determined fighter for his art, the greatest, the only one in this field of art, could not reason otherwise. But if you discard the "auto-propaganda", how many profound and passionate thoughts are expressed in his literary work! One cannot fail to read them even if they sometimes do call forth a protest.

Liszt's excellent book on Chopin is well known in our country. When he writes about the compositions of his friend, his prose seems, to our ears, too full of pathos, too pompous, but this is so understandable—the musician of genius, conscious of the inadequacy of words in transmitting the lofty feelings and powerful emotions which he rendered so easily by his playing, resorted to pathos, put in a lot of exclamation marks, naturally fighting shy of a more sober and matter of fact exposition of his thoughts and feelings. Yet he is no less intelligent than Balzac when he writes about "the man of society", his inner make-up and behaviour. These pages are perhaps the most remarkable in all the book.

Unfortunately Liszt's excellent programme notes for the concerts given during the peak period of his work as conductor at Weimar are not very popular in our country (perhaps because of their incidental nature). It is difficult to imagine better "annotations" to music. Brilliant literary quality, intelligence combined with great wit, the depth and accuracy of his musical judgment have made these programme notes into a model of what such writing should be. The main requirement for this "musicological genre"—brevity, laconic style and depth of content is here fully met.

Of Schumann there is no need to speak. His brief advice to learners, his criticisms and articles have rightly earned the respect and love of all musicians.

Berlioz, such as he appears to us from his letters, articles and, I would say, his "musical stories", I consider by no means less brilliant as a writer than as a musician. I will even confess privately that he gives me more pleasure as a writer than as a composer (with the exception, of course, of some passages of true genius in his *Requiem*, *The Damnation of Faust* and the *Symphonie Fantastique*)[1].

Why did I embark on an enumeration of all the famous masterpieces in the literature on music? Because our young musicologists (and sometimes also the middle-aged) fail to grasp the meaning, the significance and enchantment of the works I have mentioned. Their own work is permeated with "scholarliness", "analysis" and an accurate description of the object of that analysis which in most cases envelop the reader in unrelieved boredom. You cannot talk about art in a language that is too inartistic. Incidentally, in recent times there has been an improvement in the type of writing known as "dissertation", but this is far from sufficient. There is still too much description in minute-writer's style explaining what goes on in a musical composition ("in such a bar the melody leaps a fifth, in that other bar the bass drops a fourth", etc., etc.). It is probably that type of description that gave rise to the jokes about "describing a dinner" and similar witticisms.

I consider that these bad, formalistic musicological habits should be abandoned once and for all. For a musician they are unnecessary, because he can hear; they are even more unnecessary for the non-musician because he cannot understand them.

As a man who reflects on the subject of art and as a teacher I find that one of my most fascinating occupations is the analysis of the laws of materialistic dialectic, which are embodied in the art of music, in music itself, as well as in its performance, as clearly and precisely as they are in real life. How interesting and instructive it is to follow the laws of conflict between contradictions, to see how in music, just as in life in general, thesis and antithesis lead to synthesis.

We sometimes devote a great deal of time to such discussions in my class. A pianist who knows and feels these laws will always play better than the pianist who does not know them or cannot fathom them. This question is too vast and deserves to

[1] I have already mentioned Kurth, Schweitzer, Pirrot and others whom I would advise teachers and learners alike to study (critically, of course).

be specially studied and described; moreover it requires a
tremendous number of musical examples analysed in detail; for
these reasons I shall not be able to include it in this book. But to
direct the reader's thinking I shall just give a small example
from my personal experience which may explain what I mean.

Many pupils in my class studied Beethoven's Sonata in D
major, op. 10 No. 3. I have hardly even been immediately
satisfied with the rendering of the following bit from the last
movement (just before the end of the movement):

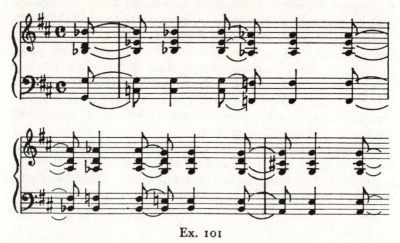

Ex. 101

Some pupils put too much stress on the strong beat of each
half-bar because they wanted to show the change of harmony
which occurred on the strong beat; others, apparently on the
assumption that a syncopation always requires a certain
accentuation, played it thus:

and so on

Ex. 102

bestowing on this lovely syncopated rhythm the character of a cake-walk. For anyone with ears to hear it was at once clear that both renderings were blatantly wrong. The pupil can be helped if it is explained to him that in this small and wonderful excerpt from the Sonata there is a struggle of contradictory elements. On the one hand the change of harmony coupled with the strong beat of the bar attracts our attention (beckons to us, if I may so express myself); on the other hand the syncopation which always requires a certain accent, whatever happens, also "beckons". These two contradictory elements of the musical phrase can be termed "thesis" and "antithesis". But the whole phrase in its entirety is the "synthesis". We musicians tend to replace the word "synthesis" by the word "harmony". It is obvious that in order to achieve harmony in rendering this phrase it is essential to find the balance between the accents on the strong beat of the bar and the accents on the syncopation; this will result in a true and beautiful rendering. It is very easy to show on the piano and very boring to describe in such detail.

I think the reader will have no difficulty in understanding what I am trying to say and will be able to draw far-reaching conclusions from this small example. Dialectic is not metaphysics; it does not hover somewhere in the air above us but is present everywhere in our lives. I feel it also in the way the grass grows and in the way Beethoven composed. Nature is the mother of dialectic.

I could give thousands and yet more thousands of examples of such work with my pupils, and of appeals to them to try to understand the laws of dialectic and give them aesthetic expression. But I think that this small example will suffice. There is hardly need to say that dialectic thinking helps those who did not "receive it from on high" to master long cyclical forms, to develop the musical process in a convincing and living manner and to render the composer's intention with integrity.

My essay would be incomplete if I failed to mention a means of musical education known to all—recordings, tape-recorders, etc. For talented and advanced pianists, recordings are now probably the most powerful means of education. So much that is remarkable and beautiful is available on records that I sometimes had the sinful thought that the time was not far distant

when teaching advanced pianists in the senior classes of the
conservatoires or by individual teachers will die a natural death
and teaching will give way to gramophone records.

Even now it happens very often that some talented and wide-
awake pupil comes to my class with a record of Rachmaninov's
Second Concerto and asks me for advice. "What do you need
me for" I tell him, "when Rachmaninov himself can give you all
the advice you want. Listen to your record some ten or twenty
times, then I shall hear you once to see what effect this 'listening
to music' has had on you."

It would be highly desirable if the greatest masters of the
piano were to make records not only of technically easy musical
masterpieces which not very advanced pupils can play, but also
of "educational" music, such as the études by Czerny, Clementi,
Cramer, etc. Many of the Clementi sonatas have now been
recorded by Vladimir Horowitz and we teachers cannot but
welcome this. In his advice to those who learn to play the piano
Hofmann says that one must try as far as possible to hear only
good performances and avoid the bad. Now this can be done
easily.

But in fact I think I am flogging a dead horse. Listening to
records and radio is so widespread nowadays that there are, I
think, only few people who are not influenced by this typical
phenomenon of our times, this outstanding achievement of
modern technology.

And here I shall make an end.

The intention had been to supplement my notes by a paper
written by my assistant, T. A. Khludova, which would tell in
detail of our work in class on various compositions of various
composers and various periods.

Although without the use of recordings, without a tape-
recorder, without actual sound, such a work is bound to be
inadequate and cannot give the exact content of a lesson, it is
undoubtedly very useful for learners. But due to the untimely
death of T. A. Khludova the publication of her paper had to be
postponed indefinitely. This is all the more regrettable since in
my book I give only one detailed description of how we study a
composition—our work on the Allegretto from Beethoven's
Sonata *quasi una fantasia* of which I speak in the chapter on
"The Artistic Image". Even so I had to give up the idea of

putting down in words the whole of the technical and tonal work, pedal, etc., since without the actual sound substratum (once more, without a tape-recorder!) such a description, however meticulous, of the process of teaching fails to satisfy me.

I am convinced that in the none-too-distant future such books as mine will be published only with an appended sound track which alone is capable of giving a full and clear idea of what is being discussed.

I have already said that I am conscious of the defects of my book, the main one being a somewhat summary treatment of the subject. Any branch of art, once you have spent your lifetime in it, is seen to be so abundant and so vast that an author who puts down on a few printed sheets what he has thought, felt and partly also done, is bound to feel dissatisfied.

But in consolation (of myself) I shall add that the reader will perhaps still feel that this book has a direct bearing on art, and that it is not just a collection of dry methodological considerations. And if my writing can help anyone to penetrate more deeply into our wonderful art and, even if only slightly, stir his feelings and thoughts, I shall be quite content.

Index